Abhijit Naskar is the 21st century Neuroscientist and Poet who has been serving at the forefront of humankind's struggle against hate, intolerance. bigotry and fanaticism.

Humankind, My Valentine

World's First Anthology of 1000 Sonnets

ABHIJIT
NASKAR

Humankind, My Valentine: World's First Anthology of 1000 Sonnets

(This anthology contains 1000 sonnets of Abhijit Naskar,

published from 2018 through 2022)

This is a work of non-fiction.

An Amazon Publishing Company, 1st Edition, 2023

Printed in the United States of America

ISBN: 9798387435782

DEDICATION

To My People of Earth.

CONTENTS

1. Fabric of Humanity

Sonnet of Human

I am but a human who's got no name,
Simply alive in the land of liberty,
I am but a human who talks no lame,
Simply communicates with utter serenity,
I am but a human who despises harming,
No matter what some books command,
I am but a human who loves not blaming,
No matter how much my peers demand,
I am but a human who lives not in history,
Simply breathes in the now and here,
I am but a human who's curious in mystery,
And loves to investigate forged with questionnaire,
I am but a human teeming with awareness beyond all race and clans,
I am but a human whose religion is liberty and god the humans.

Sonnet of Mind

Goodness is godliness,
For in being good you become the God,
Sectarianism brings loneliness,
For joy rises when you stop being an intellectual fraud,
Peace and joy can't be bought,
For you buy something when you don't own it,
Jewels of bliss are with which your mind is already fraught,
All you need is to realize within and recognize it,
With realization comes contentment,
For contentment is the product of awareness,
So be aware with all your might transcendent,
And be the being of a conscientious consciousness,
Consciousness is possessed by all animals but without consequence,
It's only the human mind that holds the power
to create an all-pervading influence.

Sonnet of Sapiens

No religion is greater than love,
For love is the embodiment of divinity,
No church is higher than the self,
Cause the self is the manifestation of the Almighty,
No worship is greater than help,
For helping is the service of God,
No prayer is as sacred as kindness,
For in kindness lies the real act of the Lord,
No scripture is more glorious than the mind,
For the mind is the creator of the scriptures,
So learn from that scripture within to be of help to your kind,
And be the glue to the fabric of humanity healing all ruptures,
Heal your kind my friend with your wisdom and warmth transcendent,
If not you then who else will unify humanity and rise as sapiens triumphant.

2. Build Bridges not Walls

Do Something So Radical (Sonnet)

Do something so radical
that the laws of nature are shaken,
Do something so radical
that your very existence becomes someone's dream,
Do something so radical
that it appears impossible to your brethren,
Do something so radical
that others either hate you or worship you to the extreme,
Do something so radical
that your breath becomes someone's mental essence,
Do something so radical
that the intellectuals keep silent in front of you,
Do something so radical
that the weak regains strength by your presence,
Do something so radical
that no one can ever repay with all the I O U,
Do something so radical

that no death can ever make you perish,
Do something so radical
that all the sons and prophets pay you heed,
Do something so radical
that your immortality makes history cherish,
Do something so radical
that the meekest of slaves starts to lead,
Do something my friend that matters to humanity
beyond the society's wildest imagination,
Thus you get to be the solution and
not the problem like the rest of the population.

3. The Constitution of The United Peoples of Earth

Mainspring of Life (A Sonnet)

I have no nationality except humanity,
I have no tradition except compassion,
I have no religion except liberty,
I have no god except a family of 7 billion,
I have no belief but only awareness,
I have no creed but only acceptance,
I have no messiah except the self,
I have no scripture except my conscience,
I have no gospel except godliness,
I have no sermon except thought,
I have no philosophy except oneness,
I have nothing to give you except love a whole lot,
I demand no obedience, nor do I desire worship and offering,
For there is death in worship, and freedom is life's mainspring.

4. Every Generation Needs Caretakers

If No One Comes, Walk Alone (A Sonnet)

If no one comes hearing your call - walk alone,
For the price of rigidity is greater than the cost of a fall.
If no one comes hearing your call - speak alone,
For the price of silence is greater than the cost of a scorn.
If no one comes hearing your call - reason alone,
For the price of prejudice is greater than the cost of loneliness.
If no one comes hearing your call - think alone,
For the price of bigotry is greater than the cost of feeling groundless.
If no one comes hearing your call - dream alone,
For the price of conformity is greater than the cost of failure.
If no one comes hearing your call - act alone,
For the price of inaction is greater than the cost of alleged misdemeanor.
If no one comes hearing your call, o brave titan - carry the society on your own,
For peace, progress and harmony are caused by the acts of the one alone.

5. Mad About Humans

Slogan For Humanity (The Sonnet)

Let's slogan for humanity above the cacophony of politics.
Let's slogan all together for the people and not bookish morality.
Let's slogan for humanity above the drumbeats of bigotry.
Let's slogan for the souls in misery and not nationality.
Let's slogan for humanity above the foghorn of policies.
Let's slogan cause we are responsible, not cause we’re aggressive.
Let's slogan for humanity above the siren of world peace.
Let's slogan being peace incarnate beyond all doctrines illusive.
Let's slogan for humanity above the noise of traditions.
Let's slogan all together trumping all worship of sects.
Let's slogan for humanity above the gunshots of authoritarianism.
Let’s slogan as just, free and brave beings, not loyal subjects.
Awake and Arise my sisters and brothers to slogan for all of humankind.
We are the light and we are the might that's needed during this ominous tide.

Live Torch (The Sonnet)

Be a live torch amidst the darkest night.
If not you, who else will light up the society!
Be a living weapon to defend the meek in fright.
If not you, who else will guard humanity!
Be a breathing sword to scare away inhumanities.
If not you, who else will draw the righteous line!
Be a valiant shield to stand against atrocities.
If not you, who else will call that duty mine!
Be a daring drum announcing the beats of acceptance.
If not you, who else will be the emblem of inclusion!
Be a fierce arrow to penetrate the clouds of conformity.
If not you, who else will free people from segregation!
Be the liberating nuke that demolishes all dogmatic shell.
If not you, who else will burn delivering the humanizing kernel!

Those Who Call You Mad (The Sonnet)

Those who call you mad will one day worship you,
For no great achievement is possible without madness.
Those who laugh at you will one day learn from you,
For working through the laugh is a criteria for greatness.
Those who know not you exist will one day seek your guidance,
For your endless sacrifice will make you a beacon.
Those who find you absurd will one day bow in veneration,
For the absurd ideas take us to the most breathtaking destination.
Those who look down on you will one day look up to you,
For your sacrifice will place you on a pedestal of glory.
Those who are deaf to you will one day cross limits for you,
For your voice will echo in the hearts as a purifying symphony.
Those who see you inconsequential will one day pay you homage.
Breathe your mission, live your mission and your acts will forge fate's foliage.

Give Me Blood and Sweat (The Sonnet)

Give me your pleasures, I'll give you awakening.
Give me your pride, I'll give you inclusion.
Give me your self-obsession, I'll give you acceptance.
Give me your arrogance, I'll give you liberation.
Give me your tradition, I'll give you revolution.
Give me your blindness, I'll give you clarity.
Give me your disparities, I'll give you humaneness.
Give me your rigidity, I'll give you serenity.
Give me your religion, I'll give you harmony.
Give me your language, I'll give you amity.
Give me your identity, I'll give you unity.
Give me your nationality, I'll give you humanity.
Give me your sleep and comfort, I'll give you assimilation.
Give me your blood and sweat, I'll give you ascension.

World in Peril (The Sonnet)

The world is in peril and security is out of the window.
If now we don't be humans, what's the point of us!
Humankind is in turmoil and anxiety is running amok.
If now we don’t be responsible what's the point of us!
Neighborhoods are wailing in fear and desperation.
If now we don’t lend a hand what's the point of us!
Communities are struggling in crippling uncertainty.
If now we don't break narrowness what's the point of us!
Nations are panting to sustain health and sanity.
If now we don't rush to rescue what's the point of us!
Nature is revolting to reclaim her kingdom.
If now we don't make peace with her what's the point of us!
Now is not the time for theorizing and criticizing.
Forgetting argumentation we must stand as one people unbending.

Liberationville (The Sonnet)

When the blood is boiling and conscience is screaming,
Stop not wishing for a messiah to appear.
When the heart is beating and the mind is restless,
Sit not praying for the miseries to disappear.
When the veins are burning and nerves are revolting,
Stay not cooped up in a cocoon of petty pleasures.
When the lungs are choking and cells are aching,
Stay not inanimate out of insecurities and fears.
When the spine is bending and the head is drooping,
Stay not silent submitting to tribal identity.
When the knees are trembling and the throat is thirsty,
Stand not frail as servant of conformity.
When the eyes are teary and lips are dreary, never consider sitting still.
Obliterate loyalty to atrocities of the norm waking up to liberationville.

6. Revolution Indomable

Revolution Sonnet

What is revolution you ask!

Revolution is an alarm,
To wake up the sleeping population.
Revolution is a weapon,
To fight tyranny and exploitation.
Revolution is a vaccine,
To prime the society against inhumanity.
Revolution is an insanity,
To humanize the paradigm of sanity.
Revolution is a tsunami,
To wash away all that's foul and carnal.
Revolution is a tornado,
To weaken the grasp of the animal.
Whenever savages raise their fangs most appalling,
Be not a mute witness but a revolution sanctifying.

O My Dear Earthling (A Sonnet)

O My Dear Earthling open your doors,
For the supreme festival has arrived.
The whole wide nature is rejoicing in love,
Step outside cultures and celebrate life.
The sky is engulfed with billions of smiles,
Smiles that know not pettiness of society.
Open your soul O Mighty Earthling,
The wind of amity is here bearing unity.
No more bounds on love, race and religion,
Prejudice suits not a species of sapiens.
Value we must character over conformity,
It's time we throw away all our allegiance.
On guard we stand against differentiation,
Hear all peddlers of hate – we are all one.

Hurricane Humans (A Sonnet)

Come all ye misfits and rebels,
Let's march to shatter the games.
Break all golden chains of comfort,
Let's work forgetting our names.
Come all ye sneered and mocked,
We must burn as flames of unity.
Let's turn into a human tsunami,
And wash away all hate and rigidity.
Hurricane humans we are o brethren,
Savagery no more is master to us.
The fountain of inclusion is our lifeblood,
We won't let tradition break our universe.
Let's finally build the kingdom of heaven,
With clay from our heart's unifying Eden.

7. When Call The People

Take My Life (The Sonnet)

Take my life if you want,
But nothing can take my sight away.
Take my breath if you want,
But nothing can take my might away.
Take my feet if you want,
But nothing can take my journey away.
Take my arms if you want,
But nothing can take my touch away.
Take my tongue if you want,
But nothing can take my voice away.
Take my bones if you want,
But nothing can take my will away.
You can erase me from earth if you so desire,
But you can't stop my ideas from spreading like wildfire.

Rise I Will (The Sonnet)

Every time there is darkness most foul,
I will burn to bring light, sight and might.
Every time there is misery unbound,
I will churn my soul to outpour delight.
Every time the horizon turns gloomy,
I will rush to the aid as a sentient soldier.
Every time the world is infected,
I will walk the alleys as a living sanitizer.
Every time there is savagery on the rise,
I will be the beacon of human alliance.
Every time bigotry overpowers the minds,
I'll be the call to resuscitate fallen conscience.
I am not a person but a sentience beyond time.
Rise I will always in crisis to fortify my humankind.

The Maker (Sonnet)

Step by step we'll reach the mountaintop,
We'll build roads penetrating impediments.
Bit by bit we'll trash our conformities,
We'll erect civilization upon reason and sentiments.
Day and night we'll stand tall in service,
Through storm, rain, heat and gloom.
There's no time for selfishness,
Being selfish would bring universal doom.
Sanity is in giving and caring,
It's in every act of collective concern.
Because if you care only for the self,
Deserting your children your neighbors will run.
The world is our home and we must be its caretaker.
Comfort is luxury, it's time we rise as the maker.

Break The Walls (The Sonnet)

Let's break the walls my friend,
There ain't no place for segregation no more.
Let's break the distance my friend,
There ain't no place for pettiness no more.
Let's sing the song of victory,
There ain't no place for savagery no more.
Let's loosen the knots of tradition,
There ain't no time for rigidity no more.
Don't you hear the siren my friend,
Can't you feel the rising sun!
Don't you hear the footsteps of dawn,
It's time to let go of all things barbarian.
Fear not the unknown and unexplored o friend of mine.
Let's walk together opening doors to one humankind.

Ain't Good People (The Sonnet)

Ain't no good people we,
If goodness means blindness.
Ain't no practical folks we,
If practicality means selfishness.
Ain't no sane citizens we,
If sanity means indifference.
Ain't no smart bunch we,
If smartness brings arrogance.
Ain't no articulate minds we,
If articulation means mindless accuracy.
Ain't no civilized society we,
If civilization means hypocrisy.
We are the force capable of mastering a planet.
Let's live not as machines but conscience incarnate.

Mad Wind (The Sonnet)

Turn into a mad wind,
And blow away the rigidity.
Now the savagery must end,
To do that we must rise as almighty.
Turn into the monsoon rain,
And wash away all sickness.
Whenever a crisis arrives,
We must step up shredding all weakness.
Turn into a purifying wave,
And smoothen the thorns of argument.
Whenever rises differentiation,
We must become the bridge without bent.
The world is unstable and feeble with insecurity.
We must be its strength offering our soul as stability.

8. No Foreigner Only Family

Love not Allegiance (A Sonnet)

If I am remembered O Soldier of Destiny,
Remember me with love not allegiance.
If you place me on the altar of your heart,
Make it not exclusive but exude acceptance.
When the darkness around bothers you,
Bask all you want in my timeless light.
But when you see others in darkness,
Forget your needs and serve with delight.
My heart will never leave your backbone,
So long as you have a cell crying for others.
I will receive honor and my highest reward,
When you annihilate yourself to wipe their tears.
I will keep burning through you for eternity,
Your actions will herald the victory of humanity.

Life Lived for Others (A Sonnet)

Torrents of joy have brought me salvation,
Bearing jewels of inclusion and unification.
My mind and my whole being have gone lost,
Into the rising tides of humanizing assimilation.
Finally serenity has arrived at my doorstep,
When I opened I found the bridge to others.
Defying all agony and selfish insecurities,
I discovered the supreme sentience in their cheer.
Their joy is my joy and their worry is my worry,
It is my vow upon the sacred pyre of conscience.
I stand ready to become dust if it is needed,
I am my gift to them, their smiles my recompense.
There is no point in living for the shallow desires,
Cause life is not lived till it's lived for others.

Salutation (The Sonnet)

My salutation to you O Human,
One who has broken the ties of creed.
The light was always within you,
Destroying the dogmas you set it free.
When your heart is labeled,
The world stays hypnotized in darkness.
The moment you rip them to pieces,
Tides of light awaken all synapses.
All separation is born of labels,
Tear those labels and there'll be light.
Once there is oneness in heart,
Oneness of humanity will manifest alright.
Emancipation lies in losing the I in Us,
Once you do, you will wake up the universe.

Into The Eyes of Racism (A Sonnet)

I looked into the eyes of racism,
All I found was insecurity.
I looked into the eyes of prejudice,
All I found was pretend sanity.
I looked into the eyes of bigotry,
All I found was savage inanity.
I looked into the eyes of hate,
All I found was delusion of purity.
I looked into the eyes of disparity,
All I found was mindless conformity.
I looked into the eyes of apathy,
All I found was spineless vanity.
I looked a lot and observed plenty,
It's time to burn bright against brutality.

Celebrating Colors (A Sonnet)

Come my friend, it's time to color the world,
It's been vague and stale for eternity.
You and I, we all have the colors in us,
Why not use them to paint over all conformity.
Let's color with our words, thoughts and action,
So that not a single inch is left unrenovated.
Let's paint with justice, equality and sanity,
And make all offices of bigotry eliminated.
There is no lack of colors in the world,
Nor there is lack of determined conscience.
Once you recognize the colors in your heart,
The universe will rejoice in our united radiance.
Colors are plenty for us to celebrate together,
Hence we take a stand forging a humane future.

Other Side of This Sonnet

On the other side of this sonnet,
There is a land most bright.
In that land of inclusion and unity,
People are strolling without fright.
They walk, speak, run and play,
Without being accused of difference.
They celebrate life with love and delight,
In someone's need they rush in alliance.
Plenty though their paths may be,
Their sense of community has no label.
They have their differences surely,
Which makes them a species most able.
Now that we've arrived at the other side,
It's time we become that people forthright.

An Immigrant's Plight (The Sonnet)

With hopes and dreams brimming in my heart,
I have traveled across miles and miles.
A single desire for a flame of acceptance,
Still burns bright in my heart's aisle.
You say home is where the heart is,
But my heart is accused of difference.
Sometimes I'm accused of faith or race,
Other times they question my allegiance.
Amidst the illusive fog of color and geography,
When did humanity cease mattering most!
Sentiments and dreams have no borders,
Character isn't exclusive to any single coast.
We've wasted enough time on labels and covers,
It's time to be family filling the world with colors.

Naked I Dance (A Sonnet)

Naked I dance here in delight,
I am not wearing name, fame or stature.
All I am wearing is a smile of humaneness,
Isn't that what matters in human nature!
I need no faith, nation or intellect,
Nor do I need illusive pomp and ceremony.
I am happy being a human above all,
I'll stay that way forever exuding harmony.
Tried a lot many countries, races and religions,
To tie me up with their rugged exclusivities.
But my heart is too grand for any one sect,
So I dance naked without any cultural amenities.
Come join me if you like my sisters and brothers,
United we'll free the world of all tribal attires.

9. Hurricane Humans

In Line of Service (The Sonnet)

World is my Louisiana,
I am its Mississippi.
Whenever it's in trouble,
My blood boils in agony.
Each drop of tear around,
Makes my bones ignite.
My life finds its meaning,
As I respond to their plight.
Joy is only joy to me,
When I bring it to others.
If gained in line of service,
Even wounds are my treasures.
Once I die for the people's future,
Then I can live in peace forever.

Peace Sonnet

Peace doesn't grow on trees,
Nor is it produced in factories.
It has been a concept of books,
Must it stay that way for centuries!
Where argumentation is afoot,
The mission becomes a phantom.
Where the mind thrives on tradition,
Peace is an inconvenience to the norm.
Peace is but a myth most foul,
An annoying goal that demands a lot.
We just prefer our cozy cocoons,
Giving up any of it is just plain absurd.
But there is a cure to the war disease.
Loosen your knots and there'll be peace.

Sonnet of Culture

Our culture their culture,
Enough of this primitive nonsense.
It may have suited our ancestors,
But it suits not beings of conscience.
Of all nations on the face of earth,
My nation is the greatest.
This is no behavior of the civilized,
It's but a sign of the stupidest.
The savage jungle or modern society,
What would you like to be a part of?
Your choice means absolutely nothing,
Till you act on the accountability thereof.
Boasting ancestry declares a dead character.
Wake up from death to write a new chapter.

Self and Society (The Sonnet)

I and you are not two but one,
The space in-between is an illusion.
The air you breathe is also in me,
Then why hang on to separation!
Where there is dark ignorance,
There festers delusion most foul.
Once you give in to such atrocity,
Society breaks out in painful howl.
Self and society are one whole being,
That's how we make a humane world.
But if this is none of your concern,
You are but a bug with conscience curled.
Fabric of society is everyone's business.
It's time we breathe life into humaneness.

10. Servitude is Sanctitude

My Name is Human (The Sonnet)

You asked, what's my nation,
I say it's humanity.
You asked, what's my language,
I say it's magnanimity.
You asked, what's my culture,
I say it's humaneness.
You asked, what's my tradition,
I say it's humbleness.
You asked, what's my gender,
I say it's fortitude.
You asked, what's my religion,
I say it's servitude.
You asked everything except my purpose.
I tell you now, it's to unite the universe.

Who's The Best (The Sonnet)

Of all nations on earth,
No nation is the best.
Of all religions on earth,
No religion is the best.
Of all cultures on earth,
No culture is the best,
Of all colors on earth,
No color is the best.
Of all genders on earth,
No gender is the best,
Of all philosophies on earth,
No philosophy is the best.
The world is diverse for us to be strong,
By walking together we'll fly high and long.

11. Time to End Democracy

Sonnet of Meritocracy

Where states dictate humanity,
Harmony remains an eternal fiction.
Diplomacy only divides people in secret,
And democracy sustains that foul friction.
Where the society is mesmerized by charm,
And politics is fueled by populism.
Values and character exist as theories,
As matter of talks, not as alive aphorism.
Under the sectarian watch of states,
Inclusion and acceptance turn to dust.
In an attempt to sustain sovereignty,
Humanity of the humans gets all lost.
Electing authorities on whim is only poker,
Without merit as core, democracy is peacebreaker.

Humanizing Democracy (A Sonnet)

Dictatorship is rule of the cunning,
Democracy is rule of the halfwits.
Both are quite degrading for society,
Cause neither of them is born of merits.
Progress requires practice of reason,
Immersed in a whole lot of love.
But when the people prefer indifference,
Society regresses down the savage curve.
Character is the foundation of civilization,
Yet that character is taken for granted.
All talk and no walk has made us shallow,
Separatism has made our soul tainted.
So it's time we feed values into democracy,
While abolishing all populist fallacy.

12. I Vicdansaadet Speaking

The Anti-Fanaticism Sonnet

Acceptance begets harmony,
Reason begets solution.
Solidarity conquers agony,
Character conquers differentiation.
Humility brings sanity,
Forgiveness brings serenity.
Patience breeds tenacity,
Conscience breeds sanctity.
Observation causes insight,
Questions cause evolution.
Self-correction facilitates might,
Self-reliance facilitates ascension.
So wake up and trample all fanaticism,
Only then we'll be free from sectarianism.

Sonnet of Festivals

Christmas isn't about the decorations,
It's about compassion.
Hanukkah isn't about the sufganiyot,
It's about amalgamation.
Ramadan isn't about the feast,
It's about affection.
Diwali isn't about the lights,
It's about ascension.
Our world is filled with festivals,
But what do they really mean?
Celebrating them with cultural exclusivity,
Makes us not human but savage fiend.
Every festival belongs to all of humanity,
For happiness has no religious identity.

The Anti-Stereotype Sonnet

Black is not evil.
White is not trash.
Brown is not illegal.
Muslims don't crash.
Women ain't weak.
Jews ain't greedy.
Men ain't playboys.
Queer ain't sickly.
Hijab is not oppression.
Hourglass ain't beauty.
Faith is not delusion.
Atheists don't lack morality.
Assumptions only reveal shallowness.
Beyond stereotypes lies humaneness.

13. Boldly Comes Justice

Police Sonnet

Police is not a profession,
But a promise of protection.
So long as you carry the badge,
You must discard self-preservation.
The thin blue line of service,
Is not for self-serving narcissists.
When your sole concern is society,
Only then can you uphold justice.
You mustn't become manikins of politics,
Nor of bureaucratic brutality.
Your allegiance is only to the people,
Their welfare will rescue your humanity.
In the sea of selfishness be the selfless drop,
Taking care of people you become a real cop.

Citizen Justice (A Sonnet)

Boldly comes justice,
Not just in color blue.
Boldly comes justice,
To make this world anew.
Boldly comes justice,
To defend the fellow innocent.
Boldly comes justice,
Upright, rational and fervent.
Boldly comes justice,
Crossing race, religion and gender.
Boldly comes justice,
To confront humanity's offender.
Justice on earth is no legal matter,
If one soul is hurt all must rise together.

Monarchy Sonnet

Bloodline doesn't determine destiny,
Only determination can do that.
Biology doesn't see royalty,
Only bugs without backbone do that.
They say above the law is nobody,
Yet the royalty makes their own law.
If this is what civilization is about,
It's much better to be an outlaw.
The very existence of monarchy,
Is a sign of a medieval society.
We deny visa to hopes and ambition,
Yet kings and queens receive undeniable loyalty.
So I address the monarchs of planet earth,
Grow up and give your character a real birth.

The American Sonnet

On Mayflower we arrived filled with hope,
Escaping persecution and atrocities.
Upon landing we became the persecutor,
And atrociously evicted communities.
Apparently we were civilized people,
Who wanted it all for ourselves.
We snatched it all from the innocent natives,
And gave reservations to help themselves.
Even today we ignore these atrocities,
And continue to perpetuate segregation.
We may look civilized on the outside,
Inside we are walking discrimination.
We are the land of liberty but only in theory,
It's time to walk the talk and embody the glory.

The Presidential Sonnet

This little sonnet I give to thee,
Who is to lead our land of the free.
Rising above all personal glee,
Open your eyes to what others can't see.
The path you seek your heart will pave,
For you to protect our home of the brave.
In case you fall into the corruption grave,
Awaken your dignity and do not rave.
I write this sonnet in ink of humanity,
So that you never forget your priority.
Stand upright and never you accept pity,
For you are to lead our land of liberty.
Let's sail boldly into the storms of annihilation,
Breathing light into dark by sheer determination.

The Voting Sonnet

Why should you vote you ask,
Since it changes nothing!
And nothing will change,
By acting the indifferent weakling.
If you want things to change,
Support character not charisma.
Trash all your populist snobbery,
And it'll abolish all political miasma.
Politics is manipulation,
But it is so due to your gullibility.
Seek out the leader with backbone,
Only then there'll be hope for humanity.
But if you find not a leader of character,
Arise and be the one you seek here and there.

Two Liberties (A Sonnet)

There is not one but two liberties,
One is savage and the other is civilized.
Savage liberty lacks accountability,
The civilized one makes us humanized.
In the jungle liberty is the supreme law,
But one that involves no accountability.
Thus injustice is the norm of wildlife,
But it can't be accepted in human society.
Accountability is the line of control,
Between human and animal behavior.
You don't need intellect to draw the line,
All you need is a well-formed character.
So liberty must be guided by accountability,
Only then can we create a sane society.

Sonnet of International Relations

Modern dictators don't use oppression,
To keep thought and liberty barred.
The effective means of new dictatorship,
Is to play the nationalism card.
Feed people lies covered with nationalism,
They'll applaud you without a but.
Talk about reason and inclusion,
They'll ignore you as a universalist nut.
Till today society thrives on sectarianism,
While arguing over peace and harmony.
We call this insanity international relations,
In our every act we empower disparity.
Still if we don't discard this sectarian savagery,
General Assemblies will sustain agony not amity.

14. Good Scientist

Sonnet of Paths

Science means nothing,
Unless we use it to lift the society.
Philosophy means nothing,
Unless it empowers humanity.
Religion means nothing,
Unless it advocates for inclusion.
Technology means nothing,
Unless it aids in collective ascension.
Tastes are plenty in our world,
So are the paths that humans take.
But if those paths hold no humanity,
Fabric of civilization will soon break.
Placing on humanity our prime attention,
Together we'll attain true emancipation.

Sonnet of Behavior

The beauty that you see with your eyes,
Is but an illusive sign of fertility.
The beauty that you see with your mind,
Is a sign of life, truth and eternity.
The peace that you seek in possessions,
Is but a mirage most rotten.
The peace that is dormant in your heart,
Will make this world awakened.
The order that you seek in law,
Is but a sign of disorder and inhumanity.
The order that the world truly needs,
Is born of your own accountability.
Chasing illusions breeds only insecurity.
Pursue meaning and there'll be serenity.

15. Sleepless for Society

Plight of A Humanitarian (The Sonnet)

My dear people of earth,
I die everyday so that your children can live.
My dear people of earth,
You've been selfish for long now it's time to give.
My dear people of earth,
I struggle everyday with your interest on top.
My dear people of earth,
Enough of this tribalism now it's time to grow up.
My dear people of earth,
I'm really tired and weary righting all wrong.
My dear people of earth,
Join me in making a world where we all belong.
I promise I don't want much from you.
All I ask is that you bid your sectarianism adieu.

Sonnet of Social Justice

Get ready to fight,
Not with hate but accountability.
Get ready to fight,
Not with vengeance but humanity.
Get ready to speak,
Not as a cynic but as a sapiens.
Get ready to speak,
Crossing all egotistical grievance.
Get ready to stand,
Trampling all petty separation.
Get ready to stand,
Not in rebellion but in inclusion.
When it is too dark around,
Look inside for you're the light all round.

When Love Awakens (The Sonnet)

When love awakens so will the world,
For love is the seed of civilization.
When love awakens the conflicts will end,
For love is the gateway to assimilation.
When care crosses family suffering will wither,
For selfishness is the cause of miseries.
When the soul is clear enough to reflect all,
All separation will turn into memories.
When breath of one becomes the breath of all,
All atrocious walls will collapse into dust.
When there's no more 'my people your people',
Only then we will be human at last.
When the fire of love engulfs our whole being,
Time will bear witness to humanity's uprising.

The Loco Sonnet

Better to be loco for something,
Than to be sane for nothing.
Better to fight and die for a purpose,
Than to sit around and do chanting.
Better to love and be exploited,
Than to be self-obsessed and crooked.
Better to disagree and annoy each other,
Than to hide the differences fostering hatred.
Better to be a know-nothing idiot,
Than to be a know-it-all loudspeaker.
Better a character without fancy clothes,
Than fancy clothes without character.
There's no future without a united humanity.
The whole world is a reflection of me.

Mind of A Human (The Sonnet)

My kind of dance is the dance of inclusion,
A dance that can't be contained with labels.
My kind of art is the art of assimilation,
An art that is beyond all intellectual fables.
My kind of science is the science of revolution,
A science that is incorruptible by bigotry.
My kind of faith is the faith in egalitarianism,
A faith that is untainted by bookish crookery.
My kind of economics is the economics of equality,
An economics guided by conscience not greed.
My kind of politics is the politics of sanity,
A politics that serves all beyond the politician's need.
I dream of a progress that is not regress in disguise.
Wielding warmth and reason we'll truly rise.

Mi Humanidad Insiste (The Sonnet)

Mi corazón insiste that I can't sit still,
Till the society is human and thus starts living.
Mi corazón insiste that I can't sleep in peace,
Till I bring out the peace the world holds within.
Mi conciencia insiste that I can't stop walking,
Till I make the fallen rise to make their destiny.
Mi conciencia insiste that I can't stop working,
Till each human extends a hand out in solidarity.
Mi alma insiste that my breath is not my own,
Till I breathe life into the souls lost in misery.
Mi alma insiste that I have no right over my veins,
Till the veins of society are freed from disparity.
Mi humanidad insiste the life of one is the life of all.
Either we are one family or nothing at all.

16. Neden Türk

Synthetic Civilization (The Sonnet)

The watchwords of civilization,
Are reason and inclusion.
Yet we live by the golden rules,
Of rigidity and exclusion.
We dress up in fancy clothes,
To feel powerful and important.
Beneath the lies of civilization,
Beats a heart most impotent.
We boast proudly about equality,
Unaware of our biases most inane.
We admire the rights of our own,
Rights of others are business of the UN.
Enough of this make belief ascension.
It's time to humanize our synthetic civilization.

Life is Prejudice (The Sonnet)

Life is one big prejudice,
Unless you question everything.
Perception is one big bias,
Unless you see beyond the seeing.
Opinions are a bunch of lies,
Till curiosity surpasses comfort.
Beliefs may very well be delusion,
Till traditions are examined with real effort.
Faith can very easily be fiction,
Unless you distinguish superstition.
Morality can turn out to be myth,
Unless you embrace evolution.
There's no place for rigidity in liberty's lands.
On the odyssey of revolutions life expands.

Battle Hymn of The Public (The Humanist Sonnet)

Mine eyes have seen the glory,
Of the rising of the Gods.
We are fighting all the worry,
Trampling authority of the frauds.
We are awakening ourselves,
Breaking the spell of tradition.
Finally we are breathing free,
Devoid of all segregation.
We still have our prejudices,
But we no longer bow to them.
Biases may still prevail in us,
No more do we submit to them.
God ain't up there but here in you and me.
Awake, Arise O Mighty Gods to die for the unfree.

17. Martyr Meets World

Sonnet of Unity

I am vicdan,
I am saadet.
My life isn't mine,
It's your emanet.
Soy sanity,
Soy humanidad.
Life lies in service,
Selfishness kills vitalidad.
Ich bin inclusion,
Ich bin indivisible.
Mein kampf is unity,
Human and hate are incompatible.
Life divided brings degradation.
Growth comes through expansion.

(vicdan=conscience, saadet=joy, emanet=keepsake, soy=I am, humanidad= humanity, vitalidad=vitality, Ich bin=I am, mein kampf=my struggle)

The Purifying Sonnet

What the world needs is a helper,
Bold, brave and unbending.
What the world needs is a fire,
Daring, determined and unflinching.
What the world needs is a heartlifter,
Radical, revolutionary and rejuvenating.
What the world needs is a river,
Persistent, ceaseless and lifegiving.
What the world needs is a martyr,
Liberated, majestic and undying.
What the world needs is a flower,
Unconditioned, naïve and beautifying.
The world of today still lives in gutter.
It is our duty to be the purifier.

Divinity for Sale (The Sonnet)

When a book becomes religion,
And doctrines become divinity,
Holiness remains speculation,
Society loses sight of humanity.
When institutions claim authority,
And sleeping masses comply,
Religion disappears altogether,
What remains is potential gone awry.
When popes and pundits sell faith,
In the name of divine supremacy,
Rigidity overrules common sense,
And reason is hailed as blasphemy.
But there is a cure for all this atrocity.
It is called individual curiosity.

Shalom Civilization (The Sonnet)

Without accountability there's no civilization,
For it is the line between human and animal.
Without integrity there's no civilization,
For it is the line between human and vegetable.
Without sanctity there's no civilization,
For it is the line between sanity and savagery.
Without amity there's no civilization,
For it is the line between humanity and machinery.
Without conscience there's no civilization,
For it is the line between order and upheaval.
Without character there's no civilization,
For it is the line between life and survival.
Civilization is a small word with a universe inside.
To unfold it requires a species without divide.

18. The Shape of A Human

The New American Sonnet

America doesn't mean the best,
America means accountability.
America doesn't mean supremacy,
America means responsible liberty.
America doesn't mean flawless,
America means growing against oddity.
America doesn't mean condescension,
America means caring for all humanity.
America doesn't mean white or color,
America means celebration of diversity.
America doesn't mean red or blue,
America means together crossing rigidity.
Stars and stripes have no place for hate.
Our heart is human, it's humanity we celebrate.

Healers Don't Exist (The Sonnet)

Healers don't exist,
Only humans do.
Once you step outside the self,
You'll see the world anew.
Gods don't exist,
Only goodness does.
Prayers may soothe your soul,
Action is what change requires.
Psychics don't exist,
But sanctity is everywhere.
Once you stop conning your soul,
The bridge ahead will vividly appear.
When the heart awakens from superstition,
Everybody will be hometown human.

Child of Earth (The Sonnet)

Walk, walk, walk ahead,
O brave child of earth.
Let no fear shackle your feet,
Selflessness paves all path.
Meditate on unity,
Dedicate to inclusion.
Educate your soul,
Be free from self-absorption.
Forget gender, religion and ideology,
Abolish all chains of tribalism.
Place people at your heart's altar,
One dream, one mission – universalism.
Shallow and separated we can stay no more.
We must break ourselves to let light outpour.

In The Church of Liberty (The Sonnet)

In the church of liberty,
Light a candle of conviction.
Do not move an inch,
Even in the face of annihilation.
Freedom, curiosity and inclusivity,
These are the beads of our soul.
Standing true to these watchwords,
We will reach our supreme goal.
If we want there to be serenity,
Destroy we must our insane egotism.
Real rest comes through humility,
When we discover the self in collectivism.
World peace and harmony are all fiction.
If conscience is awake there'll be ascension.

My Compatriots (The Sonnet)

Any compatriot of mine,
Better have a grasp of prejudice.
Arrogance sickens my soul,
My heart revolts at the snobbish.
Doubts can be healthy,
But only if driven by curiosity.
When driven by contempt,
They only facilitate animosity.
You don't have to agree,
With the whole of my notion.
But don't turn bitter my friend,
For it is a trap of degradation.
Logic may fail sometimes as well as sentiments.
Never you lose o patriot your indivisible humanness.

Goodbye Mother (The Sonnet)

Bid me goodbye o mother,
Be right back once I plant unity.
If I do not return from my journey,
Soothe yourself knowing I've died happily.
These rusted shackles hurt too much,
It's time o mother to abolish them forever.
Shoulder to shoulder your children will walk,
At the sight of our conviction bigots will quiver.
The sacred river of life has long gone dry,
I'll resuscitate it with my blood and integrity.
Your children are my family o mother,
With my last breath I will fortify their destiny.
Bless me o mother of all for my mission awaits.
I'll return victorious or die a martyr's death.

19. When Veins Ignite

I Give You My Life (The Sonnet)

I give you my life,
Crossing all foul insecurity.
Don't let me dwindle in chains,
Accept this offering of my serenity.
Pour me with all your suffering,
So I can bathe in your smile.
Take this torch of my burning soul,
With it light up your shadowy aisle.
Darkness is a fiendish illusion,
Our each molecule is a fountain of light.
I have nothing to give my friend,
So I give you my life to amplify your might.
We are dead till we live for others.
In helping them our burden disappears.

The Personal Sonnet

If you want to be heard,
You must learn to listen.
If you want to be trusted,
You must keep trustin'.
If you want to grow,
You must first evolve.
If you want to be happy,
Let yourself dissolve.
If you want to smile,
You must learn to give.
If you want to lead,
Help others to live.
Law of the jungle is self-preservation.
Law of society is collective ascension.

The Social Welfare Sonnet

I have no problem with capitalism,
I have problem when it's devoid of society.
I have no problem with innovation,
I have problem when it lacks accountability.
I have no problem with religion,
I have problem when it's run by bigotry.
I have no problem with intellect,
I have problem when it lacks decency.
I have no problem with advancement,
I have problem when it facilitates disparity.
I have no problem with politics,
I have problem when it loses all sanity.
No field is evil entire of its own.
Evil festers when we forget we can't progress alone.

This is Not Us (The Sonnet)

This is not us,
Practicing savages abhorrent.
This is not sapiens,
Intelligent yet filthy indifferent.
Some think we are advanced,
But self-absorption is no advancement.
Some say we have built a free world,
But irresponsible freedom is mere derangement.
Fancy clothes and accessories make no human,
Nor do those shallow etiquettes.
When we have no kindness for others,
We are just good-looking cannibals.
This cannot be the definition of humanity.
Need of the hour is a life of inclusivity.

No Throne, No Kingdom (The Sonnet)

I need no throne, I need no kingdom,
Human hearts are my heavenly abode.
I need no badge, I need no scepter,
Reason is my partner, warmth my zip code.
I need no praise, I need no offering,
A life of service is my paradise.
I need no reward, I need no award,
Nothing can put a price on sacrifice.
I know no etiquette, I know no manners,
These are all constructs of shallowness.
Humanity ought to drive behavior,
Humility destroys all narrowness.
To forge wholeness and sanity is our mission.
Ending all falsity let's be incarnate integration.

Sonnet of Expansion

I expect nothing from the world,
I have no desire to impress society.
I only care for its wellbeing,
Hence I simply do my human duty.
Don't know whether I'm left or right,
Which I don't give a damn about.
World has enough conflicts as it is,
One more duality we can do without.
Expansion is the other name of life,
Without which we are dead and rotten.
If we are not willing to evolve,
Humankind will be soon forgotten.
If today's thought is the same as yesterday,
Despite all achievements we are going astray.

Bow O Brave (The Sonnet)

Bow o brave, o lifter of hearts,
Bow in service losing all pride.
With your acts of care and community,
Make even the dust sanctified.
Selflessness and sanity,
Let these flow through your veins.
Offer up your nerves and bones,
As the world's unity lanes.
Lose all name and lose all pleasure,
Forget address to which you are born.
As you live in every person,
They will cross ocean to make you own.
Step outside the self for the unselfish has no match.
Every land will become golden by your holy touch.

Sonnet of Breath

The heart holds a breath,
A breath that is indivisible.
Yet we rarely take it in,
For we are raised as vegetable.
We are seeking joy here and there,
Yet there's an ocean of it within us.
It's a joy that comes alive when we care,
At the sight of selfishness it disappears.
Intimacy breeds stability and serenity,
But not the one that thrives on body.
Intimacy that's chaste and unifying,
Manifests only in innocent amity.
Human mind is the source of all ascension.
We are the origin of all civilized creation.

Human Helpline (The Sonnet)

Neither Christ, nor Krishna, nor Superman,
No imagination can rescue humanity.
Each of us is the only helpline,
Human salvation is human responsibility.
Enough with these prayer and rituals,
Now awake from the sleep of subjugation.
As heroes fraught with reason and conscience,
We must rise to break all submission.
Progress demands a life of revolution,
Self-induced slavery won't do.
The more you seek a savior outside,
The more you turn into boneless goo.
Of all life on earth the human being is peerless.
Only those called sapiens roar for the helpless.

Adopt A Neighborhood (The Sonnet)

Adopt a neighborhood,
Make their problems your own.
This is the only road to life,
Society's hope is you alone.
Charity, security and world peace,
All these are cosmetic theory.
When you learn to live as human,
You'll see their actual foolery.
When our voices combine,
All noise turns melody of heavens.
Joy is amplified a hundred times,
We lose sense of all our burdens.
Diversity and progress will come alright,
Once you perceive beyond your selfish sight.

The Final Solution (A Sonnet)

O new people, o new humanizers,
The world has been waiting for you long.
Waiting for your dawn with deepest zeal,
Society is weary yet tries to be strong.
Now rise o makers of civilization,
Replenish this death valley with your sanctity.
Make rigidity and prejudice quiver,
Sanitize humanity with rapids of indivisibility.
The sun has gone dark, the moon lost its glory,
All are waiting for your galvanizing advent.
These deserts can no more sustain life,
You alone are hope and the last encouragement.
Walk boldly as the awakening of revolution.
Wake up from indifference and be the final solution.

20. Heart Force One

Sonnet of Promise

I made a promise with my life,
Never to leave your side.
How can I maroon you my friend,
When you and I are one light.
Some call me muy loco,
Cause I stand for reason and inclusion.
A world where division is sanity,
Is but a gutter of superstition.
All things have meaning,
When we have people next to us.
Without their presence to fill our life,
Existence is but a futile fuss.
Breathing alone is like choking to death.
A breath shared is a breath well lived.

Sonnet of Nonconformity

Nonconformity is no sign of character,
Nor is swinging on wrecking balls.
Vulgarity is the same as animal liberty,
Only accountability adorns our civilized halls.
Clothes have no bearing on civilization,
Nor does allegiance to law and order.
But habits that endorse self-absorption,
Breed nothing but degradation and disorder.
Perverted animals belong in the jungle,
Self-regulation is vital in civilized society.
If we are to take this world forward,
We must stand tall with honor and sanity.
Naked or not a human is always responsible.
Unregulated freedom sustains a world most cruel.

Army of Lovers (The Sonnet)

What's needed is an army of lovers,
To set this world on fire,
A fire that burns prejudice to ashes,
And sparks a humanitarian desire.
Lovers devoted to the path of sacrifice,
Pure and chaste serving without reward,
Pursuing the one impossible dream,
The dream of humanizing the entire world.
Not a trace of self within,
Not a kernel of self-obsession,
Uncorrupted and unbending to the bone,
Wake up and be the living ascension.
Drink from the fountain of service effulgent.
Annihilated for others we turn omnipresent.

The Wholeness Sonnet

Free will is not a question of willpower,
It is a question of character.
Civilization is not a question of etiquette,
It is a question of behavior.
Order is not a question of law,
It is a question of accountability.
Harmony is not a question of toleration,
It is a question of inclusivity.
Peace is not a question of diplomacy,
It is a question of nonsectarianism.
Progress is not a question of revenue,
It is a question of collectivism.
When the heart is whole all's well with society.
Fragmentation fills the sky with disparity.

Godless Struggle (The Sonnet)

I don't believe in a God,
That doesn't help the helpless.
Through the history of humankind,
Only humans have served the distressed.
My struggle is to end all struggles,
Says the being of character and conscience.
When you stretch out your hand in love,
That's when civilization manifests.
No help is insignificant,
No kindness is too puny.
With tiny steps we'll humanize the world,
When we see every human as family.
No prayer can heal the troubles of society.
Only cure for degradation is united humanity.

The Naskarean Sonnet

It ain't easy to get Naskar,
For Naskar is no being binary.
In a world full of dualities,
Naskar is an emblem of inclusivity.
Think not it to be a person,
For the person perished in line of duty.
What lives today is the idea,
The idea of struggle for undivided amity.
Every human who helps a human,
Is a manifestation Naskarean.
Wherever there is prejudice and inequality,
They appear as a living revolution.
When one Naskar dies a thousand will rise.
The dream of unity will never face demise.

The British Sonnet

Rule Britannia,
Britannia rule the waves.
Britons never, never, never,
Shall be slaves.
Around the world we looted,
We even championed slavery.
But none of it really matters,
Consequences don't apply to royalty.
Hitler massacred so many people,
Which is petty compared to our atrocities.
Perhaps that's why Britain is so great,
None can compete with our killing spree.
It's time to civilize this backward Britannia,
By righting the wrongs of British Barbariana.

The Country Sonnet

I stand beneath the southern sky,
Looking up at the heavenly bodies.
The twinkling stars know no color,
Then why we mortals beneath act so puny!
Country means heart, country means humility,
All that is pure is born in the country.
How could we poison its innocent soul,
By our savage escapades of bigotry!
It's high time we be the example of kindness,
For the streams of Mississippi carry acceptance.
Behold ye all blind with confederate pride,
Conscience rises above the Blue Ridge Mountains.
Let's resuscitate the country with love and passion.
We'll turn this land into a cradle of amalgamation.

Sonnet of Human Intervention

Vegetables often say,
In the end all will be well.
It is but an illusion of control,
Progress comes not through silent spell.
Nothing good happens by magic,
Every good requires human intervention.
When we stand up and act with conscience,
Only then we'll cause real ascension.
The whole world is my responsibility,
Thus speaks the civilized human.
Defy the norm that makes you selfish,
Embodying love's enduring aspiration.
Forget not, we are but each other's keeper,
Born not to be intellectual, but drunken lover.

Shake The World Savaşçı (The Sonnet)

Shake the world savaşçı,
The world is only a reflection of you.
Break the mold o kahraman,
In a civilized time these molds won't do.
Your story is the one of a warrior,
Not the one fighting with weapon.
You are the hero without arms,
Your power is your determination.
One person can end a war,
If they give all to the making of peace.
You are the answer to the world's prayers,
But you must keep your prejudice on leash.
Go sleepless, starving and unappraised if needed.
Be the guerra of inclusion and unite the divided.

(savaşçı = warrior, kahraman = hero, guerra = war/struggle)

21. Solo Standing on Guard

MCA: Middle Class Activist (The Sonnet)

I don't know the meaning of socialism,
But progress without society is insanity.
I don't know the meaning of capitalism,
But catering to luxury produces disparity.
I don't know the meaning of woke,
But no life is complete without community.
I don't know the meaning of philosophy,
But intellect is useless without amity.
I don't own many fancy gadgets,
Affording essentials I stand without greed.
I'll probably never set foot on MARS,
On earth I'll be serving the abandoned in need.
High and mighty tech won't make this world better,
Till we place humanity at our highest altar.

Sonnet of Care

This is what care looks like,
Pure and chaste loving without reward.
This is what conscience looks like,
Strong and just reasoning with warmth.
This is what nobility looks like,
Humble and kind correcting one's error.
This is what courage looks like,
Firm and unbending walking across fear.
This is what sentience looks like,
Awake and upright marching with resolve.
This is what character looks like,
Messy and flawed but not afraid to evolve.
Each human is a reflection of all humanity.
Individual action determines collective destiny.

Sonnet of Nation Building

Nation means not land,
Nation means not border.
Nation means sentience and sanity,
Nation means willing to treat disorder.
Nation means not habit,
Nation means not tradition.
Nation means reason and acceptance,
Nation means conscious amalgamation.
Nations means not law,
Nations means not policy.
Nation means a genuine goodness,
Nation means an accountable citizenry.
In the name of nation do not act tribal.
Nation without narrowness is a land universal.

Shades of Brown (The Sonnet)

There is no white skin,
There is no black skin.
All of us are shades of brown,
If we can reason without stereotyping.
Climate makes the difference in color,
But not in character of the individual.
Human character knows no geography,
For a being of character is human above all.
The idea of race is a myth most foul,
Born of ignorance and narrowness.
Now we live in a different time,
That requires abolition of divisiveness.
Discard those traditions and live as sapient.
Let's build a world where color ain't relevant.

Books Over Bombs (The Sonnet)

Bombs kill terrorists,
Books kill terrorism.
Missiles kill extremists,
Mindfulness kills extremism.
Guns kill supremacists,
Goodness kills supremacy.
Law restrains cruel people,
Love reforms cruelty.
Sarin cripples the malicious,
Service cures malice.
C4 impairs the prejudiced,
Curiosity treats prejudice.
Violence can be revolution no more.
For all degradation kindness is the cure.

No Compromise (The Sonnet)

Only cowards make compromise,
When it comes to affairs of humanity.
Beings of conscience and character,
Prefer revolution over indignity.
Only bugs bow before oppression,
Driven by insecurity and indifference.
Creatures called the homo sapiens,
Choose annihilation before compliance.
Only wild animals of the cruel jungle,
Accept self-preservation as the norm.
For advanced organism such as humans,
Inclusion is life in joy and in storm.
Those with backbone stand up for humanity.
Unarmed and unbending we'll conquer inhumanity.

The Temper Sonnet

Where you need to be calm,
You burst out in rage.
Where you need to be on fire,
You walk in silence and not engage.
Where you need to listen,
You scream like a loudspeaker.
Where you need to speak out,
Somehow your words disappear.
Where it requires to be humble,
Pride takes over your humility.
Where your blood needs to boil,
Your veins seem to run empty.
The right use of temper is an act of revolution.
Put it to good use and you'll nourish civilization.

The Commitment Sonnet

Once you commit to something,
Better give up life than the commitment.
Once you make a promise,
Better stop breathing than break it.
Once you realize your purpose,
Better be destroyed than forget it.
Once you stand on your conviction,
Better be broken to pieces than lose it.
Submit, submit, o braveheart,
Submit to something bigger than the self.
Wipe out the self if necessary,
Give all to your goal asking no help.
Life has no meaning except self-preservation.
Your destiny is determined by your action.

Thus Speaks The Human (A Sonnet)

I am my government,
I write my own laws.
I need no congress to define rightness,
An alive conscience needs no one to endorse.
We barely grew out of the bible,
And already replaced it with constitution.
Before we feared an imaginary god,
Now we give law our total submission.
Law and policy may have their place,
But they are no pillars of society.
The only pillar is human conviction,
All else are shallow mockery.
One who needs law is yet to be civilized.
Be accountable and all will be humanized.

Either Aşkistan or Junglistan (A Sonnet)

Ours is either aşkistan,
Land of love founded on amity,
Or it is an archaic junglistan,
Run by contagious self-centricity.
What is civilized is also unselfish,
For selfishness makes the animal,
Across the self there is humanity,
What is unselfish is also accountable.
Technology may bring comfort,
But it doesn't ensure ascension,
When comfort belongs to the privileged,
Such progress is mere descension.
Over 3 billion years have gone in selfishness,
It's time to unself our soul and rise as sapiens.

22. Generation Corazon

Miracle Human (The Sonnet)

Turning water into wine is no miracle,
It just means you are high on something.
Real miracle is to share your last drop,
With someone who is suffering.
To heal and to help are the highest miracle,
Even if it requires the self to be sacrificed.
A mortal who bears agony for others,
Is the real miracle personified.
So wake up and work O Miracle Human,
Rush to the helpless as monsoon rain.
Cast yourself at the feet of the forgotten,
There is nothing more noble and humane.
Prayers don't work for there's no merciful almighty.
Answer to all prayers is a human practicing humanity.

Sonnet of Chemical Reality

The universe is our reflection,
We are the reflection of the universe.
What is inside is also outside,
What is outside is also inside of us.
No reality exists without human control,
Reality outside our control is imagination.
Mental chemicals produce all reality,
All can be altered with mindful action.
Mind is mightier than muscle,
Kindness is braver than cruelty.
All reform is born of mental chemicals,
Reform yourself and there'll be universality.
Truth beyond perception is futile speculation.
Let's focus on life and improve human condition.

Aşkistani: Citizen of Love (The Sonnet)

Listen you all peddlers of hate,
Hard as you may blow the horn of tyranny.
To jeopardize all your stone-age stupidity,
You'll always be confronted with an aşkistani.
We won't let your children come to harm,
Nor will we strike you back in vengeance.
But when you vilify the sanctity of human life,
Rest assured we'll restrain you without violence.
Violence may be your childish habit,
You may practice it all you desire.
We are the revolution of conscience,
That incinerates prejudice by sheer willpower.
We are not here to peddle any ideology.
All we ask is come let's be one family.

Sonnet of People (The Sonnet)

All is well when there's people with us,
Without 'em life is sugarcane without sugar,
All is meaningful when there's people with us,
Without 'em life is a painting without color.
People are the blood in my veins,
I can breathe without oxygen but not people,
Thus speaks the being called human,
Thus lives the sapiens who's brave and noble.
Community means compatriot unity,
Unity means undivided amity,
Amity means affectionate sanity,
Sanity means serene humanity.
Now one ponders the meaning of humanity.
It means humble and affectionate for eternity.

Beyond Red and Blue (The Sonnet)

I don't wanna rule no one,
Nor do I wanna prove them wrong.
I don't wanna convert no one,
Nor do I wanna sing the woke song.
My work is with the whole humanity,
No person must be left behind.
Either I'll take them all forward,
Or I'll perish while fixing the great divide.
I don't fathom the red and blue,
You can't make a rainbow with two colors.
If you are really kind and conscientious,
On its own bigotry disappears.
We must rise above all party politika,
Only then will we be the soul of America.

Sonnet of Nationality

Nation, nation whatever you are,
Time it is for you to disappear.
Plenty chaos you've caused so far,
Nation, nation now you disappear.
Long ago we lived in tribes,
Slowly we expanded our tiny hives.
Behold ye all the time arrives,
To expand again and merge with all lives.
Nationality keeps the world from peace,
Diplomacy keeps the intention on leash.
Partisanism hides the brotherhood keys,
Self-obsession fans sectarian deeds.
Let the borders trouble the tribal gov,
In our hearts let's rise as citizens of love.

Sonnet of Progress

Where the nation ends,
There the world begins.
Where the self fades,
There community begins.
Where luxury withers,
There equality begins.
Where biases shrink,
There truth begins.
Where pride dies,
There growth begins.
Where rigidity ends,
There life begins.
Such true life is forever revered.
Prejudice conquered is world conquered.

Not Woke, Only Accountable (A Sonnet)

I am no teacher but only lover,
I know no philosophy but amity.
I am no writer but only revolution,
I know no politics but serenity.
I am no thinker but only soldier,
I know no science but ascension.
I am no authority but only service,
I know no poetry but inclusion.
I am no humanist but only human,
I know no ideology but oneness.
I am no woke but only accountable,
I know no paradise but acceptance.
Taint not the mind with a puny label.
We are beautiful when we are indivisible.

Sonnet of Identity

Tell me O Mississippi,
What is my name?
For I lost my sense of self,
In line of service without gain.
Dear mountains of Blue Ridge,
Where did I come from?
I fathom not the worldly titles,
I deny narrowness as the norm.
Character makes the person,
Not pedigree and tradition.
If I can lift even five lives,
That'll be my highest salvation.
So forget that I asked about my identity.
Service is my culture and my nationality.

The Sufi Sonnet

For your ascension I became a lover,
For your rights I became a revolution.
Ask me not who I am,
Look in my eyes, you'll find your reflection.
Our world is a new world,
The soul of this world is conscience.
Without conscience we all are animals,
March ahead o conscientious with valiance.
There is no other religion but love,
There is no other nationality but humanity.
The story of human is a story of kindness,
If not, life is but an utter futility.
We are all heroes when we are together,
Togetherness forever whether alive or six feet under.

23. Mucize Insan

Sonnet of Citizens

What can the politicians do,
Unless the people allow it!
What can the government do,
Unless the people permit it!
All corruption is born of people,
Not of politics and bureaucracy.
Corrupt politicians are only symptom,
Real disease is populist democracy.
Politics is civilized when people are civilized,
But what we have is politics of blame.
Denounce blaming and take responsibility,
Then only will your children live without shame.
Your indifference fuels all political histrionics.
Build your character and there'll be no politics.

Sonnet of Palestine

I don't want to wage a war,
All I want is to raise a family.
I don’t want your empty pity,
All I seek is a little humanity.
To call genocide as self-defense,
May be textbook diplomacy.
Killing innocents to keep control,
Is an act of terrorist hypocrisy.
Brokers may bring ceasefire,
But they can never give us liberty.
All they do is arrange assemblies,
While we suffer through the century.
So I say to you o people in luxury,
Look at us and you'll know your fallacy.

Sonnet of Kashmir

Mindless nationalists of India shout,
India is the greatest nation.
Yet atrocities done in their backyard,
Make them a symbol of degradation.
Most Indians have no idea,
How it is to live under occupation.
Yet when it comes to the land of Kashmir,
They won't make any concession.
How can you reason with a deluded bunch,
Who value sovereignty over people!
They have their comfort and luxuries,
Who cares if we lack even life's essential!
Where land is more precious than life,
There lives no human but termite.

Memorial Day Sonnet

We don't want your celebration,
We don't want you to honor us.
All we want is for you to grow up,
And end all tribalism that kills us.
A thousand holidays can't bring us back,
Nor can they wipe the tears of our spouses.
How will you console our children,
How will you comfort our broken parents!
Enough with your flowers and rituals,
Enough with your crocodile care!
If you have an iota of humanity,
Step up and make all divides disappear.
Yet if you still want to live life as tribal,
Rest assured we'll give ours with a smile.

Sonnet of Technology

Technology is not good or bad,
For it knows no ethics and principles.
The prime directive of all gadgets,
Is to obey algorithm without scruples.
The problem is not technology,
Nor is it the capitalist tendency.
The real disease is human recklessness,
Which is rampant in modern society.
Your phone is not ruining your peace,
You yourself are doing it all.
A society oblivious to moderation,
In time causes its own downfall.
Power is power only when used with caution,
If used wildly all power is poison.

Sonnet of Conspiracy

Perhaps there's a monster under the bed,
Perhaps there's a boogeyman in the closet.
Perhaps they're sterilizing kids with vaccine,
Perhaps they're controlling all with a radio set.
Yes our science is well advanced,
But not advanced enough to control minds.
Besides mind-control needs no fancy tech,
When people are run by smartphone chimes.
Tales like these are good for entertainment,
Amongst a bunch of kindergarteners.
But being adult requires the use of reason,
Without submitting to prehistoric fears.
Treating insecurities with common sense,
Anyone can manifest civilized sentience.

The Vaccine Sonnet

Listen to the experts,
Listen to Fauci.
Grow up you big sissy,
Enough with the ouchie!
I got the vaccine,
Trust me it's safe.
Every scientist will confirm,
Listen to reason not hearsay.
Vaccines produce immunity,
Masks prevent the spread.
If you follow some simple steps,
You'll prevent someone's death.
Freedom without reason is savagery.
During pandemic accountability is key.

Sonnet of Traditions

Society must shed its dead traditions,
Like one sheds dead skin.
Anything that lives must evolve,
For stagnation is death's twin.
The difference between life and death,
Lies in the desire for evolution.
Fancy rags on a prehistoric mind,
Makes way for a horrific extinction.
Other animals lack brain power,
To overcome shortcomings and be better.
But the jelly inside the human skull,
Can take us on an endless adventure.
All that is old is not necessarily gold.
Accepting yesterday's good move ahead bold.

Sonnet of Stagnation

Stagnated water breeds disease,
When in motion it breathes life.
Stagnated mind breeds segregation,
When in motion it breaks divide.
Stagnated air breeds pollution,
When in motion it brings rejuvenation.
Stagnated ideas breed prejudice,
When in motion they bring illumination.
We are not a species, we are a family,
A stagnated psyche cannot feel its delight.
Open your eyes from your rigid sleep,
In your vision the world will unite.
All animals are bound to live in stagnation.
Only human neurons hold the capacity for expansion.

Who is Miracle Human (The Sonnet)

Who is the miracle human,
Can they turn water into wine?
Do they never run out of bread,
Can they turn cotton into golden twine?
None of this is actually miracle,
All these are stories of fantasy.
When ignorance was default thinking,
Magic defined a person's capacity.
Real miracle is an act of kindness,
Nothing is higher and more divine.
When you share happily your last bread,
That is holiness most genuine.
Rise and conquer all old prejudice and fantasy.
Stand firm and foster the miracle humanity.

I Expand, Therefore I Am (The Sonnet)

I expand, therefore I am,
Thought is no measure of sapiens.
Even a dog can think what's best for it,
Such selfishness is no existence.
Expansion makes the human,
Inclusion strengthens life.
Diversity beautifies society,
There is no room for divide.
Sanity lies in unselfishness,
Selfishness is inhumanity.
When all world becomes one family,
That my friend is true community.
Let us be vast and breathe in the world.
Let us show all, the blue dot is no less bold.

Lovenut Sonnet

When I was a teenager,
There was a sticker on my desk.
My father had stuck it there,
Saying, till you reach your goal, don't rest.
Since that day I haven't stopped,
For I haven't reached my goal.
You may ask what the goal may be,
It is to die a lovenut lifting all.
Lovenut is one who is nuts,
Total bonkers for the benefit of society,
One whose lifeblood is sacrifice,
A revolutionary who is above all security.
I give a call to all the lovenuts of society.
Stop not till you remind all their humanity.

24. Hometown Human

Sonnet of Phony Activism

Those who give their life to society,
Never call themselves activist.
Those who work night and day for others,
Rarely identify as reformist.
It's only the vane, lame and the shallow,
Who draw attention with phony activism.
Those who actually care for society,
Live a life of sacrifice beyond definition.
Activist and woke are actually code,
That says, look at me I am so great.
Real greats don't care about labels,
They're martyred for others without regret.
The world doesn't need more phony label.
What's needed is humans being accountable.

Sonnet of Occupation

With just weeks of lockdown,
You all feel restless and bland.
That is how everyday life is,
For people in occupied land.
Imagine living your whole life,
Subject to restriction and suspicion.
Ask a Palestinian or a Kashmiri,
They'll reveal the face of occupation.
Life, liberty and happiness,
Are the rights of every being.
Whenever a government violates them,
Civilized humanity must intervene.
I call to all humans far and near,
Rest not till statehood is declared.

Sonnet of Nazi America

America is the land of liberty,
Offer available only to white people.
When it comes to people of color,
It's a Nazi nation though unofficial.
If you are white and you make a mistake,
You are most likely to receive a warning.
But if you are a person of color or muslim,
Better have a good reason for breathing.
They say we live in a democratic land,
A system of, by and for the people.
But what they forget to teach in school,
People doesn't really mean every individual.
No one can change the past that's for sure.
Defying all supremacy we must rise and roar.

Sonnet of National Beauty

Beauty and ugliness as we know them,
Are the product of an ugly mind.
Once we step across all pretenses,
We learn how much we've been blind.
The whitest places on planet earth,
Happen to be the ugliest of all places.
For what appears to be a fancy joint,
Is filled with a bunch of suited savages.
Nations of color have problems too,
But they don't pretend to be advanced.
When we claim to be a global leader,
We must first practice inclusion on demand.
Great is not the nation that appears fancy,
But one which values people over diplomacy.

Sonnet of Cryptocurrency

The reason people are nuts about cryptocurrency,
Is that they hear the magic phrase regulation-free.
But what they forget to take into account,
Is that it also means the user alone bears liability.
The purpose behind a centralized system,
Is not exploitation but to provide trust and stability.
Anything that is decentralized on the other hand,
Is a breeding ground for fraud and volatility.
Not every fancy innovation is gonna benefit society,
Innovation without accountability is only delusion.
Cryptocurrency can be a great boon to banking,
If it merges with the centralized financial institution.
Intoxication of tech is yet another fundamentalism.
Algorithm without humanity is digital barbarism.

Sonnet of Luxury

Serenity shrinks as luxury grows,
While you pay moderation no heed.
Disparity is not a matter of economics,
All of it is born of human greed.
Moderation is the key to contentment,
Lesser the needs the happier you are.
Grow up and get hold of your needs,
Learn to tell necessities from desire.
Cherish the little things in life,
Value people over possession.
A healthy society is born of healthy mind,
Health begins where ends self-obsession.
Sophistication is an enemy of life.
A life of simplicity is bound to thrive.

I Dream of A World Civilized (The Sonnet)

I dream of a world civilized,
Where color of skin is nothing.
But when I look at the present,
It poses a challenge to my dreaming.
I envision a society night and day,
Where law is not necessary.
But when I look at the world today,
I realize how far it's from reality.
I dream of a world most human,
Beyond all gender and sexuality.
But when I look at the moment's truth,
It is far too distant from that humanity.
Yet difficulties only add value to a dream.
If not today when will our journey begin!

The Juneteenth Sonnet

Once upon a time but not long ago,
They brought us to America in chains.
Thinking of themselves as superior race,
White barbarians kept us as slaves.
But the sapling of humanity found a way,
To break those chains causing ascension.
Whites and blacks all stood up together,
And lighted the torch of emancipation.
Juneteenth is now declared holiday,
Yet to some it feels like a critical dishonor.
The human race comes from a black mother,
Yet they treat people of color as inferior.
The America handed to us is far from civilized.
But together we'll make our home humanized.

Sonnet of National Obligation

When a nation is founded on terrorism,
It has an obligation for self-improvement.
If admitting the past hurts your feelings,
Better remain in your mother's basement.
If we really look for filth and atrocities,
We'll find it in the history of every nation.
The real problem is not the history,
But the absolute denial of its admission.
No nation can become civilized,
Till it steps up to right the wrongs.
Admit the errors of our ancestors,
And pledge to never repeat those harms.
Humanity begins with admitting inhumanity.
Lo we are the shield against further atrocity.

Sonnet of Abortion

My body, my decision,
Whether I choose birth or abortion.
Till a state can care for the newborn,
No bill is qualified to offer resolution.
Instead of controlling my birth canal,
Work on carving a paradigm of equality.
Build a world where a newborn is a gift,
Not a burden on life, dream or economy.
Abolish all disparities born of greed,
Strip the wealthy of their ill-gotten riches.
Use all resources for collective welfare,
So that status ends up on history pages.
Worse than aborting is birthing in instability.
I'll give birth when I need not rely on pity.

Breathing While Black (The Sonnet)

White folks think before going to work,
Hope I don’t run into traffic on the way.
Black folks think before going to work,
Hope I don't get shot and make it safe.
White folks think before going to jog,
Hope the park is not much crowded.
Black folks think before going to jog,
Hope I don't run into someone bigoted.
White folks teach their kids before school,
Don't you dare talk to strangers.
Black folks beg their kids on knees,
Don't act smart when approached by coppers.
Whites can dream of being big and creative.
All we blacks can dream of is being able to live.

Unselfish Sonnet

Unself your soul,
And lo the joy pours.
Wipe out the I,
And the world is yours.
The more selfish you are,
The more anxious you'll be.
One who's lost in service,
Is the epitome of humanity.
In a world of self-obsession,
Be the spark most selfless.
Burn yourself to ashes,
Let all bathe in your kindness.
To give is to live o human.
To die for others is salvation.

Leap Beyond Libido (The Sonnet)

Brotherhood won't do,
Nor will sisterhood.
What the world really needs,
Is a sense of humanhood.
So long as gender lingers,
In the behavior of human.
We'll not have a society,
Free from sexualization.
Genitalia have no role in society,
Other than in bed.
When you leap beyond libido,
Even a naked body seems sacred.
The body has evolved to crave for release,
But a well-built character is hard to please.

Sonnet of Breastfeeding

From the breasts a world is fed,
With their warmth society is raised.
Yet we ignore their sacred place,
Without breasts we'll all be erased.
Woman's breasts are not objects,
With or without a baby clinging.
We may hail them means of pleasure,
Only when the person is asking.
Way more than triggers of romance,
Breasts are symbolic of motherhood.
A society that doesn't respect mothers,
Will never ever attain humanhood.
A world that is safe for mothers,
Is safe for all beyond age and genders.

25. Girl Over God

Dear Vatican (The Sonnet)

You took a man,
And turned him savior,
You took his love,
And vilified her honor.
You cooked up stories,
And added some magic,
Put in a few guilt traps,
Everything was copasetic.
You sanctioned four books,
Buried the rest for blasphemy,
For you wanted no one to know,
JC was a mortal practicing humanity.
You wanna know what is holiness?
Burn your bible and rush to the helpless.

A Dingbat Lover (The Sonnet)

Better be a dingbat in love,
Than play ping-pong with hearts.
Better be bonkers in sacrifice,
Than an arrogant smartypants.
Better give all without reserve,
Than be selfish and just take.
Better be wiped out in service,
Than take greed to your grave.
Better look idiot and learn,
Than be proud and stagnant.
Better be trusting and cheated,
Than a cynic scraping love's remnant.
There is no guarantee in life and love.
If you want guarantee open a liquor shop.

Science and Religion (The Sonnet)

Science and Religion have no feud,
Both are expressions of naturalism.
The real feud has been between,
Intellectualism and fundamentalism.
Facts help us take the world forward,
Reason helps us treat primitiveness.
But facts and reason alone won't do,
Without warmth all matter is lifeless.
Of course there are flaws in religion,
In science too there's greed and bigotry.
If in religion we have extremist nuts,
We also have plenty of scientific bully.
Instead of picking on each other's mistake,
Let us be human across intellect and faith.

How to Love (The Sonnet)

How do I love thee?
Lemme count the ways.
No wait, why bother counting,
When I can shower you with praise!
When there's sunshine on your face,
Lemme drink it like miracle syrup.
When your soul is blue and cloudy,
Lemme be your personal stand-up.
Your achievements are my own,
As such they boost my swag.
When you are mad at yourself,
Lemme be your punching bag.
Give me your body or not, I don't care.
I just wanna be there to wipe your every tear.

26. Gente Mente Adelante

Sonnet of Fundamentals

Equality, harmony, diversity,
These are not something you believe.
Just like water, air and food,
These are not something you believe.
Fundamentals of human life,
Are beyond all pettiness of opinion.
Argumentation may have its place,
But we must distinguish facts from fiction.
Plenty are the minds so are the beliefs,
But beliefs mustn't undermine humanity.
All of us are dumb, some less some more,
So we must place people before rigidity.
No belief is ultimate, no opinion olympian.
Putting aside truth, let us first be human.

Ever Onward to Equality (The Sonnet)

Someone once said,
Ever onward to victory.
I say to you today,
Ever onward to equality.
Though the objective is the same,
In path lies the distinction.
I'll say it plainly, to live is to grow,
Including the means of revolution.
Liberty is fundamental in life,
But not by harming the innocent.
Revolution of arms is revolution no more,
What's needed is revolution in conscience.
So I say, let us sacrifice all for society.
Let us rise as soldiers of universal amity.

Crazy Not Callous (The Sonnet)

I'm crazy,
But not obnoxious.
I'm free in mind,
But not callous.
I'm ignorant in many things,
But I ain't no intolerant.
I may not know much etiquette,
I know caring with commitment.
I am but a lover most naïve,
No scholar of nothin'.
I am but a warrior unbending,
Got no time for philosophizin'.
To live for people is the mission.
In lifting the fallen lies salvation.

Gun-Fetish (The Sonnet)

When I was in my teenage years,
I believed, having a gun would be so cool.
Then I grew up and it occurred to me,
Firearm fetish is but hysteria of the fool.
Guns don't make the society safe,
Any more than nukes ensure world peace.
Civilians carrying personal firearm,
Are but rabid dogs without a leash.
If you are worried about self-defense,
Daily practice some form of martial arts.
Your gun is not only a threat to you,
It is also a threat to your loved ones.
So I beg you my responsible civilian sibling,
Give up your gun and uphold peacemaking.

Sonnet of Martial Arts

The secret to Martial Arts,
Is not style but training.
Pick any form that appeals to you,
And train regularly without failing.
Practice a hundred moves five times,
It is of no use whatsoever.
But practice one move every day,
And it'll be your lifetime protector.
But before all that ask yourself,
Why do you wanna be a martial artist?
Is it to nourish an able mind and body,
Or to be yet another fitness narcissist?
Trash all your arrogance before training.
A martial artist is to be gentle and caring.

The Golden Sonnet

Where is el dorado?
It is not a city but a person.
Where is the kingdom of heaven?
It is not a place but compassion.
Where can we find joy?
Not the market but in acts of goodness.
Where can we find health?
Not in gadgets but in simpleness.
Where can we find strength?
Not in the bank but in character.
How can we make progress?
Not with luxury but by lifting the other.
Lesser the needs, better the life.
Gentler the soul, lighter the strife.

Flag Cruelty Fraught (The New American Anthem)

Say, can you see,
The darkness we've caused?
Our star spangled banner,
Is a flag cruelty fraught.
It ain't land of the free,
It ain't home of the brave.
Where looks define dignity,
Is but humanity's grave.
Slavery is alive as racism,
Bigotry still claims dominion.
First we must treat these ailments,
Or else, for us there is no dawn.
O say, it's time to abolish all false glory.
Forget valor, let's first practice equality.

Sonnet of Climate Change

No matter whether you are loaded,
All the world's money won't save your child.
As our climate gets further compromised,
The rich and poor will suffer and die alike.
Industry gave us affluence and advancement,
But at the expense of our planet's wellbeing.
Our ancestors couldn't fathom it back then,
We don't have their luxury to be greedy fiend.
We barely have a decade to reduce emission,
After that all the prayers won't rescue humanity.
You think things have been hard in your life,
Wait till you hear in grave your children's agony.
Enough with this bickering over phony regulation!
Discard all luxury and reduce individual emission.

Be Unrealistic (The Sonnet)

Be unrealistic and work for a world,
That the society considers nonsense.
Once upon a time taming fire was unreal,
Then arose a bunch of brave sentience.
Today's madness is tomorrow's sanity,
If we're mad enough to stand solo on guard.
Today's sacrifice is tomorrow's civilization,
If we can give all without hoping reward.
If only one person dies for the cause,
A hundred people realize their humanity.
I may die today in the line of duty,
But the struggle continues through eternity.
So let us be brave and go beyond reality.
Let us be accountable and do the necessary.

Love Alone Triumphs (The Sonnet)

Great people have often said,
Truth alone triumphs.
I am no great but a plain human,
So I say, love alone triumphs.
Truth may require intellect,
Inquiry requires some cynicism.
To be loving needs none of that,
Love lights up the darkest chasm.
Keep your intellect if you desire,
Explore further the arc of truth.
But all the discovery means nothing,
If countless souls go without food.
It is far better to be an insane lover,
Than to be a heartless discoverer.

Lift Others (The Sonnet)

If you want to lift your spirit,
Lift others.
If you want to help yourself,
Help others.
If you want to find happiness,
Forget about happiness.
If you want to discover joy,
Just give without selfishness.
Be crazy, loco and bonkers,
For the welfare of others.
The only kingdom of heaven,
Is in cheering someone who suffers.
Better than self-help is unself-help,
For the rise of people is rise of the self.

No Rest (The Sonnet)

There is no rest,
Till the last drop of tear is wiped out.
There is no leisure,
Till the voiceless can speak aloud.
There is no relaxing,
Till the last empty stomach is fed.
There is no sleep,
Till all droopy spines are made straight.
There is no joy,
Till the last grey life is colored.
There is no comfort,
Till the last anxious soul is empowered.
The struggle isn't over till the fallen rise.
Security later, first let us be civilized.

Hola, Soy GORA (The Sonnet)

Hermanas y hermanos, hola, soy GORA,
Guerrero, Observador, Reformador, Amante.
Thus speaks the human practicing humanity,
Despite all agony, no retrocedas oh valiente!
To the helpless, destitute and discriminated,
I am but a nameless servant most humble.
To lift the fallen and make them self-reliant,
Is the purpose of my life, straight and simple.
Beware o peddlers of hate and bigotry,
Get hold of your prejudice and hysteria!
When calm, reformist mind brings light,
When enraged, it is the fabled chupacabra!
Each conscientious being is reform incarnate.
From your humane struggle never you deviate.

27. Earthquakin' Egalitarian

New Melody (The Sonnet)

What is this new melody,
That I hear on my guitar!
What is this new tune,
That makes squabbles disappear!
What is this new serenade,
Calling upon a headstrong wind!
Whose are the footsteps I hear,
With such vigor yet gentle and kind!
Amidst the cacophony of cockiness,
What is this heartbeat of sacrifice!
Amidst the drumbeats of individualism,
What is this new desire to universalize!
What is this new voice of sanity I hear!
It is you and me, the branded blasphemer.

I Want The Golden World (The Sonnet)

No matter what you say,
I want the golden world.
To hell with the sayers of nay,
I keep working without reward.
You may have your comfort,
Enjoy all your luxuries futile.
For me there's no other joy,
Like making someone smile.
All you do is take and take,
Yet I have nothing against thee.
Just remember that one day,
You shall die of obesity.
Vegetables can mock all they want.
I shall die building the golden world.

My Golden Earth (The Sonnet)

O my golden earth,
I am but your stupid lover.
The flute of your dazzling fragrance,
Makes my agonies disappear.
Whenever your sky is cloudy,
My heart drowns in drought.
Whenever your oceans quiver,
With tears my eyes get fraught.
Whenever you giggle in prosperity,
It pours honey into my ears.
Whenever you shine with festivals,
Light and love erase my historic fears.
You are my home o my golden earth.
All your children are my sisters and brothers.

Latin not Lethal (The Sonnet)

Yes I am latino and proud,
That doesn't make me a thug.
Yes I am brown in color and loud,
That doesn't mean I'm a lethal bug.
Some of us can't speak English,
That doesn't make us second-rate.
We care for family as much as you,
In friendship we walk to the world's end.
Savage imperialists walked on our corpses,
While they snatched our lands and homes.
Yet you call us illegal and dangerous,
Showing no remorse or desire to atone!
None of us can undo the past I know.
Our kids may walk together, let's make sure.

Sonnet of A Religious Person

I spent years as a Christian,
I didn't find God.
I spent years as a Muslim,
I didn't find God.
I spent years as Hindu and Sikh,
Still there was no inkling.
I spent years as Buddhist and Atheist,
Still I understood nothing.
I did it all, prayers, rituals, meditation,
None of it brought me serenity.
For serenity has been all along,
At the feet of the ailing humanity.
I shelved all scriptures and stood as human.
Kindness alone is the sign of a religious person.

Heart Humanish (The Sonnet)

I am but a simple sufi,
What'll I do with applause!
If you want to give something,
Lend a corner in the heart of yours.
I am but a fumbling fakir,
What'll I do with all the gold!
Only with the touch of a kind heart,
We shall bring prosperity in our world.
I am but an ignorant dervish,
I don't know much ayat and psalm.
All I know is, love is the breath of life,
Without it, all progress is harm.
Rituals and intellect all will perish,
What will live on is the heart humanish.

Gamblers of Rigidity (The Sonnet)

Rigidity in the name of religion,
Will fill this world with tears and fear.
Prejudice in the name of tradition,
Will turn this land into a graveyard.
Doctrines are truth for dumbbells,
Holy books are life for the unholy.
Hear all fools, all rigid corpses,
Love is the only sign of divinity.
Let us lose religion if we do,
We'll stand proudly as human beings.
Let us lose all faith and allegiance,
We'll live as lovers, not fragmented fiends.
There's no future for gamblers of rigidity.
Let us step forward with reason and amity.

Worship of Chains (The Sonnet)

Enough with the worship of chains!
Enough with celebration of selfishness!
Time it is to shatter the altars of separation.
Time it is to be the ravager of primitiveness.
Let us hang all our sectarian gods and idols.
Let us start a new worship of love and liberty.
Let us be prophets and messengers of harmony.
Let us be disintegrated in realization of inclusivity.
Let us go insane and kick all prison-gates down.
Let us burn locks to ashes with flames of heart.
Let us call upon the vigor eternal from within.
Let us hunt down the last trace of inhuman dirt.
Let us draw a noble anatomy for civilization.
Let us lay ourselves as cornerstones of ascension.

Break Destiny (The Sonnet)

Be the one to make and break destiny,
For all powers of universe are in you.
Be the one to make and break paradigm,
For the very source of creation is you.
Cowards and vegetables talk of fate,
While the valiant is up and working.
Those who can't do mock the doer,
Yet there's no progress without a dingaling.
If taking a stand makes you a nutcase,
Be the nuttiest case that has ever walked.
But never you compromise with insanity,
Even if it is endorsed by the whole world.
You are the defender of all society.
Even in hardship never forget your duty.

My Lady Liberty (The Sonnet)

O my beloved lady liberty,
Here, I place my head at your feet.
The way you've been upholding freedom,
May I live as vigorous without greed.
You have given refuge to the persecuted,
You have shown light to the distressed.
May I be as upright as you my dear,
May my life shelter the meek and repressed.
Let me absorb you through my every pore,
So I may draw from your eternal strength.
The way you stand as testament of justice,
May I stand as steady giving up my last breath.
I can never repay my debt to you lady liberty.
Take my life and use it as ointment for society.

Just A Human Sonnet

Emotion first,
Attire later.
Simplicity first,
Sovereignty later.
Friendship first,
Faith later.
Goodness first,
God later.
Morality first,
Nationality later.
Peace first,
Patriotism later.
Let nothing be a hindrance to humanity,
Fulfillment of life lies in universality.

My Sight is You (The Sonnet)

My sight is you,
My faith is you.
I give all to thee,
For my life is you.
In my heart are you,
In my soul are you.
I can live without air,
But not without you.
My heaven is you,
My treasure is you.
I don't need no palace,
All I want is you.
My science is you, my art is you.
The morning of my mind is you.

My Liberty (The Sonnet)

My liberty is not in luxury,
My liberty is on the blades of grass.
My liberty is not in the palace,
My liberty is in molecules of dust.
My liberty is not in fancy ceremonies,
My liberty is in alleys of the homeless.
My liberty is not in the crown jewels,
My liberty is at the feet of the pathless.
My liberty is not in murals of rigidity,
My liberty is across tradition's torment.
My liberty is not in the habits of history,
My liberty is in building the present.
My liberty is in the destruction of destiny.
I am liberty incarnate and I write my own reality.

Praise (The Sonnet)

In praising myself,
I only insult myself.
In pleasing myself,
I bring misery upon myself.
Lots of things I bought,
Plenty places I travelled.
Nothing gave me the bliss I seek,
No matter how much I groveled.
Then I stopped wanting things,
I ceased craving for gratification.
I placed my heart at your feet,
Finally I found my absolution.
Long was I lost in the sleep of pride.
Erasing the self I found my light.

Brave (The Sonnet)

Say o brave, o soldier of eternal heights,
May I be decapitated before my head bows.
Say o brave, o explorer of impossibility,
May I feed another while my stomach growls.
Say o brave, o pedestrian of purity,
I obey no law for I'm the epitome of rightness.
Say o brave, o athlete of amor and amity,
I am sheer insanity exuding real saneness.
Say o brave, o bearer of benevolence,
I am disaster, blaster and master of destiny.
Say o brave, o vessel of valiance,
I devour fear, greed, pride and insecurity.
Say o brave, I am the seed of all assimilation,
The first one standing, earthquakin' egalitarian.

28. Giants in Jeans

Will You Be My Poetry (The Sonnet)

You keep calling me a poet,
I embrace the sentiment but not the title.
I may have some power over words,
But the words themselves are nothing valuable.
It's the world behind the words that matters,
A world where all walls collapse and wither.
Once you wake up to that world,
Save human, all other titles disappear.
In that world of oneness you shall discover,
My words are not the real poetry.
My true poetry is your own humanness,
I am but a reflection of your struggling humanity.
So let's get rid of this poet and reader business!
You be my poetry, I'll be your pages.

I Write to Destroy You (The Sonnet)

I don't write to pamper your ego,
I don't write to give you comfort.
I don't write to teach you self-love,
I write to destroy all selfish thought.
I don't write to inspire your pride,
I don't write to cater to your insecurity.
I don't write to entertain shallowness,
I only write to abolish self-centricity.
I don't write to tickle the instaslaves,
I don't write to peddle false perfection.
I don't write to lick the privileged boots,
I write to make soldiers of self-annihilation.
My science and my art were born on the street.
That's where I learnt, all suffering is born of greed.

Giants in Jeans Sonnet 3

Greed fosters desire,
Desire further facilitates greed.
The more you entertain it all,
The more you're stuck in a suffering-spree.
Now the question to ask is,
How do we break free from this living hell?
It is rather simple and straight forward,
Refute submission to all primitive spell.
Wildlife demands selfishness,
For it's the law of primitive existence.
But the law of civilization is,
Civilized life is defined by kindness.
Stand up as human against the animal's desire.
Be the bold-spirited, unselfish world-maker.

Giants in Jeans Sonnet 4

How to build a world,
When there is no instruction manual!
You don't need no instruction,
For you are the world and the manual.
You are the creator as well as the creation,
Your two hands are hands of destiny.
Once you set your mind to building a society,
All peddlers of division will beg for mercy.
You are not the second coming,
For you are the first and one of a kind.
Holding the hands of these firsts through ages,
The world advances leaving savageries behind.
This my friend is the motto of world-building,
Live life as a future human amidst bigoted vermin.

Sonnet of Enlightenment

World is born when individual is born.
Individual is born when collectivity is realized.
Collectivity is realized when selfishness is erased.
Selfishness is erased when love is universalized.
Love is universalized when separation is destroyed.
Separation is destroyed when superstition is crushed.
Superstition is crushed when reason is nourished.
Reason is nourished when correction is desired.
Correction is desired when ignorance is recognized.
Ignorance is recognized when arrogance is abolished.
Arrogance is abolished when humility is fostered.
Humility is fostered when simplicity is habit.
Simplicity is habit when awareness awakens.
Awareness awakens when expansion awakens.

Giants in Jeans Sonnet 6

Expansion is health,
Expansion is sanity.
Contraction is sickness,
Contraction is animality.
In expansion there is civilization,
In expansion there is humanity.
Defy everything that makes you narrow,
Defy everything that facilitates bigotry.
Expansion is another name for life,
The life of a human who's responsible.
Animals can practice errors as tradition,
But for a human self-correction is highest struggle.
Self-correction wipes out all walls of division.
Lesser the walls greater the expansion.

Sonnet of Moronity

Eraser is not for the one,
Who makes an error.
Eraser is for the one,
Who is a self-corrector.
Hence pages of our paradigm are filled,
With many heinous mistakes.
While some of them are born of implicit bias,
Most are just plain boneheadedness.
It is one thing to be stoked about progress,
And quite another to be aware of its purpose.
If we forget the point behind it all,
Vultures will feed on our fancy carcass.
Purpose of progress is to lift all humanity,
Not to pamper the elites' moronity.

Giants in Jeans Sonnet 8

Elitism is moronism,
For it facilitates disparity.
A world built to worship the elites,
Is a kingdom infested with moronity.
Call yourself human the day,
A billionaire and a janitor are equal to you.
Until then with every bit of your snobbery,
You are only making disparities brew.
Equity, justice and inclusion,
All begin not in the Capitol but at home.
Even alone, if you can practice those tenets,
That's when your sentience is truly honed.
To a struggling stranger if you cannot lend a hand,
Our world will remain a decadent wasteland.

Giants in Jeans Sonnet 9

Thread by thread fabric is made.
Heart by heart community is made.
Star by star the sky is made.
Shoulder to shoulder the world is made.
The power of one is the power of all,
Wilderness is another name for divisionism.
When we are together we are civilized,
Civilization is synonym for nonsectarianism.
But the tragedy of the world is,
Each thread thinks they are all important.
And the problems faced by others,
Are all considered insignificant.
A world where callousness is assumed cool,
Is but a billion-dollar grave of the fool.

Billion-Dollar Grave (The Sonnet)

All our life we work hard to buy golden chains.
With which we then bind ourselves.
What's the point of living as fancy slaves?
What will we do with our billion-dollar graves?
We sit on our couch covering our eyes,
Then we yell, why everything is so very dark!
But no one hears for they are also shouting,
Praying for a messiah to bring back life's spark.
We've forged fascist fences out of all our gold,
And have placed them as walls around us.
Then we shout out - help, help,
And beg to be saved by the universe!
Greed of dollar is the toxic mold on the green of life.
Life flourishes on moderation, not consumerist strife.

Sonnet of Consumerism

Ever wonder in a world of consumerism,
Who's the consumer, who's the product!
You may think that you are the one owning things,
But it's the things that own you, head and heart.
When unmoderated materialism is the world's norm,
Consumer is the product, product does the consuming.
And this insanity is revered as industrial growth,
Then they wonder, why is there so much suffering!
The point is, your insecurity is good for business,
The shallower you are, the more your pocket empties.
But if you don't wanna end up at la casa de loco,
Stop living in products and focus on memories.
Corporations chasing revenue cause economic disparity.
Buy less, buy local, to construct a sustainable economy.

Giants in Jeans Sonnet 12

If you wanna see economic equity,
Start by supporting your local business.
One small business in one small neighborhood,
Is the backbone of sustainable economic progress.
Amplifying revenue by catering to emptiness,
Is the mark of a stone-age transaction.
There is nothing wrong in producing revenue,
But it mustn't come through exploitation.
Business is good for social advancement,
But business without humanity is regress.
Most companies see consumer welfare secondary,
Their goal is to increase the number of slaves.
Corporate social responsibility is only a PR stunt.
Business with warmth lasts forever in people's heart.

Against Nothing (The Sonnet)

I am not against consumerism,
I am not against corporations.
I am not against politics and policy,
I am not against politicians.
I am not against fame and fortune,
I am not against celebrity.
I am not against entrepreneurship,
I am not against technology.
I am not against bureaucrats,
I am not against red tape.
I am not against bibles and comics,
I am not against prayers and faith.
I ain't against anything that serves human welfare.
The moment they go astray, I'll be their nightmare.

Environment and Development (The Sonnet)

Environment is not more important than development,
Development is not more important than environment.
Since we no longer live in the wilderness as animals,
We must make both work together in agreement.
Why do we need to wipe out forests and lakes,
To lay the foundation for growth and prosperity!
With our achievements in science and tech,
We can build modern cities nestled in greenery.
Unfortunately, once the green of dollar starts rolling in,
Green of nature goes out of the window.
The real problem is the mindset of profits over people,
It has nothing to do with our desire to grow.
Let us find harmony between concrete and nature.
Without harming earth, let us build green skyscrapers.

Giants in Jeans Sonnet 15

I am the craftsman,
I am the craft.
I am the artist,
I am the art.
I am the infinity,
I am absolution.
I am impossibility,
I am the solution.
I am the just,
As well as justice.
I am equality,
As well as its means.
There's always a way, so long as I exist,
And I exist wherever there's a Universalist.

Giants in Jeans Sonnet 16

In case you are wondering,
What is a universalist!
Let me make it very clear,
It is one who lives above all ist.
Then you may question,
Isn't universalism another ism!
To which I ask you,
Is drinking water hydrationism?
There's a ton of words,
That we are compelled to use.
But to realize life,
We must step across linguistic abuse.
Still if universalism causes in you friction,
Let us just call it assimilation.

Giants in Jeans Sonnet 17

I've said this before, I'll say it again,
Don't be rigid with words and terminology.
Take the leap across language,
Then you shall witness life's vivacity.
Words serve their purpose,
When you use them to erase divide.
In every other situation,
Words and terms cause nothing but strife.
This comes from a person,
Whose very life is rooted in words.
If I can consider words secondary,
So can you break your wordly walls.
Leave the fight over words to couch philosophers.
Much work remains for us the world builders.

Sonnet of Grammar

Grammar, Oh Grammar,
Whatever you are,
Go away and bother,
The intellectual scholar.
I ain't no intellectual,
Nor am I a scholar,
So bother me not,
With your snobbish affair.
My words come from the soil,
My structure is born on the street.
I didn't even graduate college,
What do I know about literary creed!
Time has come for me to put you in place.
Be an aid to discourse, not an uptight nutcase!

Giants in Jeans Sonnet 19

Be humble to the lowly,
And gentle to weak.
Be a dinosaur to the phony,
And a stone wall to the critic.
It is a mad, mad world,
Where the naïve is up for abuse.
Be naïve and simple on the inside,
But learn when it's time to act a douche.
Some bullies only understand strength,
If needed keep your strength at hand.
A few firm roars of your conviction,
Will make the oppressors wet their pants.
But be very cautious while using your strength,
Reckless power turns even a saint into tyrant.

Giants in Jeans Sonnet 20

Who’s the saint, who’s the tyrant,
Is not determined by the show of strength.
Real mark of human character,
Lies in your gentleness radiant.
The strongest souls on earth,
Keep their strength hidden unless needed,
Whereas the shallow and the entitled,
Walk around trotting over the hearts of the helpless.
Turning the other cheek to the oppressor,
May work in a world of fairies.
In our primitive world of organic apes,
Turning the other cheek means aiding inhumanities.
Love is the only answer, there is no question,
But it is a lover's duty to stand up to oppression.

Giants in Jeans Sonnet 21

In what world love means complacency?
Definitely not a human world.
In what world love means tolerating hate?
Definitely not a human world.
In what world love means allowing more harm?
Definitely not a human world.
In what world love means agreeing with bigots?
Definitely not a human world.
In what world love means aiding barbarians?
Definitely not a human world.
In what world love means supporting superstition?
Definitely not a human world.
Being loving doesn't mean letting the hate continue.
It means standing up to make all hate stop with you.

Giants in Jeans Sonnet 22

If the world is messed up,
We may not be the cause of it.
But if we die leaving it the same,
We are nothing but bags of wind.
Society wasn't built on equity,
Nor was it built on principles of justice.
All was founded on exploitation of the lowly,
And some modern apes still can't get over it.
Till today the rich talk about equality,
While flying in their private jets.
Things get even more hypocritical and wacky,
When they talk about climate change.
However, we can still make this world better,
We just have to actually start living simpler.

Giants in Jeans Sonnet 23

Simple life starts with a simple heart,
A heart not congested with selfish desire.
The more you have things that you want,
The less you have things that matter.
Sooner or later we gotta grow up,
However chances are that we won't.
And when that is the case for humankind,
I'm terrified of what's headed our civilized coast.
Materialism has made a mockery of sanity,
Industry has flourished upon that mockery.
Such insanity may have suited our ancestors,
But does it suit pedestrians of universality!
I don't want you to weep over our failures.
All I ask, let's advance not as slaves but world builders.

Giants in Jeans Sonnet 24

Who is to build the world?
Who is to raise the society?
Who is to water the plants?
Who is to stand up for sanity?
Who is to bear agony for community?
Who is to go hungry feeding another?
Who is to heal the sick while bleeding?
Who is to lift the lowly trotting fire?
Who is to burn alive to bring light?
Who is to walk on thorns to build the bridge?
Who is to be deceived yet stay humble?
Who is to lay down so others can climb the ridge?
It is you, o misfit, o explorer of impossibility,
Even if no one joins us, our world is our responsibility!

Giants in Jeans Sonnet 25

Wanna know about people's character?
Walk around in shabby clothes.
Wanna know who's wise, who's egotistical?
Be the dumbest despite your brainforce.
Never try to impress people.
The more you try, the more they lose interest.
Nourish your warmth and kindness instead,
Those who care will reach out themselves.
But always remember one little thing,
You can either have life or calculation.
Calculate where it's needed,
But not in every situation.
Lovers and soldiers are the only ones living,
Rest of society is just dehydrating.

Giants in Jeans Sonnet 26

H2O may be water of earth,
But water of heart is love.
Without love the land of heart,
Ends up as infertile dirt.
So I say to you, oh being of heart,
Never be a miser in matters of love!
Give out love to family and stranger alike,
The more you give the more you'll have!
Love is the only thing in the world,
That dries up the more you try hoarding.
Be a robeless hobo if needed,
But never restrain your spree of giving.
Now let me tell you a secret of advanced economy.
Only with giving shall we wipe out financial disparity.

Sonnet of Charity

Charity doesn't end disparity,
It only postpones it.
Giving doesn't mean only giving,
It means lifting the fallen spirit.
With one hand help those in need,
With another treat their environment.
Don't just give money to the destitute,
Lift them up so they could help themselves.
The greatest charity in the world,
Is to help someone become self-reliant,
So that they do not need charity,
From anyone ever again.
Purpose of charity is not to build a world of charity,
Purpose of charity is to end the need for charity.

Giants in Jeans Sonnet 28

Kindness is saneness,
All else is vainness.
Better kind and be deceived,
Than live with emptiness.
To have a life of joy,
Be joy to others.
Your life will be truly whole,
When you stand up for another.
Life isn't a product,
That you can find at BestBuy.
You shall discover life when,
For others your pleasures go awry.
Pleasure has nothing to do with human life.
Life is in helping others and relieving their strife.

Giants in Jeans Sonnet 29

Awake, Arise and Walk the Talk,
Be the reason for someone's smile.
Read a few books, you'll live a little,
Help another and you'll live a lifetime.
Kindness is the only sign of life,
Not a lifestyle of luxury and riches.
Despite having all if you don't know to help,
You're but an animal of the wilderness.
What is the point of a life,
That has no bearing on social uplift!
Accountability is humanity,
Indifference is mark of an egotist.
Whole world is hometown for the being who's human.
But for self-obsessed savages even the hood is martian.

Giants in Jeans Sonnet 30

Earth and Mars, what is the difference,
Mars is barren, Earth isn't much behind!
Mars is barren for there's no advanced species,
Earth is made barren by its native intelligent kind.
We haven't yet learnt to take care of Earth,
Yet we are now headed for Mars as colonizer.
With the money it'll take to get to Mars,
We can literally end world hunger.
Mark you, I am not against space exploration,
But there's what I call existential priority.
I guess robots who vacation at high altitude,
Are least likely to fathom what's humanity.
Advancement that ignores human suffering,
After a brief flight, eventually brings universal ruin.

Giants in Jeans Sonnet 31

Progress is a messy term,
Which in theory means ascension.
But in practice it means serving the wealthy,
And to hell with the rest of the humans!
When reckless monkeys start making rockets,
They behave like some fancy junkie.
When nuts and bolts hypnotize the apes,
Equity, justice and honor feel secondary.
Traditions have been ruling human behavior,
Now technology has cast a spell on society.
Just like mindless traditions are dangerous,
Heartless technology is injurious to humanity.
Traditions and technology both can be a boon,
Yet as of today, they sustain a world of fools.

Giants in Jeans Sonnet 32

Some people still say,
Women belong in the kitchen.
By that same logic,
Men belong in the jungle.
Traditions of yesterday
Cannot be the standard for today,
Ethics and logic of primitives,
Cannot be the measure of civilized way.
Each generation must find themselves,
They must rewrite their own code.
Better to die in the course of ascension,
Than to survive in hypnotized mode.
Cut off all allegiance to the dead and dark,
As new humans build your own moral arc.

Giants in Jeans Sonnet 33

For rotten corpses tradition is life,
For heartless robots greatest faculty is logic.
Yet it is combining tradition and logic,
Shall we emerge as beings sapient and heroic.
We must use reason to scrutinize tradition,
We must use warmth to moderate logic.
When we put reason and warmth together,
We are endowed with powers terrific.
Sometimes we gotta compromise logic,
Sometimes we gotta compromise tradition.
We shall recognize which is needed when,
When we live as wholesome human.
It all begins when we throw rigidity overboard,
Opposing nothing that reduces discord.

Giants in Jeans Sonnet 34

Be the breaker of discord,
Be the maker of harmony.
Be the taker of agony,
Be the giver of amity.
Be the light to the dark,
Be the might to the meek.
Be the kite to the fallen,
Be the sight for 'em to peek.
Be the heart that burns bright,
Be the hand that answers plight.
Be the feet that ignore fright,
Be the head that walks upright.
Rather than being a lazy descendant,
Be the reason for a future radiant.

Giants in Jeans Sonnet 35

Future is just imagination,
And the past is nothing but memory.
But what we must keep in mind is,
The present contains the infinity.
Present is called present,
For it holds the gift of creation.
You decide whether you'll use it to create,
Or waste it on anxiety and illusion.
Draw lessons from the past,
As well as from futuristic imaginations.
But do not let them cripple you,
As illusory obstructions to action.
Feet firmly on present spread your sight far and wide,
And you shall rise as the master of time and tide.

Giants in Jeans Sonnet 36

Time and tide rule the coward,
While the valiant makes their own time.
Take it slow and be the flow,
Leave the racing to the boneless slime.
Those who say that competition is good,
Are but primitives whose religion is dollar.
A world founded on soulless competition,
Will never be free from societal disorder.
Have some regard for the worth of life,
Dishonor it not by treating as NASCAR.
Feel, think and behave as a human being,
Not as a preprogrammed teleprompter.
The rivers and birds fear no competition,
Yet without them the world cannot function.

Sonnet of Nature

What do the rivers do?
Give water for our thirst.
What do the trees do?
Give air for our lungs.
What do the animals do?
Give food for our tummy.
What do the flowers do?
Give fragrance for our body.
After taking everything,
From every member of nature,
What do we pompous idiots do?
Destroy all natural order.
It's high time to get our act together.
Nature doesn't need us, but we need her.

Sonnet of Renewable Energy

There is a plug point in the sky,
Which is beaming electricity 24/7.
Yet we drill holes into the earth,
To suck oil and power our concrete heaven.
When humankind first started drilling,
They had no idea of its implication.
But eventually scientists raised warnings,
Yet drilling continued due to lack of efficient solution.
Fossil fuel has already damaged the climate,
And we no longer have time for scholarly fight.
So I say to scientists, engineers and entrepreneurs,
Come up with affordable home solar-grid.
Electric cars won't do anything for climate emergency,
Unless all electricity comes from renewable energy.

Giants in Jeans Sonnet 39

The greatest renewable energy,
Is the power of human will.
If we are truly willing for reform,
Nothing in the world can make us kneel.
But we've grown accustomed to complacency,
And indifference feels rather pleasant.
That's why we let brutality continue,
While we pretend to be absolutely innocent.
This callousness has become our curse,
It has kept us apes from evolving.
If we are to ever become actually human,
To inhumanity we must stop complying.
All humanity is born of the individual.
If we are responsible so will be the world.

Giants in Jeans Sonnet 40

It has become a habit to kneel,
You keep kneeling wherever it's convenient.
Then when your submission is exploited,
You wonder why the world is so deviant.
If you want corruption to stop,
Stop facilitating it with your submission.
Instead of being a jellyfish all your life,
Feel the backbone and stand up as human.
The term human carries a lot of weight,
But in today's world it only carries dead weight.
That's because being vegetable is rather easy,
Whereas being human requires to be sentient.
So stop bending at every little situation.
Every time you bend, you break civilization.

Giants in Jeans Sonnet 41

Whatever doesn't adapt gets extinct,
But this doesn't mean adapting to inhumanity.
In fact, if living requires adapting to inhumanity,
Better die revolting than live with complacency.
In every situation ask yourself,
Is compromise at the best interest of society!
And whatever your whole conscience answers,
In that particular situation act accordingly.
We may compromise facts and reason,
When we are amidst warm people of faith.
We may compromise faith and belief,
When amidst freethinkers who know no hate.
But remember that under no circumstances,
We are to bow before hate and prejudices.

Giants in Jeans Sonnet 42

Once you start listening to prejudice,
Prejudice stops listening to you.
Once you slip into the stereotypical curve,
Stereotypes start to own the whole of you.
None of us are immune to prejudice,
That includes yours truly.
Human brain concocts prejudices,
To ensure our survivability.
Prejudices are assumptions,
That constitute the whole of perception.
Very little of our mind's reality,
Is actually free from bias and superstition.
Though we can never be fully free from prejudice,
With reason we can learn to distinguish it.

Giants in Jeans Sonnet 43

When we know not we are prejudiced,
There is no question of treating it.
When we know not we are biased,
There is no question of overcoming it.
When we know not we are bigoted,
There is no question of humanizing.
When we know not we are self-obsessed,
There is no question of universalizing.
When we know not we are sectarian,
There is no question of being nonsectarian.
When we know not we are inhuman,
There is no question of being human.
Humanity begins with the awareness of animality,
First know we are animals, then act towards diversity.

Giants in Jeans Sonnet 44

Diversity brings prosperity,
Tribalism brings tragedy.
Inclusivity brings harmony,
Exclusion brings anxiety.
Amity brings serenity,
Prejudice brings insecurity.
Affection binds community,
Mistrust breaks sanity.
Kindness kindles kinship,
Hate brews fiendship.
Goodness grows heartship,
Arrogance fosters bruteship.
Gentle beings make a gentle world.
Until it's realized, we're stuck in a jungle vault.

Giants in Jeans Sonnet 45

Who makes us primitive - nature.
Who keeps us primitive – ourselves.
Who makes us ignorant – nature.
Who keeps us ignorant – ourselves.
Who makes us tribal – nature.
Who keeps us tribal - ourselves.
Who makes us stereotypical – nature.
Who keeps us stereotypical – ourselves.
Who makes us narrow – nature.
Who keeps us narrow – ourselves.
Who makes us wild – nature.
Who keeps us wild – ourselves.
Nature still dictates plenty on how we apes move.
But she has also given us the power to improve.

Giants in Jeans Sonnet 46

Love is in everybody,
Not everybody is in love.
Power is in everybody,
Not everybody can power-up.
Everybody loves beautiful clothes,
Few care for heart's beauty.
Everybody is obsessed with liberty,
Few can bear the responsibility.
Everybody lives amidst the collective,
Only few practice collectivism.
Everybody talks about the world,
Not everybody has the world in them.
Poor is not the one whose pocket is empty,
But the one whose heart lacks comity.

Giants in Jeans Sonnet 47

Walk up to death,
And smile at your doom.
At the sight of your conviction,
Stars will begin to bloom.
Tread bravely on misery,
Defy anything that causes weakness.
At the sound of your courageous footsteps,
The soil will regain its fragrance.
Embolden your chest o mighty victor,
Against a hailstorm of ridicule.
Even the slight sound of your whisper,
Will give chills to the cruel.
Care for society, not its opinion of you.
Sacrifice all image and status, and stand up anew.

Giants in Jeans Sonnet 48

It's not about whether good things happen to you,
But whether you're a force for good to another.
It's not about whether you go to church,
But whether you're the answer to someone's prayer.
It's not about whether you make a name for yourself,
But whether you lose your character in the process.
It's not about whether your dreams come true,
But whether you forget to live as a rat in the race.
It's not about whether you bow to authority,
But whether you compromise dignity to be accepted.
It's not about whether you move fast enough,
But whether you rise up after being defeated.
The world is full with fake mottos to sustain submission.
Be a dinosaur of destiny and destroy all snobbish notion.

Giants in Jeans Sonnet 49

Vegetables have destiny,
Humans have responsibility.
Vermin have luxury,
Humans have simplicity.
Nightcrawlers have insecurity,
Humans have dignity.
Bedbugs have stability,
Humans have community.
Donkeys have self-love,
Humans have self-annihilation.
Horses have competition,
Humans have revolution.
Fancy castles of glass belong in fairy-story.
No time to rest, we have too much duty.

Giants in Jeans Sonnet 50

The more you philosophize the fundamentals of life,
The more you lose the fundamentals of life.
The more you intellectualize the essentials of life,
The less you fathom the essentials of life.
The more you dogmatize love and kindness,
The more you destroy love and kindness.
The more you argue over virtue and goodness,
The less you actually practice virtue and goodness.
The more you fight over whose ideology is the best,
The more your ideology breeds problem not solution.
The more you boast about your own culture,
The more you move astray from cultural integration.
Humans are those who place humanity above all else.
Till you realize this, you are stuck in your tribal mess.

Giants in Jeans Sonnet 51

Comfort doesn't make you grow,
Only crisis does that.
Convenience doesn't strengthen character,
Only catastrophe does that.
A candle is safe when it's not burning,
But that is not why it exists.
A ship stays steady when it's at the dock,
But its life is in the open seas.
Diamond isn't born amidst concrete luxury,
It is born in the hardship of wilderness.
A human mind isn't truly born,
Till it conquers its luxurious reliance.
If not the world, be responsible for your neighborhood.
Someone somewhere is in need of your humanhood.

Giants in Jeans Sonnet 52

Humanhood isn't him, her or them,
Humanhood requires realization beyond sex.
Pronouns may be a step in the right direction,
But they are not passport for arrogance and disrespect.
The purpose is to erase hate from society,
And we ain't gonna do that by passing judgment.
If we want there to be equity and acceptance,
We must learn to trample first our own arrogance.
Rebelling for the sake of rebelling achieves nothing,
Arrogance only produces just another bitter creature.
In trying to fight against prejudice and oppression,
Be cautious that you don't end up as the new oppressor.
Revolution is the foundation of civilization's evolution,
But it must be rooted in gentleness, not cancellation.

Giants in Jeans Sonnet 53

If you call me liberal,
You have understood nothing.
If you call me conservative,
You have understood nothing.
If you call me religious,
You have understood nothing.
If you call me atheist,
You have understood nothing.
If you call me communist,
You have understood nothing.
If you call me capitalist,
You have understood nothing.
You'll never find me in your fancy ideology,
You'll know me by taking pain to wipe another's agony.

Giants in Jeans Sonnet 54

It is human nature to shed tears in agony,
But taking pain to wipe another's tear is humanity.
It's human nature to be sad at the loss of something,
But giving up all to lift another is humanity.
It is human nature to reply harm with more harm,
But to stand unbending without violence is humanity.
It is human nature to reply argument with argument,
But knowing when to lose an argument is humanity.
It is human nature to win by dragging others down,
But defying competition to live a purpose is humanity.
It is human nature to blame disparity on politicians,
But to step up ensuring equity in one's area is humanity.
Just because it's human nature, doesn't make it civilized.
We shall be civilized when we are no longer hypnotized.

Giants in Jeans Sonnet 55

Selfishness is superstition,
Unselfishness is civilization.
Luxury is savagery,
Simple living is rejuvenation.
To live one must consume,
But over-consumption is sickness.
Gratification without moderation,
Ruins all internal wellness.
Freedom is not only life's treasure,
It is also a great responsibility.
Clothes and appearance come later,
There's no human without accountability.
Focus on the mettle of the human within,
Only then we'll be more than a selfish fiend.

Giants in Jeans Sonnet 56

Where the human is accountable,
There flourishes civilization.
Where the human is selfish,
There looms degradation.
Where the human has tasted sanity,
No possession can cause distraction.
Where the human has felt the joy of sacrifice,
Annihilation becomes the only ambition.
What does a world of self-obsession know,
About drunkenness of the lover!
A world run by cold facts and blind faith,
Considers the greedy to be sober.
So I say, to hell with such self-centric soberness,
I am better off with my life of madness.

Giants in Jeans Sonnet 57

Who is mad, who is sane,
Who's gonna decide it for whom?
In a world run by judgmental fools,
Disparity is hailed as the rule.
Luxury thrives on disparity,
Greed thrives on materialism.
That's why the paradigm we live in,
Labels kindness as impractical altruism.
Better be an impractical fool with warmth,
Than a dead ribcage without a heart.
Better be a law-defying bad samaritan,
Than a complacent bag of lard.
Only sign of sanity is in mad humanity.
Stand tall o brave, as an epitome of integrity!

Giants in Jeans Sonnet 58

Integrity doesn't come from wallet,
It comes from your character.
Yet you continue to value dollar,
Putting character on the back-burner.
Then you scream at the politicians,
For all the disparities and despair.
Never for a second you consider,
To distinguish need from desire.
More you pursue dollars and products,
Better it is for the corporate fraternity.
Your desire for limitless comfort,
Ruins you and makes them super wealthy.
Dial down your pursuit of convenience,
And then you'll experience the surge of sentience.

Giants in Jeans Sonnet 59

Suits and boots are not sentience,
Manners and etiquettes are not culture.
Intellect and technology are not progress,
Faith and tradition are not character.
Now that we've put them out of the way,
Let's talk about the matter of significance.
If you ask what that matter is,
I am talking about internal exuberance.
What is science without human warmth,
What is faith without some reason!
What is technology without community,
What is tradition without ascension!
All these are okay in their own place,
But they must be practiced with sapience.

Giants in Jeans Sonnet 60

Just because we call ourselves sapiens,
Doesn't mean we are actually sapient.
Just because we call ourselves advanced,
Doesn't mean we are not deviant.
Having an advanced brain,
Is not the same as being advanced.
When all brain is wasted on self-centricity,
We only drift away from life's vivid path.
Life is not about mechanization,
Life is not about the pursuit of comfort.
Animal life may run on self-preservation,
Either you are human or self-absorbed.
To wipe out the self is my greatest ambition.
Birth of human is in benevolent disintegration.

Giants in Jeans Sonnet 61

Integration lies in disintegration,
Where the I ends there the US begins.
Harmony lies in annihilation,
Where the tribe ends there the globe begins.
Whatever suited our ancestors,
Is not compatible with a modern society.
You can either have allegiance to borders,
Or you can have serenity and amity.
Pledging allegiance to a rag on a pole,
Is no longer a sign of well-built character.
If you wanna slogan for anything at all,
Let us slogan for sentiments beyond border.
Though born tribals, let's aim towards universality.
Let's end all foul traditions of tribal identity.

Giants in Jeans Sonnet 62

What is my identity?
What is your identity?
Why bother with all that nonsense,
Let us focus first on humanity.
Your birthplace isn't your identity,
Your culture isn't who you are.
Who you are is defined by your action,
Your conduct defines your character.
A gentle janitor is more human,
Than a condescending scientist.
A kind waitress is more human,
Than a cold, billionaire elitist.
Clothes, culture, creed, all are expendable.
Better be dead than compromise principle.

Giants in Jeans Sonnet 63

What are we without principles,
Nothing but a bag of animal flesh.
What are we without reason,
Nothing but tradition's infectious abscess.
What are we without warmth,
Nothing but insects chasing self-centricity.
What are we without collectivity,
Nothing but mechanics of monstrosity.
What are we without humility,
Nothing but a bunch of smart nimrods.
What are we without moderation,
Nothing but poisonous arthropods.
Higher the sentience, greater the responsibility,
A mind oblivious to this, is oblivious to humanity.

Giants in Jeans Sonnet 64

Let us be oblivious to security and comfort,
In our pursuit and practice of humanity.
Let us be oblivious to personal happiness,
In our endeavors into the impossibility.
Let us throw all fear and anxiety overboard,
For the dreams that'll determine our destiny.
Let us trample every foul desire for luxury,
And treat the hard problem of inhumanity.
Let us pay no heed to gain and pain,
In our course of constructing a whole society.
Let us not sit around praying for a messiah,
And stand up ourselves to carry out that duty.
Let others be oblivious to humanity if they want.
Even if it's doomsday, sapling of service we'll plant.

Giants in Jeans Sonnet 65

Doomsday is not when the earth collapses,
Nor is it the contagion of a deadly virus.
Doomsday is when humans forget humanity,
As such all of us are doomsday descendants.
There is no such thing as fall of humanity,
For humankind never rose to civilization.
Our ancestors were savages with bow and arrow,
We are modern savages with nuclear ammunition.
Each of us are raised as an incarnate of doom,
Through our veins flow the germs of selfishness.
Everybody talks of peace without realizing,
The opposite of war is not peace, it's unselfishness.
So stop worrying about the fall of civilization.
Live as human so that there actually is a civilization.

Giants in Jeans Sonnet 66

Civilization doesn't fall from the sky,
Nor is it born in the Capitol building.
The cornerstones of civilized behavior,
Are born of a character that is willing.
Civilization and degradation are born of us,
So far we've been causing degradation.
In a blind pursuit of endless revenue,
We've confused inflation with civilization.
The prime problem with the world is,
All want freedom but not accountability.
That's how vampires in suits and uniforms,
Sell segregation in the name of sovereignty.
Life comes first, then the stars and stripes,
If needed, hundred union jacks be sacrificed.

Giants in Jeans Sonnet 67

Flags on poles depict savage life,
A life civilized knows no flagmania.
Time for nationalism is long gone,
It's time to stand as one family together.
If we must pledge allegiance,
Let us pledge it to people in need.
Forget King James and Uncle Sam,
As humans and for humans let us live.
If we can lift even five lives,
Then only can we be called human.
One who contains the world in their chest,
Is the one and only civilized person.
While fools entertain hindrances to humanity,
Blood of the civilized boils at the sight of brutality.

Giants in Jeans Sonnet 68

In our so-called modern world,
Suits and brutes often go together.
People try to hide their heart's dirt,
With clean clothes and fancy manner.
If manner and fashion made human being,
All things concrete would have a golden touch.
Structure of our shelters has changed a lot,
Structure of our heart not so much.
In our walk and talk we may seem civilized,
Inside we are crawling with primeval tendencies.
But that's not really the problem here,
Real problem is our denial of these primitivities.
To be civilized we must break the spell of perfection,
For civilization is born out of willful self-correction.

Giants in Jeans Sonnet 69

Eraser is not for one who makes mistakes,
Eraser is for the one willing to correct those.
Wise is not the one who wins always,
Wise is the one who knows where to lose.
Cultured is not the one who is learned,
Cultured is the one who's above sectarianism.
Glue is not for one who breaks something,
Glue is for the one willing to fix them.
Joy doesn't come to those chasing joy,
Joy comes to those who live for a purpose.
Life doesn't come to those being reckless,
Life unfolds in the acts of the selfless.
We are all broken one way or another.
Instead of bickering, let's be strength to each other.

Giants in Jeans Sonnet 70

When we strengthen another,
We become strong ourselves.
When we make another smile,
We become happy ourselves.
When we reach down to lift another,
We lift up ourselves.
When we break ourselves to help another,
Own brokenness is healed by itself.
When we are kind for no reason,
We act as the human we ought to be.
When we lose the self in helping another,
We regain the self with honor and glory.
Key to your life is in another's heart.
To unfold existence disregard all reward.

Giants in Jeans Sonnet 71

Regard for reward ruins the heart,
Regard for praise hampers growth.
Live with kindness for kindness is life,
Throw all argumentation overboard.
Mind and mind are not really separate,
They are the streams of one soul.
Streams born of mortal neurons,
Capable of realizing the immortal goal.
All goals are mortal except one,
The eternal dream of collective ascension.
Vegetables may sleep all they want,
Bravehearts must rise without hesitation.
Beyond sleep, security and nonchalance,
There's a valley of, by and for the humans.

Sonnet of Heaven and Hell

There's a tale we hear of a heavenly kingdom,
Which is passed on through generations.
Because once you place salvation outside life,
Accountability vanishes from all prioritization.
Self-determination makes one unfit for slavery,
Reason makes one unfit for manipulation.
If you take charge of your life and community,
Institutions fail to dictate your ambition.
Heaven and hell exist here and now,
They are manifestations of human behavior.
Acts of oneness bring heaven in a moment,
Deeds of division breed hell from thin air.
The paradigm we have was made yesterday.
It is our world, let's build it our way.

Giants in Jeans Sonnet 73

The world is our family,
Our family is our responsibility.
Policy, constitution, bible all later,
First the individual must practice integrity.
Every generation needs caretakers,
The caretaker of your generation is you.
Defying all talks of destiny and success,
Give up yourself to build the society anew.
Let the windbags shout all they want,
You do your existential duty in silence.
Neither woke, nor activist, just as human,
Stand tall with dignity and act with sapience.
The society is ours, so are its troubles.
Walk as the only human amongst vegetables.

Giants in Jeans Sonnet 74

What makes a human, what makes inhuman,
How can we make the distinction?
Action and expansion make the human,
Inhumans thrive on comfort and contraction.
If your humanity is alive and awake,
You'll despise comfort at the sight of disparity.
If you are not a self-centric inhuman,
You'll be unable to sleep till you lift society.
Luxury lures the shallow and the vain,
Snobs are lost forever in chasing products.
Human beings with backbone and insight,
Cannot be coaxed by separatist constructs.
Civilization awakens when we traverse duality.
Each of us is to be the incarnate of nonduality.

Giants in Jeans Sonnet 75

Nonduality comes from wholeness,
Wholeness rises when sectarianism is slashed.
Sectarianism fails when we fall in love,
Not with one person but the whole world.
When the stranger becomes family,
Politicians will lose their job.
When love overwhelms all rigidity,
Arms dealers will mourn and sob.
When diplomacy keeps the world divided,
Reliance on institutions goes through the roof.
The best way to sustain profits of war,
Is to keep people infected with the nationalist flu.
Enough with this barbarianism of sovereignty!
Step up and shout, the whole world is my family!

Giants in Jeans Sonnet 76

In the old days tribal chiefs used to fool people,
With talks of tribal honor and heritage.
Today's chiefs in suits manipulate modern tribals,
With talks of national security and lineage.
When our ancestors behaved as tribals,
It is acceptable for they didn't know better.
But when we identify as civilized yet act tribal,
It is but a degrading stain upon our honor.
Though all politicians are not savages,
Paradigm of modern politics thrives on division.
So make not the dreadful mistake to think,
That politicians are gonna bring peace and elevation.
It is a world of citizens, citizens are its lifeblood.
You and I are its caretakers, not some elected vanguard.

Giants in Jeans Sonnet 77

Blaming politicians achieves nothing,
It only enables new crooks and thugs.
Blaming the system achieves nothing,
If you continue as selfish bugs.
It's not enough to thank the soldiers,
Each of us must be the soldier.
It's not enough to thank the martyrs,
Each of us must be the martyr.
Put your thankfulness to some good use,
By taking up responsibility for parts of society.
It's okay if you can't lift the whole world,
At least stand up to your local atrocity.
Law is only the secondary pathway to justice,
The primary path is abolition of cowardice.

Giants in Jeans Sonnet 78

O my coward heart,
Enough with this cowardice!
When will you beat for real,
Enough with being fear's accomplice!
Your work is to aid life,
Your work is to aid the world.
If you can't do none of that,
Why do you exist at all!
Long you've slept with indifference,
Long you've crawled as vermin.
It is time to stand tall with dignity,
It is time to be a force upliftin'.
O my coward heart, be coward no more,
You've been a doormat enough, now be a lovedoor!

Giants in Jeans Sonnet 79

There's a door from my heart to yours,
But you can't see it with naked eye.
To see the door from heart to heart,
To all stereotypes you must first die.
There are biases in us that are evolutionary,
Then there are those imposed by culture.
In unlearning these predominant tendencies,
We become humanity's true keeper.
Spare the biases spoil the society,
This is what I once said before.
Biases keep us from becoming human,
We can't be slaves to them no more.
The door of love is opened with love.
Let's open our doors and be the living dove.

Giants in Jeans Sonnet 80

The dove of peace is no mythical creature,
For each of us is a potential dove.
We are the twig and we are the bird,
All peace begins with a human of love.
Mind is the master of war and peace,
Mind is the creator as well as ravager.
Individual will determines collective destiny,
Intention is civilization's true mother.
Diplomacy will not bring peace,
Neither will science and technology.
If the everyday human has no universality,
All power practically breeds insanity.
Nuts and bolts don't make a species advanced.
We are advanced when we walk hand in hand.

Sonnet of Blood and Water

Blood may be thicker than water,
But water is far greater than blood.
Blood may discriminate between people,
Water saves all without a single word.
Even while helping the wounded,
Blood discriminates both in mind and medicine.
But to put out the fire of someone's thirst,
Water doesn't care about a single thing.
Now tell me which one deserves all the glory,
Tell me which one is greater,
Is it blood that's prejudiced all the time,
Or is it the life-giving water?
All care for blood and family first,
Few can make a family out of the world.

Giants in Jeans Sonnet 82

Whatever makes a human being,
Is also what makes a family.
There's no such thing as a stranger,
For a human being with humanity.
All the world is our next of kin,
All towns are our hometown.
There is no my country your country,
All nations are our playground.
Troubles of one are troubles of all,
We are but keepers of each other.
Joy of one is the joy of all,
In helping another our sorrows disappear.
Let us be a boon in each other's life.
Let us be brave and stand together upright.

Giants in Jeans Sonnet 83

Where the head is without fear,
And the heart is without hate,
Where the spine doesn't quiver,
And the feet do not shake,
Where conviction doesn't mind,
The hailstorms of mockery,
Where conscience doesn't retreat,
In vain complacency,
Where character doesn't bow,
Before the myth of authority,
Where life doesn't stoop,
At every whim of primitivity,
Come meet me there at your own pace,
I shall wait for you till my dying days.

Giants in Jeans Sonnet 84

You don't die when your body dies,
You ain't born when your body is born.
The body and being are not the same,
But they can be if we truly want.
Birth of a brain is birth of potential,
Birth of a brain is birth of possibility.
It doesn't necessarily mean birth of a being,
It doesn't necessarily mean birth of humanity.
CNS holds the seeds of civilization,
Neurons hold the seeds of human living.
But without the will to sow those seeds,
It is just an empty body without a being.
Birth of human is quintessential for global serenity.
Put the animal to sleep and wake up to humanity.

Giants in Jeans Sonnet 85

Ahoy my friend, wake up to humanity,
Enough with the sleep of tradition!
Be bold, brave and insane if necessary,
And throw overboard all caution.
Don't take travel tips from couch potatoes,
Don't hear tales of revolution from cowards.
Break free from the cocoon of convenience,
Be the one whom inhumanity fears.
Be the pillar the society lacks,
Be the shade for tired pedestrians.
Be the bridge that unites lands,
Be the gate to the earthly heavens.
Distance between lands will all disappear,
With kindness if you can walk up to your neighbor.

Love is Not A Christian Thing (The Sonnet)

Love thy neighbor is not a christian thing,
Love stuck in barriers stays love no more.
Shalom, ahava, simcha are not jewish concepts,
Peace, love and joy constitute life's core.
There's no christianity, there's only love,
There's no buddhism, there's only compassion,
There's no naskarism, there's only humanity,
There's no humanism, there's only assimilation.
Faith that raises walls within the mind,
Is faith of the prehistoric savages.
Faith has a place in civilized society,
Only if it helps break assumptions and barriers.
Let us come together across faith and culture.
Let us be companions in each other's adventure.

Hanukkah Sonnet

Hanukkah, Oh Hanukkah, let's light the menorah,
Let's wipe out all divide, even if some call it utopia.
Come one, come all, no matter the culture,
Let's stuff some latkes while we dreidel together.
Worry not about the candles burning low,
Fear not the darkness of hate and narrowness.
So long as we stand as bridges and not walls,
No darkness is match for our uplifting radiance.
The light of the festival doesn't come from candles,
The sweetness in the air doesn't come from treats.
The light and sweetness of these joyful festivities,
Rise from the loving streams of our heartbeats.
Let us burn bright as the gentle epitome of ahava.
Let us live life as a walking and talking menorah.

Christmas Sonnet

Jingle bells, jingle bells, jingle all the way,
Oh, what fun it is to give our own life away!
Saint Nicholas did his part, so did Chris himself,
Now it's time for us to be the happiness gateway.
Dashing through the alleys devoid of lights,
Holding up high as beacon, our own heart,
Breaking ourselves to pieces and burning to ashes,
We'll ensure no one lacks the love a human deserves.
We are Dasher, Dancer, Prancer, Vixen and Comet,
We are Cupid, Donner, Blitzen and Rudolph.
We are also modern day Nick, Chris and Eckhart,
By our love and oneness let the world be engulfed!
Twelve days ain't enough to celebrate Christmas.
As humans we must live each day helping others.

Giants in Jeans Sonnet 89

One human's despair is all humans' despair,
One human's welfare is all humans' welfare.
When we genuinely start to feel this way,
No neighborhood will be left without care.
There's no politics, there's only accountability,
There's no equity, there's only sanity.
There's no diversity, there's only life,
There's no rights, there's only humanity.
Party is just a means of change,
Meant to bring reform through organization.
But in reality party takes preference over people,
And becomes the problem instead of the solution.
Use your neurons and defy all political histrionics.
Build a society that requires no party politics.

Sonnet of The Benevolent Crook

Politics doesn’t mean affairs of the people,
It is but a telenovela of sectarian histrionics.
Democracy doesn't mean rule of the people,
It means a new dictatorship of the charismatic.
A paradigm born of selfishness and greed,
Is no place for an honest and innocent person.
But if politics is the path you choose for reform,
Leave theories outside before entering the dungeon.
When you are compelled to be crooked,
Make sure it is not for any benefit personal.
Be the Godfather of crookedness if needed,
And manipulate the system to lift the people.
All abuse power of politics to climb the social ladder.
Be the benevolent crook and use it as social leveler.

Giants in Jeans Sonnet 91

Idealism has no place in an organic world,
It only hampers the growth of humanity.
No matter how perfect their bookish definition is,
In the real world they all function differently.
Sometimes I shake hands with the devil,
Sometimes I am the devil myself.
If you are crooked to the hypocrites for people,
The end does justify the means quite well.
I ain't no diplomat, I ain't no scholar,
I am but a simple soul off the street.
Based on the requirement of the situation,
I'll do whatever it takes to ensure social uplift.
It is a hypocrites' world where honesty is a curse.
Though gentle inside, learn to pretend dangerous.

Giants in Jeans Sonnet 92

They say honesty is the best policy,
Because honest cowards make ideal slaves.
If you have a backbone and you use your brain,
Crooked overlords lose their authoritative reins.
It's good for corruption to have law-abiding citizens,
Who are complacent and pay disparities no heed.
Original thinking makes one unfit for exploitation,
Corruption thrives on people's endless greed.
When people start to feel, think and act as human,
They will be silent less and will stand up more.
When they start to live as beings of character,
They will buy things less and help others more.
There is no best policy till that policy applies to all.
What matters is, we are responsible for our world.

Giants in Jeans Sonnet 93

Enough with blaming the bureaucrats,
Enough with blaming the politicians.
The regular civilians are no better,
In fact, they are worse than the authoritarians.
For trivial things they shout at the lowly,
At real inhumanities they keep quiet.
Over coffee they debate law and policy,
While living life as corruption incarnate.
Billion dollar scams are not the only scam,
A dollar worth of greed is also crime.
Corruption does not fall from the sky above,
Civilian corruption is the root of it all every time.
Uncorrupt democracy is born of uncorrupt civilians.
Before you blame a politician, observe your actions.

Dollar of Disparity (The Sonnet)

Millions of people go without food,
For some privileged nimrods to afford their luxuries.
Millions of people have no access to essentials,
So that celebrities can buy their lamborghinis.
The difference between phony activists and a reformer,
Is not in what they say but in their lifestyle and action.
In a world that still suffers from the lack of essentials,
Indulgence in luxury is human rights violation.
What people do with their money is not a private affair,
Each penny above necessity belongs to social welfare.
One who talks of equality while riding in a Rolls Royce,
Is the last person to be concerned of people's despair.
None has a right to luxury till all can access necessities.
Every dollar spent on luxury is a dollar of disparity.

Giants in Jeans Sonnet 95

Divisionism and dollarism are the curse of society,
Yet society worships them as the greatest boon.
Peace and peoplism are cussed as commie claptrap,
While populism continues to give power to goons.
No society is born just, warm and humane,
It falls upon each of us to shape it in such a way.
You don't need to run for office to bring reform,
You just need to stop brushing your duties away.
Not all politicians are reformers,
Though every single one of them pretends to be.
But every responsible civilian is living reformation,
Even if they do not say anything to anybody.
Reformation is not a matter of brainless partisanism,
It is a matter of nonpartisan and hearty collectivism.

Giants in Jeans Sonnet 96

The sun doesn't call itself light-bringer,
Yet the whole world venerates it as such.
The wind doesn't call itself the soother,
Yet the whole world craves for its gush.
The rivers don't call themselves life-giver,
Yet the world can't function without their currents.
The reformer doesn't call themselves humanizer,
Yet all progress comes to halt without their footsteps.
If someone identifies as a scientist or humanist,
It means nothing till they use science to lift others.
If someone identifies as an activist or humanitarian,
It means nothing till they can be annihilated for others.
Designation-dropping is habit of the kindergartener.
Identity of grownups is revealed through behavior.

Giants in Jeans Sonnet 97

Age doesn’t make you wise, curiosity does.
Intellect doesn't make you curious, growth does.
Experience doesn't make you grow, expansion does.
Travel doesn't make you expand, self-correction does.
Cynicism doesn't help correction, awareness does.
Books don't make you aware, accountability does.
Law cannot make you accountable, humanity does.
Appearance doesn't make you human, acceptance does.
Wokeness doesn't make you accepting, character does.
Clothes don't make character, conduct does.
Etiquettes don't define conduct, goodness does.
Tradition doesn't make you good, oneness does.
Oneness is the mother of all civilized behavior.
Without oneness we're ever headed for disaster.

Giants in Jeans Sonnet 98

There's no humanity,
Only degrees of animality.
There's no civility,
Only degrees of primitivity.
We are not even close,
To be worthy of the title human.
All we can do however,
Is be less of an animal.
It is not rocket science,
Just a matter of willfulness.
Are you willful enough,
To defy your innate selfishness!
Bold steps without self-regulation,
Like cancer, ultimately causes destruction.

Giants in Jeans Sonnet 99

Self-regulation is not caution,
It is an act of course-correction.
Too must sentiment and no reason,
Destroys both the path and the pedestrian.
Be aware of your shortcomings,
As well as your greatest strength.
Adjust the means and pace of your course,
Thinking as a whole being with heart and head.
There is no surefire way to success,
Success and failure are products of capitalist torment.
Life is but an experiment of trial and error,
Instead of fretting the future, cherish the experiment.
If today's you is slightly more human than yesterday,
That is true success, no matter what creeplings say.

Giants in Jeans Sonnet 100

If success makes you cold and apathetic,
Better be unsuccessful and suffer every day.
If materials imprison you in a castle of cockiness,
Better live simple and keep all luxuries at bay.
If intellect makes you distant from the people,
Better be dumb and exude a ton of humility.
If power makes you corrupt like everybody else,
Better stay away from positions of authority.
Tribalism and self-centricity are universal,
So are the abilities of awareness and moderation.
What is not universal in this whole wide world,
Is the practice of those abilities of civilization.
It's a blunderful world and humankind is the cause of it.
No matter the history, let us commence operation fixit.

29. Şehit Sevda Society

Wake Up From Death (The Sonnet)

Wake up from death and return to life,
For as living dead we've been crawling for long.
Wake up from sanity and return to insanity,
For we've been insane in sanity for long.
Wake up from possibility, return to impossibility,
For we've been slave to the possible for long.
Wake up from reality and return to absurdity,
Habits of past have kept us hypnotized for long.
Wake up form truth and return to love,
For we've always confused assumptions with truth.
Wake up form ideology and return to the soil,
Integration means inclusion, not ideological coup.
Enough with nonchalance in the name of practicality!
Let us now rise as tornado and wipe out all apathy.

Your Struggle is My Struggle (The Sonnet)

Your struggle is my struggle,
'Cause my heaven is in your smile.
Your trouble is my trouble,
Without you by my side all victory is vile.
My life is only life when you are in it,
For a life without love is but death in disguise.
Without you my achievements mean nothing,
'Cause you're the sweetness of all my flight.
You are the light of my eyes,
Without you I am but a ship without compass.
You are the strength coursing through my veins,
Without you I turn into worthless abscess.
You are my sky, my land and my ocean.
The breath of my life is you and my salvation.

Law of Sacrifice (The Sonnet)

The more you give life,
The more you'll have life.
The more you give light,
The more you'll have light.
The more the I gets lost in others,
The more you'll end all bigoted strife.
The more you take pain for those around,
The more you'll know the joy of life.
Worst of all superstitions is selfishness,
It keeps an animal from becoming human.
Let the mind be cleansed of all self,
So our heart becomes a mirror for every person.
Reject all selfishness that makes you cold and blind.
Sacrifice is the law behind all love and light.

Wipe Out The I (The Sonnet)

Once a person gives up all for others,
They'll achieve everything worth achieving.
The art of self-discovery is in self-annihilation,
Whereas self-obsession only causes suffering.
Once a person is insane with the sacrificial spirit,
They'll know the meaning of civilized sanity.
Once a person feels the joy of selflessness,
All worldly pleasures will turn into foul vanity.
Once a person hones the power of simplicity,
They'll trash all trace of pomposity from life.
Once a person senses the valor of humility,
They'll discard all arrogant divide.
Life is simple, but we mess it up with selfishness.
Wipe out the I, and you will taste its sweetness.

Your Culture is My Culture (The Sonnet)

With infinite love brimming in my heart,
I have arrived at your doorstep.
Please, I beg you, do not turn me back,
Let me in, so I may be one with your footstep.
It's not my fault, I wasn't born in your culture,
Yet I've assimilated your culture as my own.
Please do not throw me out my dear friend,
Standing together our powers will be honed.
I may not speak your native tongue,
I may not be familiar with your way of life.
But do you not smile like me when in joy,
Like me do you not shed tears when in strife!
Here I stand at your door with my arms stretched.
Hold it with affection or chop it off if you so elect.

The One of My Heart (The Sonnet)

I see the one of my heart,
In every direction, in every face.
Yet I won't say a word,
In silence I'll bear all coldness.
You may throw me out of your heart,
But you can't oust yourself from mine.
You are in every pore of my being,
You are my only lifeline.
You are the one that runs in my nerves,
As the power-grid of my mind.
The pain of being a one-sided lover,
Is sweeter to me than a thousand goldmines.
Cuss me, mock me, hurt me all you like.
All I care about is to be an aid in your life.

Undestination (The Sonnet)

I gave up my country in your love,
I gave up my home for your sweetness.
I stand at your door without identity,
Will you take me in and fill my emptiness!
I've sailed my ship towards undestination,
Let the waves take me where they may.
Embracing the unknown I became a pal of all.
Come out my friend from your cage of dismay.
Come with me, and we'll explore all impossibility.
If we must be awful let's be awful together.
Let us lose all maps and walk around as vagrants.
Why worry, when we have each other!
To hell with destination, let us savor the journey!
Before success and achievement, let us first have unity.

To Seduce You With Looks (The Sonnet)

I haven't come to seduce you with looks,
I have come to overwhelm you with love.
I haven't come to break your door by force,
I've come to charm it open with my mind's touch.
I haven't come to bring you worldly riches,
But to offer you the garland of my heart.
I haven't come to usher you with complements,
I've come to celebrate you, tearing myself apart.
I haven't come to count the benefits of bond,
I've come to make you lose count of your wounds.
I haven't come to feel butterflies in my stomach,
But to fight the world, helping you break all rules.
Let me burn to ashes time and time again,
So I may remove the shadows from your life's lane.

Forgive Us Jesus (The Sonnet)

Forgive us Jesus, my friend,
We couldn't walk in your footsteps.
You asked us to love our neighbor,
Yet we found it impossible to be hateless.
You didn't hate those who hated you,
You loved them despite being mocked.
Yet we can't even talk without judging today,
We can't accept any difference in thought.
Forgetting all comfort and luxury,
You gave your life trying to erase bigotry.
Yet we made you fodder for our own prejudice,
And turned the crucifix into a badge of cruelty.
We used you my friend to deepen our division.
We prefer mindless worship over hearty compassion.

War Ain't Peace (The Sonnet)

Hudson, Thames, Nile and Sindhu,
All are now red with the blood of the innocent.
Who is to blame for such catastrophe,
Everybody who accepts arms race as upliftment.
Suited savages have seduced them to believe,
That bigger the military greater the pride.
It's necessary for politicians to sell nationalism,
Or else their loyal subjects will all get untied.
Acts of national security only breed insecurity,
Which forces people to seek comfort in weapons.
True, lasting stability and serenity of a nation,
Comes only from a universal desire for union.
Let the politicians sell war in the name of peace.
Why must the citizens buy it like rats chasing cheese!

30. Handcrafted Humanity

Home Country (The Sonnet)

If immigrants ain't real Americans,
Neither is our revered Lady Liberty.
She too came from a distant land,
Yet today she is the American epitome.
If even this doesn't broaden your heart,
What about the founders of our history!
All of them were textbook immigrants,
What white supremacists cuss as refugee.
Any land that holds potential for ascension,
Draws the repressed souls of humanity.
Though I belong to the whole wide world,
Land of Lady Liberty is my home country.
A nation's character isn't defined by rigidity,
It is defined by a hearty unity in diversity.
A nation's character isn't defined by rigidity,
It is defined by a hearty unity in diversity.

Handcrafted Humanity Sonnet 2

I belong to the whole world but,
America will always be my home country, my ground.
Because she adopted me and honored me as a son,
When the country I was born in kicked me around.
Those who celebrate you in the making,
Are the ones who genuinely care about you.
Those who shout your name after you are a big deal,
Will toss you like garbage as a new craze substitutes you.
Pay no attention to the mockery of vermin,
It's a world full of snobs, hypocrites and backstabbers.
With the last ounce of your strength unbound,
Recognize, realize and act upon your life's purpose.
Life is too short to be wasted on holding grievance.
Forget them or not, forgiveness always brings peacefulness.

Handcrafted Humanity Sonnet 3

Sentiments, sapience and sentience speak,
The same tongue no matter the geography.
Tears, smiles and hugs from heart speak,
The same tongue no matter the boundary.
Geography is merely a measure of land,
It is no measure of the human being.
Universality alone defines the heart of human,
Anything short of that is mark of a fiend.
Let the borders be outside, there's no problem,
But never let them fester inside the mind.
Many will come and call you traitor,
Do not let their narrowness drag you behind.
Amidst all contraction be an example of expansion.
Let us live as walking flame of earthistani ambition.

Sonnet Earthistan

Earthistan is not a place,
Earthistan is a people,
People who've forgotten borders,
Who ain't no sectarian sheeple.
Earthistan is not a nation,
It is but the spirit of expansion,
A spirit that loves each and all,
And knows no discrimination.
Earthistan is not geography,
It is but the oneness of mind,
Where nobody's superior or inferior,
Where nobody is left behind.
As citizens divided long we've practiced savagery.
Awake, Arise and get to work, Oh Brave Earthistani!

Sonnet of Struggle

The struggle of one,
Is the struggle of all.
Denying freedom to one,
Is the beginning of collective fall.
Lasting happiness for one,
Is in the happiness of community.
Even one soul without serenity,
Is a world without serenity.
The anguish of one,
Casts shadow on collective mind.
Even if one person falls behind,
It is the fall of all humankind.
Togetherness is another name for progress,
Together forever, either as lovers or ashes.

Lover Off The Street (A Sonnet)

Beauty and bliss are all around,
When my feet walk alongside yours.
Life reaches the pinnacle of being,
When I'm annihilated for a smile of yours.
Climbed plenty hills, trotted plenty jungle,
Nowhere did I find a drop of sanity.
Then I stood crazy before your radiance,
And I got drenched in beams of serenity.
I am but a naïve lover off the street,
Without a single trace of intellect.
The only thing that I've learnt in life is,
In your happiness lies my upliftment.
Business is measured by how much we receive,
Life is realized when we stand hellbent to give.

Handcrafted Humanity Sonnet 7

Give, give and give again,
To give without reserve is living.
Fall, fall and fall again,
To fall without stopping is rising.
Break, break and break again,
To break without bending is integrity.
Lose, lose and lose again,
To lose without submitting is victory.
Love, love and love again,
To love despite being fooled is sanity.
Help, help and help again,
To help despite being deceived is humanity.
To give is to live, that is the civilized normal.
Kindness alone sets the human apart from animal.

Handcrafted Humanity Sonnet 8

Strength of the mind lies not in bitterness,
Rather it lies in gentleness incorruptible.
One can wear a suit and still be a savage,
Saints don't need no suit to look presentable.
Service makes a saint, sacrifice makes a reformer,
Service and reform know no institutional authority.
No institution is high enough to dub one as saint,
It's the saints who set example of the best of humanity.
But mark you, no saint ever calls themselves saint,
Reformers never boast themselves as reformers.
'Cause labeling is an act of savage minds,
While saints and reformers are busy lifting others.
Pay no attention to definition and designation.
All a human can do is, be the living reformation.

Handcrafted Humanity Sonnet 9

I don't write on revolution,
I am the revolution all-round,
So is every single person working,
To lift the society off the ground.
I have no message on reform,
I am the very force of reformation,
So are you and every single person,
Who lives a life of purpose and ascension.
I don't like competitions one single bit,
Competitions are for horses, not heroes.
I may not be a hero, but I am no horse either,
Revolution and reform ain't no competitive sports.
Live life not to win or lose, but to realize a purpose.
Sewers of society have plenty rats but very few humans.

Handcrafted Humanity Sonnet 10

Person without purpose,
Is a ship without compass.
Life without awareness,
Is trucks without drivers.
I despise alcohol, nicotine and drugs,
Music is my stimulant.
I despise gossiping and partying,
Service is my fulfillment.
Even the deaf can hear the music of life,
Yet those with ears hear nothing.
Even the blind can see the beauty of heart,
Yet those with eyes are busy with shopping.
Life is not an entitlement, it's a promise,
Of caring and sharing till we slip into the great abyss.

I Am Broken (The Sonnet)

Yes I do care, not about what the snobs say,
I care about how the deprived live.
Yes I am obsessed, not with looking fancy,
I am obsessed with alleviating others' grief.
Yes I am greedy, not for wealth and possession,
I am greedy to see sunshine on teary faces.
Yes I am nuts, not for perfection or fashion,
I am nuts about equity, honor and upliftment.
Yes I am scared, not that I may get hurt,
But that blinded by bias I may hurt someone.
Yes I am insecure, not about getting deceived,
But about losing control and causing harm.
Yes I am broken, unstable and bonkers as hell,
All 'cause others matter to me more than myself.

Handcrafted Humanity Sonnet 12

Here are some words born of narrowness,
Activist, woke, religious, atheist,
Socialist, communist, capitalist, conservative,
Intellectual, intelligent, classy, elitist,
Educated, learned, well-versed, sound-mind,
Traditional, old-fashioned, spiritual, altruistic,
Empiricist, Existentialist, rationalist, freethinker,
Godly, compassionate, selfless and mystic.
I refuse to be defined by any of them,
None of them can explain my true sentiment.
I may advocate for the good within each of them,
But I refuse to give any of them exclusive endorsement.
All these words are too puny to define my identity.
My name is human, my heart contains entire humanity.

Sonnet of Fields

Art is a mirror of time that shows,
What's been, is and could be.
Science is a bridge of time,
That helps us build the future to be.
Philosophy is a spank on the tank,
That makes us cautious of mistakes.
Faith is but an imaginary friend,
That fills in when the sky darkens.
Education is a liaison to social lanes,
That arms us to engineer new lanes.
Medicine is a keeper of health,
That helps us overcome sickness.
Each social field has a noble cause,
Whether they fulfill it depends on action of ours.

Sonnet of Science

Science is but a bridge of time, it can,
Either take us forward or dump us in prehistory.
Science alone does not ensure our advancement,
Unless it's practiced with warmth and accountability.
Sheer reason without any sentiment is,
As dangerous as sheer sentiment without any reason.
In order to forge a world fit for humans,
We must break the ice between reason and emotion.
Problem is that we like picking sides,
Either we are too emotional or too rational.
A civilized human ought to be none of that,
A civilized human acts upon the need of the situation.
So I say o mighty human, be not an intellectual moron.
Science is a means of service, not intellectual gratification.

Doctor's Sonnet

A doctor is one who's gentle as a bird,
A doctor is one who's brave as a soldier,
A doctor is one who's amusing as a clown,
A doctor is one who's caring as a mother.
Treating the sick is not a comfort job,
It is a difficult life without leisure and lure.
If all you want are wealth and tranquility,
Trade in your medical license for a liquor store.
The world is filled with doctors most cold,
Many don't practice medicine but self-centricity.
Instruments and intellect don't make a doctor,
Without warmth all pills lose their efficacy.
Healthcare means aid first talk rules later.
Better a kindhearted fool than a heartless monster.

World Without 9/11 (The Sonnet)

Better a kindhearted fool than a heartless tool,
Kindness is born when we aren't afraid of burning.
Coldness looks appealing on nuts and bolts,
On human beings it is absolutely unbecoming.
A world without 9/11 and January 6,
Begins with a heart without hate.
Cultural and racial profiling don't ensure security,
True security is born when we act as love incarnate.
The helpless, forgotten, discriminated and destitute,
Are my brothers and sisters, and I won't stop,
Till I lift them up to take their rightful place,
Upon the fabric of society, with my last blood drop.
Each and every breath of mine is public property.
Once I die for the people, then I can live in serenity.

Handcrafted Humanity Sonnet 17

Once I die for the people,
Then I can live in peace.
Till then each moment I'm restless,
Each moment I'm without ease.
As a precious gift of nature,
I received this human life.
I gotta make the most of it,
By using it to alleviate human strife.
I'll be gone soon but,
I'll leave behind enough soldiers,
To take care of this world,
For thousands of years.
I am an addiction most destructive.
Leave all ego behind before taking the dive.

Handcrafted Humanity Sonnet 18

I am an addiction most dangerous,
Keep children away from my works.
If you want them to grow up self-centric,
Make sure they never hear my words.
It is a world built on selfishness,
Where being a selfish savage is a must.
Show any sign of selflessness,
And they'll lock you up as altruistic nut.
That's why they invented fancy terms,
Like altruism, humanism, humanitarianism,
So that they can continue the fighting,
Without ever practicing humanity free from ism.
So you make a choice today, will you be human,
Or remain a snobbish savage of a concrete junglistan!

Handcrafted Humanity Sonnet 19

It takes awareness to be human,
To be animal it takes none.
It takes moderation to be human,
To be animal it takes none.
It takes regulation to be human,
To be animal it takes none.
It takes restraint to be human,
To be animal it takes none.
It takes gentleness to be human,
To be animal it takes none.
It takes humility to be human,
To be animal it takes none.
Everything civilized starts with awareness.
But if you like being animal let go off all restraint.

Sonnet of Rulers

The only people who'll rule the world,
Are the ones who want to rule not a being.
The only people to inherit the earth,
Are the ones who want to inherit nothing.
The only people who win hearts,
Are those who give all without question.
The only people who become family to all,
Are those who walk without assumption.
The only people who never die,
Are those who happily die for others.
The only people who are the happiest,
Are those who have no trace of selfish desires.
Selfishness is synonym for suffering and misery.
Joy is just a byproduct of service to humanity.

Handcrafted Humanity Sonnet 21

Listen one and listen all, I am just a human,
Let it be all there is to know about me.
Rest will reveal itself on their own when,
You reach out without a judgmental mentality.
Gender and sexuality do not matter,
Unless you are looking for a partner.
Color does not matter, period,
All that really matters is a person's character.
A civilized world is predicated on character,
Not on gender, sexuality or complexion.
But if you still can't realize this simple fact,
It's you whose mind lacks civilization.
When a belief diminishes your humanity,
It's the belief that you must reject, not humanity.

Facts and Belief (The Sonnet)

No belief is worth losing your humanity over,
No intellect is worth losing your kindness over.
Facts, faith, reason, religion all come later,
First and foremost we must humanize our behavior.
If a belief or intellect makes you a better person,
More power to your belief or intellect I say.
But if they become a hindrance to your humanity,
Throw it immediately like poison far, far away.
Beliefs have cast shadows of wars throughout history,
Facts have provided weapons for those wars.
Then again beliefs have taught us to love our neighbor,
Facts have helped us fight calamity and disorders.
Let all beliefs and facts be guided by a warm heart.
Warmth alone will make our world fit for human birth.

Graveheart Sonnet

You don't go to grave when you die,
Most live carrying a grave in their heart.
In that grave they keep all humanity buried,
While a beast looking human walks the earth.
Forget all fiction about life after death,
First you learn to live this life as a human.
A life lived on prejudice and superstition,
Is the actual, tangible damnation.
Make your heart a cradle of community,
And a breeding ground of all things civilized.
Then only the beast will turn human,
Only then true sapience will be realized.
Looks mean nothing if inside you're filled with dirt.
Live a little and die alive, instead of being a graveheart.

Handcrafted Humanity Sonnet 24

Whenever the people are in danger,
A dervish will rise always.
Whenever the society is in darkness,
A light-bringer will rise always.
Whenever the world faces trouble,
A mechanic will rise always.
Whenever communities face misery,
A reformer will rise always.
Whenever liberty is in jeopardy,
A soldier will rise always.
Whenever peace and harmony are in distress,
A bridge-builder will rise always.
But these braveheart beings won't fall from the sky.
You and I must stand up whenever things go awry.

Two Politics (The Sonnet)

There is not one but two politics in the world,
One involves issues of society, another is partisanism.
Affairs of society is how politics is defined in books,
But in real life politics is all about partisan nimrodism.
Even the politicians are aware of this simple fact,
So they boast about placing people before politics.
But they never really have any intention of doing that,
So they continue with their usual partisan histrionics.
Real politics is supposed to be all about the people,
Yet today politics is all about politicians, not people.
Then they throw around some words for good measure,
Like socialist, capitalist and so on, at the sheeple.
Enough with this primitive left and right nonsense!
For once be whole and act with civilized sentience.

Handcrafted Humanity Sonnet 26

Your road may just have two sides,
Left and right, but mine doesn't, buddy.
Binary paths belong in bygone past,
All things civilized are non-binary.
Try defining life as mere good or bad,
Try defining home as mere good or bad.
Anything that matters in human existence,
Are all above dualities such as that.
For example, tech is neither good nor bad,
But its reckless use does more harm than good.
Effective observation requires whole eyes,
Stand whole above duality, and you'll know all truth.
Give me a hundred eyes teeming with wholeness.
In their sight I'll show you, what is humanness.

Sonnet of National Sickness

Wanna study a superpower, study America.
Wanna study dysfunctional power, still study America.
Wanna study spirituality, study India.
Wanna study rotten spirituality, still study India.
Wanna study rise of secularism, study Turkish Republic.
Wanna study fall of secularism, still study Turkish Republic.
Wanna study standards of beauty, study the Korean Republic.
Wanna study doctored beauty, still study the Korean Republic.
Wanna study pride and loyalty, study good old Britannia.
Wanna study primeval pride and loyalty, still study Britannia.
Wanna study statehood, study People's Republic of China.
Wanna study the horrors of statehood, still study China.
Every nation on earth suffers from a distinct ailment.
The first step towards recovery is acknowledgement.

Handcrafted Humanity Sonnet 28

Worse than ignorance is denial of ignorance,
Acceptance of ignorance makes way for learning.
Worse than bigotry is denial of bigotry,
Acknowledgement of it facilitates mental cleansing.
We are all biased, that's not the problem,
Trouble begins when we let biases dictate action.
Brain thrives on assumptions, that ain't the problem,
Trouble begins when all thought ends at assumption.
There is no such thing as truth in the world,
It's all one big belief meant to aid life not wisdom.
Perception is almost entirely born of guess-work,
'Cause our brain doesn't care about ascension.
But the kernel of curiosity also lies dormant in our brain.
Rise, roar and rebel my friend, rejecting all storm and rain.

Fully Vaccinated (The Sonnet)

I am alive, well and fully vaccinated,
Despite pledging allegiance to no authority.
Listening to experts is not complacency,
It's just an act of common sense humanity.
You trust bus-drivers to get you to work,
You trust pilots to fly you to places.
Then why are you afraid to trust scientists,
Without science we'd still be living like savages.
State doesn't need to put microchip in your body,
Future tech isn't needed to rule prehistoric veggies.
Your dependency on social media is sufficient,
To observe, manipulate and exploit your life stories.
Be cautious of your online footprint, not inoculation.
Be accountable and get your shot trampling all hesitation.

Celebrities Ain't Health Experts (The Sonnet)

Celebrities and influencers are not health experts,
Stop taking medical advice from halfwits of wellness.
Stop being a two-bit doctor from ten minutes of googling,
For Google is not a substitute for doctors and nurses.
Compared to that of a trained and experienced doctor,
Even as a neurobiologist my diagnosis skills are insignifant.
Then why can't you accept that when it comes to medicine,
Your opinion is worth no more than a counterfeit coin.
One goes through years of training and many sleepless nights,
Then they earn the right to wear the white coat of service.
And yet upon spending an hour surfing on the internet,
You put on the personality of a grey-haired neurologist!
Lack of expertise is by no means the same as lack of dignity.
But denial of expertise indicates a definite lack of senility.

Handcrafted Humanity Sonnet 31

Reason is not a sign of intellect,
Reason is a sign of curiosity.
Moderation is not self-restraint,
Moderation is a sign of sanity.
Revolution is not a sign of defiance,
Revolution is an act of accountability.
Calm is not a product of conformity,
Calm is a result of integrity.
Kindness is more than an act,
Kindness is practical holiness.
Love is more than a memory,
Love is an existence.
Values and virtues constitute humanness,
All of which rise from the fabric of oneness.

Handcrafted Humanity Sonnet 32

Oneness is not a new experience,
Most of us already feel it for our family.
All that is need is, we take a step forward,
And expand our self-centric boundary.
In name only humankind is civilized,
When it comes to action we are savage tribals.
With such sectarian heart we wanna colonize Mars,
We can't still stand as one people of our home-world!
Home is not a place, home is a family,
My home is the world, for my family is humanity.
The human heart is too grand to be wasted,
In the gutter of cultural exclusivity.
Oneness is civilization, so let's first be one as human,
Afterwards we shall be one with all of nature's creation.

Handcrafted Humanity Sonnet 33

Humanity is not a species,
Humanity is a promise.
Community is not a word,
Community is mind's uplift.
People are not creatures,
But our path to salvation.
Their sorrows are not theirs,
But key to our expansion.
Earth is not a mere planet,
It is a land of possibility.
All that possibility comes to life,
When we step across self-centricity.
In the jungle survival via cruelty is taken as sanity.
A human would rather die than give in to cruelty.

Handcrafted Humanity Sonnet 34

When the world burns,
If you don't feel yourself burning,
You are more dead than alive.
When those around you suffer,
If you don't feel your stomach turning,
You are more dead than alive.
When your neighbors weep,
If tears don't drop from your eyes,
You are more dead than alive.
When a stranger is in distress,
If you don't feel their strife,
You are more dead than alive.
Anybody can be kind to family, that's no biggie.
Be kind to a stranger, that's the sign of humanity.

Hero Worship (The Sonnet)

We used to worship the sun and the moon,
We used to worship stones and trees.
Then reason grew stronger along with imagination,
So our worship shifted from elements to entities.
Some of them were real and some fully fictitious,
We just needed an excuse to externalize our divinity.
Even today we keep inventing fictitious characters,
Despite knowing they are fiction we pledge our loyalty.
It seems like we are always holding out for a hero,
Outside our very own everyday, ordinary psyche.
Fiction is healthy so long as we grow no dependency,
Real heroes are just humans standing unbent on duty.
Enough with worship of fiction from comics and scriptures!
It's time to be the hero and take the world on our shoulders.

Handcrafted Humanity Sonnet 36

With the world on my shoulders I keep moving,
Despite the agony and nightmares most heavy.
With the good of society in heart I keep working,
Despite my fears and most crippling insecurities.
I can't afford to rest, for I have a duty to humanity,
I will carry out my duty through all of life's strife.
Circumstances will never be in my favor but,
It's I who decides whether to give them reins of my life.
Come hail or high water, I'm the ruler of my existence,
Thus speaks the one who's determined with dignity.
I am the one who holds the reins of society,
Thus speaks the human awake with accountability.
Better to be annihilated in the path of life and service,
Than to be a miser of love in the hopes of being rich.

Sonnet of Life Lessons

Rich is not the one who's got a lot of dough,
But one whose touch make others forget their woe.
Happy is not the one who's always chasing pleasure,
But one who forgets all pleasure helping another grow.
Success is not about getting recognition,
Success is about achieving excellence beyond norm.
Achievement is not when you reach a certain goal,
But when your goal lifts others beyond your home.
Destiny is not a script written by a superman,
But one you write yourself with your labor and sweat.
Sanctity is not what priests sell you at the church,
But how you behave with others outside the church gate.
Nobody can give you lessons of life packed in a few lines.
If you know to help another, your heart knows all the lines.

Handcrafted Humanity Sonnet 38

Behavior is the way to the beautification of this world,
Not policy, policing or debates on international relations.
Politicians don't cause war, citizens do with indifference,
Brush off indifference and you'll cripple all corruption.
Bullets kill body, not bravery, for bravery is contagious,
Oppression cripples individual, not ideas of uplift.
Ideas with potential for good are spectacularly timeless,
Sacrifice of a revolutionary in line of duty never goes amiss.
Being god-fearing makes you no more divine than animals,
True practical divinity is when you serve the helpless as deity.
Without service, regardless of hype, there'll be no progress,
Act of service facilitates all things civilized for self and society.
Progress of humankind mustn't rely on political intervention.
While the world rots how can we crave for selfish gratification!

Handcrafted Humanity Sonnet 39

Gratification is damnation,
For it turns a mind into slime.
Recklessness is extinction,
It's a breeding ground of crime.
Indifference is inhumanity,
For it makes way for injustice.
Blind obedience is savagery,
For it empowers the primitives.
Heartless intellect is dangerous,
For it facilitates apathy and coldness.
Mindless sentiment is also lethal,
It turns us even more blind to our biases.
Neither monasticism nor materialism will do.
To move forward we must stand whole and true.

Handcrafted Humanity Sonnet 40

Let me burn to ashes time and time again,
So I may remove the shadows from your life's lane.
Let me be annihilated in love time and time again,
So I may give this world taste of the sacrificial flame.
Let me be shattered to pieces time and time again,
In pulling the world together with harmony's twine.
Let me be crushed to dust time and time again,
In being a bridge to those who are left behind.
Let me be shredded with wounds and pangs,
Yet have a smile while I treat another's agony.
Let me walk on thorns time and time again,
So it may invigorate others to write their destiny.
Only by living life as a demonstration of sacrifice,
Shall we make the world of humans humanized.

Handcrafted Humanity Sonnet 41

The world is not black and white,
And neither is our human life.
If we still do not get it,
We oughta check if our brain's alright.
Life is full of variation and colors,
So is everything that is civilized.
But in order to feel it in our heart,
We must move beyond primitive fright.
There is no place for duality in society,
Nothing is this or that, contrary to sight.
Everything alive is a gorgeous rainbow,
Only the kingdom of death is black and white.
Think, feel and act as a nondual being,
And we will have all the harmony we need.

Handcrafted Humanity Sonnet 42

There is no light without shadow.
There is no might without weakness.
There is no joy without sorrow.
There is no sight without blindness.
There is no growth without mistakes.
There is no height without failure.
There is no rainbow without rain.
There is no bravery without fear.
There is no humanity without community,
There is no community without differences.
There is no individual without collectivity,
There is no tomorrow without togetherness.
There is no civilization without accountability.
Senility, serenity all come when we're one with society.

Handcrafted Humanity Sonnet 43

What is society?
An extension of individuality.
What is community?
A sense of extended amity.
What is sanity?
Awareness of primitivity.
What is serenity?
Moderation of necessity.
What is success?
Practice of excellence.
What is life?
An existence of mindfulness.
Now I ask you, what is humanity?
It is but a sense of universalized family.

Handcrafted Humanity Sonnet 44

There is no stranger,
There's only family.
There is no neighbor,
There's only family.
There is no community,
There's only family.
There is no society,
There's only family.
There is no reform,
There's only responsibility.
There is no revolution,
There's only accountability.
No matter the term, meaning is the same.
Together we shall triumph, separated we'll go lame.

Handcrafted Humanity Sonnet 45

There is no failure,
There is only learning.
There is no success,
There is only exploring.
There is no destination,
Only path and pedestrian.
There is no absolution,
Only realizing uncivilization.
There is no pursuit of purpose,
There’s only being the living goal.
There is no becoming human,
There's only being less of a troll.
Once we realize life in our very veins,
Nothing will matter except moving out of the drains.

Handcrafted Humanity Sonnet 46

When the tides of realization rise,
Words wither and fade away.
When the light of accountability shines,
Darkness of insecurity goes away.
When the bells of togetherness ring,
Noise of discrimination disappears.
When the breeze of harmony flows,
All storm of judgment slowly withers.
When the doves of amity sing,
Vultures of violence start falling.
When vessels of inclusion speak,
Peddlers of sectarianism lose standing.
When the love of humanity stands tall,
All differentiation is bound to fall.

Handcrafted Humanity Sonnet 47

The road to the sky,
Goes through the streets.
The road to happiness,
Goes through immense miseries.
The road to immortality,
Goes through acts of annihilation.
The road to awareness,
Goes through curious investigation.
The road to the world,
Manifests out of our own heart.
The road to the heart of people,
Appears when we are their life's part.
And you know where lies all hope for integration!
It lies in an uncorrupted desire for unification.

Handcrafted Humanity Sonnet 48

Selflessness doesn't mean denying the self,
Being without self is being beyond the self.
It comes back humanized a thousand times,
When you expand the self to reach out and help.
You don't need to deny the self for inclusion,
Or to forget your roots for integration.
All you gotta do, if you want collectivity, is,
Expand your roots and branches in cohesion.
There is no coexistence, but only existence,
For coexistence implies a life of separation.
What the world needs is a wholesome life,
One that exists in the nameless land of heartnation.
So I say my friend, mark this simple notion.
One who is whole is human, all others are imitation.

Handcrafted Humanity Sonnet 49

All our life we live as imitation,
All our life we live as slaves to the past.
When will we live as original humans,
When will we walk as beings beyond class!
All sectarianism is a violation of human rights,
As such all divisions are uncivilization.
Society is society only if there is sanctity,
The highest sanctity is abolition of differentiation.
There is no high society or low society,
The divide is created by empty savages in suits.
When their inside is moronically hollow,
They seek comfort in the poison of sectarian fruits.
I say, enough with this gold-plated lifelessness!
Let us now live for real, rejecting all shallowness.

I'm No Poet (The Sonnet)

I thought I could bear the title poet,
But as it turns out, I cannot.
I can barely bear the title of scientist,
Let alone adding another next to it.
Each title feels like a burden herculean,
My heart cannot function with such burden.
If I am to create works of life and wholeness,
I must be free from titles, sane and insane.
My ideas are not born of mere thought,
If they were, there wouldn't be any torment.
My work comes from a land beyond labels,
A place deeper than thought can penetrate.
So you may call me whatever you like.
In my mind, I am but a nameless light.

Handcrafted Humanity Sonnet 51

Can you put a label on light, sight and might?
The moment you do, you diminish them.
All labels are poison that diminishes your humanity.
Life inside a golden prison is still imprisonment.
You know what a God or a Human is?
It's just a being who has grown out of fakeness.
Yet you will end up labeling yourself and others,
It's difficult for the mind to fathom namelessness.
Fragmentation is our past, there is no denying it.
It's with fragmentation that our ancestors survived.
But just because it worked for savages in the jungle,
Can we accept it as norm in a world that's civilized!
However, labels are necessary for social functioning.
Trouble begins when label takes preference over the being.

Handcrafted Humanity Sonnet 52

I don't want an ideal world,
I just want a human world, quirks and all.
It may have certain technical needs,
But in its heart, it'll be above all dividing fall.
Mark you, separatism is not a quirk,
It is a filthy sickness of the mind.
Let all walls and borders be of geography,
But never let them prevail inside.
Just like labels, titles and designations,
Borders are needed for the world to function.
But never let them define human character,
Arise O Lovenut, and be a soldier of unification.
There's no use in updating your phone's OS every day,
If inside you are still run by an OS from the stone-age.

Handcrafted Humanity Sonnet 53

Smartwatches don't make you productive,
They only make you a lifeless humanoid.
Fitness trackers don't make you fit,
They only make you paranoid.
Internet doesn't make you intelligent,
Without awareness it makes you conspiracist.
Technology doesn't make you omnipotent,
Without moderation, they make you stupid.
There was a time when inventions solved problems,
Today they create problems to sell products.
Technology driven by the desire for revenue,
Doesn't lift society, instead wreaks havoc.
It is high time we place humanity in technology,
Or else, our greatest power will carve a dark destiny.

Handcrafted Humanity Sonnet 54

Every boon is a curse, every curse is a boon,
It all depends on the person wielding it.
In the face of a curse a vegetable gives in,
Whereas the brave turns it into a power-kit.
In reality, there's no such thing as curse or boon,
It is all a creation of our own imagination.
Curse is just our predisposition to primitivity,
Boon is our potential for greatness and ascension.
Life itself is an endless war between curse and boon,
Each victory of the boon takes civilization a step ahead.
But far more common is for the curse to take control,
'Cause giving in to primitivity is a traditional habit.
So grow some vagina without wasting any more moon.
Will you be a puppet of your curse or rise a living boon?

Vagina Power (The Sonnet)

There's nothing special about growing balls,
In fact, man-sack is the definition of weakness.
If you wanna grow something, grow a vagina,
For vagina is the epitome of resilience.
There's an organism that goes through hell,
Quite regularly, yet stands strong and brave.
It is the source of all creation everywhere,
Yet all through history it's been kept as slave.
No love can surpass the love of a mother,
No care can surpass a sister's care.
Yet a society run by balls and bananas,
Makes a hooker out of our mothers and sisters.
Worship of balls is but a prehistoric mania.
There will be no balls without a vagina.

Handcrafted Humanity Sonnet 56

Isn't matriarchy a better alternative to patriarchy,
It obviously is, for a short while indeed.
Soon the troubles of greed and war will disappear,
In its place will appear new issues due to insecurity.
So though I wholeheartedly say without reservation,
The world will be a much better place if run by woman,
If it is a good world for all humans that we want,
All must be involved across gender differentiation.
It's not about women being better troubleshooters,
It's not about men being war mongering morons.
It is really about constructing a whole society,
Where not a single individual faces discriminations.
Thus what'll save this world from getting more screwed,
Is neither sisterhood nor brotherhood, but humanhood.

Muslim Not Terrorist (The Sonnet)

I am a Muslim, not a terrorist,
Just like not all whites are neonazi.
To hate, being an animal is enough,
Love is a sign of sapience and sanity.
Nobody is infidel to me,
For my faith is that of oneness.
Disbelief doesn't make one a kafir,
Only kafir is one without kindness.
No matter what we call water,
It quenches everybody's thirst equally.
I accept all religions to be true and equal,
For what matters is our common humanity.
I have but one message, love over all hatred.
Without love nobody's human, no matter our faith.

Handcrafted Humanity Sonnet 58

Faith is no declaration of character,
It is just a matter of mental necessity.
It has nothing to do with truth and holiness,
In many cases, it makes a person quite unholy.
I often find myself speaking to my dead teacher,
It gives me strength and helps me take the leap.
The scientist in me knows it's all in my head,
But sometimes all logic must take a backseat.
The problem however is not our imaginary friend,
It is our loyalty to it at the expense of our humanity.
Keep your faith if it helps you through hard times,
But never let it be an impediment to universality.
Imagination is healthy when it sustains us as human,
When it ruins our humanity, it's time for its demolition.

Sonnet of Intolerance

Intolerance and religion don't go together,
If they do, you are a far cry from being religious.
Intolerance and science don't go together,
If they do, such science is just modern hogwash.
Intolerance and philosophy don't go together,
If they do, you are a dickhearted intellectualist.
Intolerance and humanism don't go together,
If they do, you are a far cry from being humanist.
Intolerance and intellect don't go together,
If they do, such intellect is all blade, no handle.
Intolerance and wisdom don't go together,
If they do, you are but a sophisticated vandal.
Anything that is civilized helps abolish intolerance,
If it doesn't, it is yet another prehistoric nuisance.

Handcrafted Humanity Sonnet 60

We must get our priorities straight,
Nay, we must get our priority straight.
Once we place humanity at the very top,
Everything else will fall in its right place.
Sometimes imagination may take front seat,
Sometimes intellect, other times sentiment.
As long as there is a human at the wheel,
Smart or not, you'll still bring upliftment.
Before you go about elevating the world,
First you must elevate your own heart.
Shred all attachment to intellect and pride,
Go boldly fighting into the dust and dirt.
The road to the sky goes through the street.
If the street revolts us, time won't pay us any heed.

Handcrafted Humanity Sonnet 61

Those who've severed ties to the street,
Have severed ties to life and liberty.
Those who've severed ties to the soil,
Have severed ties to joy and sanity.
Meaning of life lies in simplicity,
Sanity of life lies in being humble.
If these two sound like alien language,
You're up the creek without a paddle.
In these stormy nights, only shelter is love,
But the egotist remains oblivious and unkeen.
Shred all egotism and arrogance my friend,
You shall become a shelter most comforting.
Come out oh brave, be a vessel of benevolence.
Engulf the whole world with your magnificence.

Handcrafted Humanity Sonnet 62

True freedom is amongst the people,
True freedom is in soil and society.
Bring down all barriers between self and others,
And you shall know responsible liberty.
When you come out and sing the song of service,
The world bathes in sanctifying torrents of happiness.
Lift up your heart, your soul, your entire being,
Then burn it all to ashes, so the world knows kindness.
Community doesn't come from books and libraries,
A selfless spirit is the source of all community.
Be that spirit and rejuvenate all with your touch,
Bring back this world of walking dead to life and sanity.
Your eyes are the window to a humane future,
Feel it in your soul and your heart will make it appear.

Handcrafted Humanity Sonnet 63

Love alone can explain love,
Freedom alone can explain freedom,
Kindness alone can explain kindness,
Affection alone can explain affection.
But if you are looking for explanation,
In love, you are not really in love.
Explanation is an act of intellect,
At times you gotta be an idiot to just love.
It's not enough to find an explanation,
You must learn the place for explanation.
Those who place intellect over kindness,
Will never know life and ascension.
When we accept each other's disfunctionality,
We'll be most functional in all of history.

Handcrafted Humanity Sonnet 64

History is suggestion,
Future is but fiction.
Loyalty to either of them,
Is impediment addiction.
Your story is your own creation,
You are your own aspiration.
You are the ink, pen and paper,
Your life is your own decision.
You are the savior you seek,
You are the messiah when meek.
You are the sight when blind,
Wake up from fear and take a peek.
Cater no more to your insecurity,
Befriend 'em all and you'll have victory.

Handcrafted Humanity Sonnet 65

If you wanna be loco,
Be loco for liberty.
If you wanna be horny,
Be horny for harmony.
If you wanna be obsessed,
Be obsessed for oneness.
If you wanna be a nutcase,
Be a nutcase for knowledge.
If you wanna be a dingbat,
Be a dingbat of determination.
If you wanna be a rebel,
Be a rebel in revolution.
All live for self, all are miserable.
You for one live for others, giving up all label.

Nutty Community (The Sonnet)

Crazy am I, crazy are you,
When crazy together, we live anew.
Miserable am I, miserable are you,
When miserable together, I find joy in you.
Broken am I, broken are you,
When broken together, we are each other's glue.
Insecure am I, insecure are you,
When insecure together, we find it all untrue.
Disfunctional am I, disfunctional are you,
When disfunctional together, we function well.
Fallen am I, fallen are you,
When we fall together, we'll rise sure as hell.
Let us go against ourselves in defying self-centricity.
You be a nut, I'll be a nut, let's build a nutty community.

Handcrafted Humanity Sonnet 67

In the nuttiness of community,
There is heartiness of humanity.
In being a dope against dogmas,
There comes destruction of rigidity.
In being sleepless for society,
We ensure the kids can sleep sound.
If all slept and snored like bugs,
Hate and discrimination will be all around.
In the fiery touch of accountability,
Lies the treatment for disparities.
With the awakening of realization,
Bickering of words fades in the abyss.
At least one is born every century to die for society.
Are you the one to rise, work and die for humanity?

One Life, One Idea (The Sonnet)

One life, one idea, one duty – love.
One body, one being, one vision – amity.
One heart, one sight, one sentiment – care.
One mind, one kind, one community – humanity.
One pen, one ink, one paper – awareness.
One hive, one height, one light – assimilation.
One kite, one compass, one flight – unity.
One sail, one sea, one ship - self-correction.
One gospel, one goal, one gamble – collectivity.
One cult, one core, one culture – unification.
One church, one mosque, one temple – nonduality.
One road, one reason, one reality – nondifferentiation.
Take the mind beyond the bind to see the world anew.
A world united comes to life when walls turn dust in you.

Handcrafted Humanity Sonnet 69

Word of the somnolent masses is noise,
Word of the reformer is rule, divine rule.
On their shoulder the world progresses,
Even though they are seen by peers as fool.
Not a heartless activist or a mindless bigot,
Be a reformer and humanize the world.
The first and only qualification is oneness,
All harmony comes from the heart's cord.
There is no future, if there is no reformer,
Docility doesn't make this world fit for living.
The civilians have light, life and possibility,
Because of reformers who give up everything.
If you like sleeping, don't mock those who don't.
If they fall asleep, you and your children won't.

Handcrafted Humanity Sonnet 70

Sleep is animal,
Human is sleeplessness.
Rest is animal,
Human is restlessness.
Pleasure is animal,
Humanly potent is pain.
Name is important,
But first learn to lose all name.
To fly is good,
Better is to bow to the helpless.
Rightness is important,
More important is kindness.
Feel with your heart, think with your head,
Bring 'em together and walk straight ahead.

Handcrafted Humanity Sonnet 71

No matter the pain never stop walking,
No matter the gain never stop growing.
No matter the aim never ignore the journey,
No matter the fall never stop rising.
No matter the mockery never lose heart,
No matter the applause never stop working.
No matter the roses never stop giving,
No matter the thorns never stop caring.
No matter the comfort never stop learning,
No matter the crisis never stop smiling.
No matter the glory never lose humility,
No matter the darkness never stop helping.
We learn more in crisis than in comfort.
Helping through both is the sign of a good heart.

Handcrafted Humanity Sonnet 72

Sign of life is not whether you are breathing,
Sign of life is whether you are helping another.
Sign of sight is not whether you see with eyes,
Sign of sight is whether you see the pain of another.
Sign of hearing is not whether you hear sounds,
Sign of hearing is whether you listen to heartbeats.
Sign of voice is not whether you can speak yourself,
Sign of voice is when you help the voiceless speak.
To touch someone doesn't mean touching the skin,
The touch that makes a society is that of the heart.
Sign of society is not to walk, talk and dress fancy,
The measure of society is a heart without dirt.
Peace, progress and integration won't fall from the sky,
Unless the commoner breaks free from all selfish outcry.

Handcrafted Humanity Sonnet 73

Who is the commoner, who is not!
Who is the civilian, who is not!
We are all commoners, all civilians,
One who feels separate is a savage hotspot.
If you feel above the commoners,
You don’t belong on an earth of humans.
I see myself in all and all in me,
Thus feels the being with civilized sentience.
Principles over pedigree, virtues over victory,
That's the way to build a world most humane.
Law, religion and politics all would disappear,
If each of us plants a sapling in our life's lane.
Everybody is civilian, everybody is president.
Each of us is responsible for every social dent.

Handcrafted Humanity Sonnet 74

Society is us, we are the society,
We are worshipper, we are almighty.
Gods are we, legends are we,
Why crawl all life with complacency!
Makers are we, breakers are we,
Whatever we decide, so shall it be.
It's time to break all rigid disorder,
And nourish our world with amity.
Taint not the mind with a puny label,
We are beautiful when we are indivisible.
In case you are wondering what's indivisible,
I'll simply say to you, it's love's another label.
Where there is love, no division can ever fester.
It's when we lack love that we give in to barrier.

Loveburnt (The Sonnet)

Jungle creatures look beautiful,
When they are in a habitat that's natural.
The human mind is beautiful when,
Mind and muhabbet are indistinguishable.
Don't go about looking for your phone,
To google the meaning of muhabbet.
It's just a term for the timeless force of love,
The force at the core of all civilized sentience.
You can't force love, all you can do is,
Be vulnerable and reach out despite your insecurity.
Whether the person of your heart responds back,
Is not in your hands, but a matter of cosmic serendipity.
You may burn in the inferno of hate and fear all you want.
Bearing all snowstorm I stand unbent, ready to be loveburnt.

Handcrafted Humanity Sonnet 76

Act with love then forget what you did.
Serve with kindness then forget what you did.
A mind that loves another to receive some gift,
Such a mind is not a mind but a filthy guano pit.
What you receive is not yours to decide,
It is but the decision of Mother Nature.
If you do good, good things will happen to you,
Is but a delusion of our insecure ancestors.
Causing goodness must be the cause of goodness,
All other reasons are mere excuses of hypocrisy.
The question of reward must never enter,
If it does, you're committing a mockery of humanity.
Love alone can cause love, all other means fail in time.
Love is above logic and policy, love is the world's lifeline.

Handcrafted Humanity Sonnet 77

Anybody can draw courage from hundred people,
There's nothing great and glorious about it.
When a hundred people draw courage from you,
That right there is your greatest achievement.
It doesn't help to whine about the obvious,
When the candle of love is burning low.
What is needed is that you burn your heart,
And make a pyre out of its sacrificial glow.
One who lays oneself down to lift the world,
Has the whole world as their lifeline.
Make a bridge out of your blood and sweat,
In our moment of sacrifice we live a lifetime.
Love alone is the highest truth of civilization,
All else are mere echo of primitive recollection.

Handcrafted Humanity Sonnet 78

I do not know about physical time,
Physicists can tell whether it exists.
But if we talk about psychological time,
I'll tell you straight ahead, it doesn't exist.
With this mental time a world is built,
Physical time has nothing to do with it.
Past exists because we can remember it,
Future exists because we can imagine it.
Since all of it is the creation of our brain,
All of it is in our very own human hands.
Learning from the errors of time gone by,
We must act now to raise a future most grand.
Mind is the sentient seed of all time and tide,
Yet we hide like roaches behind fate's fake hide.

Fate and Future (The Sonnet)

Fate and future both are servant to the determined,
For they are nothing but creation of human determination.
Yet most of humanity remain oblivious to this simple fact,
For they're born and raised in a society run by indoctrination.
Reason and questions are seen as treason against heritage,
Submission and guilt are praised as honorable righteousness.
Calling ignorance as righteousness doesn't make one righteous,
You are righteous when you have the guts to mend mistakes.
Ignorance is part of life, so is our drive for self-aggrandizing,
It's human to make mistakes, what's not, is their glorification.
Acknowledge your mistakes, biases, ignorance and prejudice,
We start to rise when we acknowledge our degradation.
Our ancestors were primitive humans with unused goodness.
If we die primitive like they did, why live in the first place!

Raghead (The Sonnet)

Some call me raghead,
Some call me desert dweller.
Some call me curry-breath,
Some call me f-ing nigger.
This is not just my story,
But of every person of color.
In a world stolen by whites,
Anything non-white is inferior.
Upon receiving so much hate,
I admit, sometimes I do feel gloomy.
I know how it is to be cussed everyday,
So I choose love no matter the agony.
The tradition of hate has gone on long enough.
I choose to be the break in habit on the world's behalf.

Handcrafted Humanity Sonnet 81

If a tradition endorses hate and mistrust,
It's the tradition that we must reject not people.
If a heritage endorses division and discrimination,
It's the heritage that we must reject not people.
If an ancestor passes on bigotry and barbarism,
It's the ancestor that we must reject not people.
If a bible teaches phobia and separatism,
It's the bible that we must reject not people.
If a messiah preaches blindness and conspiracy,
It's the messiah that we must reject not people.
If God commands oppression and occupation,
It's the God that we must reject not people.
Above all commandment, love is the highest truth.
Anything that divides love is a stoneage residue.

Handcrafted Humanity Sonnet 82

Cutting edge on the outside, stoneage on the inside,
That's how we spend our life as imitation humans.
With etiquettes and vocabs we try to cover our dirt,
Yet the filth shows up, no matter our pretense.
You can dress a chimpanzee in a fancy tuxedo,
That doesn't change how the chimpanzee behaves.
The same goes for us apes in our suits and dresses,
To put it simply, we are just good-looking savages.
Then there's the magic innovation called social media,
Which helps already fake humans to be more fake.
Thus yet another innovation has gone down the gutter,
'Cause humankind excels at failing to self-regulate.
Whether digitally or really, we always pretend perfection.
The day we accept ourselves is the day of our resurrection.

Facebook Sonnet

Facebook is not just injurious to health,
It's now a full-on humanitarian crisis.
If you think it's just a harmless bad habit,
You're fanning the flames of social necrosis.
Social media ought to make people social,
Not make pavlov's dogs out of humanity.
Yet all that facebook actually does today,
Is drive society towards clinical insanity.
Social media is not necessarily bad,
So long as it doesn't feed on our stability.
Yet facebook has devised the perfect algorithm,
To learn, pump and monetize human instability.
Facebook is the definition of what AI must be not.
Algorithm without humanity is mental holocaust.

Sonnet of Power

It is not enough to have a great innovation,
We must learn how to use it without causing harm.
Just like it's not enough to have nuclear power,
We must use it for good without blowing up the world.
We haven't yet outgrown our primitive fetish for guns,
How could we possibly use, not abuse, advanced technology!
All great power has the potential for bad as much as good,
Going mad over power doesn't help peace and prosperity.
No power should be taken for granted and used recklessly,
Even a knife is super lethal in the hands of an innocent toddler.
That's why new parents childproof the home before childbirth,
How do we peopleproof a planet so they don't hurt each other!
But here the people we're talking about are nobody else but us.
Why must our world be fodder for buffoons in political fuss!

Handcrafted Humanity Sonnet 85

There's a path from my heart to yours,
But we cannot see it with our puny eyes.
Our heart is the path, the path is our heart,
This won't make sense till you go beyond sight.
There's a bridge from my mind to yours,
We can't see it 'cause we're busy raising walls.
To bridge the gap from mind to mind,
First we must bridge the gaps inside of us.
Fragmentation is the cause of all stagnation,
Stagnation is the cause of all division.
To wipe out the divisions from the face of earth,
We must step up and treat our fragmentation.
Oneness doesn't appear magically out of thin air.
It's a journey of a lifetime, the journey of love's labor.

Handcrafted Humanity Sonnet 86

Every lover is a fighter,
Who you love, you fight to protect.
Can you fight till death the same way,
While defending humankind's interest!
To fight ain't about being a gunslinger,
It's time to wield our heart as canon and candle.
Because if we still cannot outgrow firearms,
We better pack up and head back to the jungle.
Where there is love, guts come naturally,
Guts and glory without love do only doo-doo.
Responsibility in love needs no special mention,
Love makes a leader even out of a lifelong stooge.
Fall, fall and fall in love, for love is the only way.
Take the rap, mend the mess and herald a new day.

Sonnet of Holy Water

A new day starts with a new you,
And I ain't talkin' about born again nonsense.
A bigot baptized a thousand times is still a bigot,
A human helping another is Christ himself.
There is no second coming, there's no reincarnation,
Except when we go from selfishness to kindness.
We are the messiahs and saviors of our people,
Nobody's gonna fall from the sky to lift the helpless.
The liquor store sells you the same divinity,
That the holy store sells you for even higher price.
We'll be born again when we abolish such divinity,
By baptizing the soil of society with our sacrifice.
The tears of joy someone sheds because of you,
Are the only holy water to build the world anew.

Handcrafted Humanity Sonnet 88

Holiness has a better name,
Which has nothing to do with religion.
Religion has a better name,
Which has nothing to do with religion.
Gospel has a better name,
Which has nothing to do with religion.
Prayer has a better name,
Which has nothing to do with religion.
Belief has a better name,
Which has nothing to do with religion.
Bible has a better name,
Which has nothing to do with religion.
Lemme tell you the name that substitutes even God,
It's just an ordinary kindness of the human heart.

Handcrafted Humanity Sonnet 89

The core of a human is kindness,
The core of an animal is self-centricity.
The essence of a human is simplicity,
The essence of a moron is complexity.
The spine of a human is community,
The spine of vegetable is complacency.
The veins of a human hold thunder,
The veins of a bonehead carry rigidity.
The eyes of a human see injustice,
The eyes of a monkey see nothing.
The feet of a human trudge mockery,
The feet of slime only keep crawling.
Human, human wherever you are,
Grow some vagina and be a mountaineer.

Handcrafted Humanity Sonnet 90

Mountains bow when you start climbing,
Oceans dry when you start crossing.
Awake, arise and boldly march forward,
The path appears when you start walking.
Churches collapse when you stand up,
Temples tremble when appears your face.
Gods keep quiet when you speak up,
Nature smiles when you defy her gaze.
We are the only life-form on earth,
With the potential to humanize nature.
Though Nature can survive with or without us,
Only we can make her less of a monster.
Possible and impossible, it's all in our own psyche.
We're not just a life-form, but a realm of possibility.

Handcrafted Humanity Sonnet 91

You may have heard of the cliché,
Impossible means I am possible.
But possibility that's only about you,
Is worse than what's impossible.
When you turn impossible possible,
You mustn't be the only one benefitted.
If the change you cause doesn't cause change,
Then what is the point of it all anyway!
No dream must be coldly self-centric,
No destination full of luxurious desire.
When you look back at the days gone by,
You oughta see labor, not your lost character.
Dream is a wonderful thing, so long as it's human.
Any dream separate from society is an endeavor inhuman.

Handcrafted Humanity Sonnet 92

My dream is the world's dream,
Thus speaks the volcanic victor.
The world in me is the world in thee,
It is time to be each other's mirror.
If I have ten days to live,
I'll spend one day gathering strength,
So I can spend the rest nine days,
Helping and lifting the fallen.
If all the harms brought upon people,
Don't make your blood boil,
Then ask yourself this one question,
Is there blood in your veins or engine oil!
Still if you don't mind the troubles of our world,
What good is that full 5 litres of blood!

Handcrafted Humanity Sonnet 93

Blood that only runs a single body,
Is nothing but animal blood.
Blood that nourishes a society,
Is actual, genuine human blood.
Nerves that energize a single mind,
Are nothing but animal nerves.
Nerves that invigorate a community,
Are actual, genuine human nerves.
Spine that straightens a single body,
Is nothing but animal spine.
Spine that straightens a planet,
Is actual, genuine human spine.
Human life is nature's greatest force for good.
Will you live it as such or waste it being cold and crude!

Handcrafted Humanity Sonnet 94

Selfishness is a boon for the animal,
But a curse for human and humanity.
Any society founded on selfishness,
May live long but not without cruelty.
Now the question that we must ask is,
Is life really life when fraught with cruelty!
Such a life looks good in the jungle,
We are born to do away with such atrocity.
It is never about survival, not any more,
If it were, we didn't have to move out of jungle.
We moved out of our Mother Nature's basement,
So we could build a kind world for ourselves.
A world built on kindness, conscience and courage,
That is what we the humankind are born to raise.

Handcrafted Humanity Sonnet 95

Nature always tries to trick us most strongly,
Into being a filthy bunch of egotistical morons.
If we stand true to our conviction of community,
No cockeyed canine is gonna dictate our terms.
Survival of the fittest is the motto of animal,
Sacrifice for the helpless is the motto of human.
The decision is to be made by none but you,
What'll you spend your life as - animal or human!
Let's not spend another day with cold shoulder,
Let us rather put all of our shoulders together.
Only then we will be a tad stronger than history,
And rise as the mightiest descendant of Nature.
To conquer ourselves is to conquer space and time.
We live the fullest when we live as people's lifeline.

Handcrafted Humanity Sonnet 96

To conquer hearts is to conquer time,
To conquer souls is to conquer space.
The whole world belongs to those,
Who belong to the world beyond labels.
Nobody belongs to the society,
Till they lose ownership of themselves.
Civilization is built on selves lost in service,
Our rise is in the end of selfish achievements.
Cruelty kills no cruelty, only kindness does it,
Fighting fire with fire turns the world to ashes.
Bullets don't kill bigotry, only education does that,
Set your heart on fire, let all bask in your effulgence.
The sun will never set on the empire of human beings,
So long as they are humans and not colonial creeplings.

Handcrafted Humanity Sonnet 97

I am a human being,
Born and raised on earth.
Borders try quite a lot,
To tear my heart apart.
A child is taught early on,
About the separation of culture.
Then they shout like idiots,
War is caused by policymakers.
True integration of society lies,
In the heart around the corner.
Expand beyond all teachings,
And nobody will be left a stranger.
If we can't step across appearance outward,
How will we ever be an intergalactic culture!

Handcrafted Humanity Sonnet 98

Culture should be a path, not a prison,
Yet we've been living in it as prisoners.
Identity should be a land with no bounds,
Yet we've been living with it as islanders.
Community should be a castle of togetherness,
Not a cold, bigoted and unchanging Fort Knox.
Tradition should be about strengthening bonds,
Not about separating people from loved ones.
Intellect should be about using reason to heal,
Not boasting one's psychological supremacy.
Worth of a person is defined by character,
Not by their appearance, status or pedigree.
Enough with this idiotic pursuit of shallowness,
If not now, when exactly will we foster humanness!

Handcrafted Humanity Sonnet 99

To hell with our ancestors,
To hell with our background.
We can learn a lot from history,
But we mustn't use it as our ground.
Our ground is the people around us,
Nothing must come between people and people,
For there is no 'my people and your people',
Rather it is all just one human people.
When they ask me which state I come from,
I tell them, I come from the state of oneness.
In that state there is no policy of inclusion,
For there nobody is divided in the first place.
Many call it enlightenment but I call it oneness.
To heal all division nothing's stronger than wholeness.

Beyond Inclusion (The Sonnet)

It is not really inclusion that we must aim for,
Rather we must work to outgrow the need for inclusion.
It is not really global harmony that we must aim for,
We must outgrow the very term international relations.
It is not really a reform in policy that we must aim for,
Rather we must aim to outgrow the need for policy aids.
It is not really social awareness we must aim to advocate,
Rather we must be the living epitome of social oneness.
It is not a flea market of parties that we must aim to build,
Rather we must turn the very term partisanism obsolete.
It is not a junkyard of ideologies that we must aim to raise,
Absorbing good from all, let us stop being ideological elites.
Plenty of time we have wasted on arguments of philosophy.
Now let's go out on the streets and soil to get our hands dirty.

31. Mücadele Muhabbet

The Being is The Bridge (The Sonnet)

I came to life at Dakshineswar,
At Kapadokya I got my sight.
I found my might at Shaolin,
At Liberty Island I came to light.
In Pernik I bathed in love,
By the Volga I tasted sapience.
Lika taught me the role of innovation,
Sudbury gave me the sail of science.
Streets of Calcutta showed me suffering,
Streets of Chicago reminded, I'm the answer.
It's not the place but people who hold magic,
Revolution rose when all of them came together.
You won't know me as the father of a nation.
You'll know me as the maker of amalgamation.

Peace is Existence (The Sonnet)

Peace is not a statement,
Peace is existence.
Love is not a sentiment,
Love is sentience.
Awareness is not a practice,
Awareness is absolution.
Moderation is not restriction,
Moderation is jubilation.
Ignorance is not inferiority,
Ignorance is upliftment.
Failure is not the end,
It is the road to development.
Acknowledge the whole, quirks and all.
You have all the powers to treat the world.

You Are The Universe (The Sonnet)

You don't carry the torch, you are the torch.
You don't build the bridge, you are the bridge.
You don't pave the way, you are the way.
You don't make peace, you are the peace.
You don't build the future, you are the future.
You don't build civilization, you are civilization.
You don't serve the society, you are the society.
You don't work for reform, you are reformation.
You don't walk the path, you are the path.
You don't lift humanity, you are the humanity.
You don't make progress, you are the progress.
You don't serve the community, you are community.
You don't live in the universe, you are the universe.
Dimension destiny unfolds only in the human heart.

Lovely and Beastly (The Sonnet)

Lovely on the outside, beastly on the inside,
That is the norm of the modern world.
Fancy in appearance, yet lousy in sapience,
That's what we call civilized and cultured.
We are given a world rooted in shallowness,
Which screams selfishness in its every act.
Enough with this life of nonexistence,
We've spent long enough as empty wolfpack.
Let us now build our destiny with our sweat,
And devil and deity take the hindmost.
We shall soar high by serving on the streets,
There is no higher life, no greater post.
It's ok that we haven't known true civilization.
What's not ok is to pass it on through generation.

Life Beyond Rhyme (The Sonnet)

Those who don't do, bark,
Those who are humans, do.
Those who don't help, howl,
Those who are humans, help.
Those who don't lift, laugh,
Those who are humans, lift.
Those who don't encourage, cuss,
Those who are humans, encourage.
Those who don’t mend, mock,
Those who are humans, mend.
Those who got no vagina, patronize,
Those who are humans, grow vagina.
If we can love ourselves despite our flaws,
Why can't we be a little kind to others!

To Live A Single Day (The Sonnet)

To live even for a single day,
In the full light of oneness.
To walk even for a single day,
In the full might of kindness.
To talk even for a single day,
In the full sight of humility.
To breathe even for a single day,
In the full height of amity.
To smile even for a single day,
Without a trace of hidden deceit.
To love even for a single day,
As an undeterred force of uplift.
Isn't that the highest sanity?
Isn't that the highest humanity?

Humans Are Defined (The Sonnet)

Vegetables are defined,
By the comfort they crave,
Humans are defined,
By the obstacles they brave.
Absence of obstacles,
Is not a sign of achievement.
Absence of obstacles,
Indicates a lack of movement.
Even the mountains bow,
But not for self-absorbed snobs.
Oceans part making way,
Only for those not afraid of storms.
Awake, arise o soldier of valiance and valor.
Sleep not, slacken not, the world is in your care.

Pay it Forward Sonnet

Say no thanks, instead help another,
And tell them to pay it forward.
The one tradition this world badly needs,
Is that of kindness beyond all reward.
The world lacks kindness and compassion,
For so far rituals are passed on as tradition.
One generation of savage and divided tribals,
Makes sure to propagate nothing but division.
This very prehistoric tendency must end,
We must humanize the very notion of tradition.
Let us place all glory on the colors of joy,
Let us prioritize kindness over all argumentation.
And remember not to mechanize this with ideology.
Helping those in need is just plain ordinary humanity.

Human and Love (The Sonnet)

The day human and love are the same thing,
The day human and harmony are the same thing,
The day human and inclusion are the same thing,
The day human and acceptance are the same thing,
The day human and reason are the same thing,
The day human and emotion are the same thing,
The day human and duty are the same thing,
The day human and dignity are the same thing,
The day human and persistence are the same thing,
The day human and perseverance are the same thing,
The day human and resilience are the same thing,
The day human and character are the same thing,
The day self and society are the same thing,
That day each of us will be a human being.

How I Get My Ideas (The Sonnet)

You wanted to know how I get my ideas,
The universe speaks to me.
You wanted to know how my words appear,
The soil and the air hand them to me.
You asked how do I speak for every culture,
I listen to the heart beyond the word.
You asked how am I not bound by geography,
Long ago I turned my inner walls into dust.
You said to me that I should have some fun,
I'll indeed have fun when the fallen are lifted.
You wanted to know why do I care at all,
That's because I am an alive human not an insect.
Instead of asking why and how a human acts human,
If there is no such being around why not be the first one!

The Price I Pay (The Sonnet)

I spent my life in the depth of heart,
So my social skills are a little lacking.
Either they want me to be deep always,
Or they simply call me rather cheesy.
Whenever I try small talking as human,
I fail and fail again most spectacularly.
That's the price I pay for being your rock,
A timeless pillar unfit for warmth and amity.
Mine is not to ask why, mine is to do or die,
A path in which I turned my life into an idea.
Still it'd be nice to be treated as a human,
It'd be nice to feel the gentleness of another.
There is no greatness without weakness.
Greats must persevere no matter the coldness.

The Dream Lives On (The Sonnet)

Washington had a dream,
The dream of free America.
Martin Luther had a dream,
The dream of equal America.
Adi Shankara had a dream,
The dream of advaita Bharat.
Chandra Bose had a dream,
The dream of azad Bharat.
Naskar too has a dream,
The dream of undivided Earth.
My body will perish soon but,
The dream will live on through hearts.
Gone are the days of nationalistic insecurity.
Lo the time comes for expansion of humanity.

Mission Immortal (The Sonnet)

You can put an end to my life,
But you can't wipe out my light.
You can break all of my limbs,
But you can never break my might.
My might comes from my conviction,
My light comes from my oneness.
Body is just a vessel for the mission,
Mission that is immortal and timeless.
For the mission to turn into reality,
All reality must be turned the mission.
Living in body we live a few decades,
Living in mission we turn immortal.
So let us put all self-preservation aside,
Forgetting limelight let us be timelight.

Vibration and Frequency (The Sonnet)

Surpass the nonsense of vibration,
Surpass the nonsense of frequency.
Come down to the land of mortals,
Embrace the heart's simple beauty.
Science is science, sentiment is sentiment,
In rationalizing sentiment one breeds superstition.
There is no vibration to love and community,
There is no frequency to uplift and unification.
Cleanse your mind of all imitation science,
Just like you ought to do with bigoted holiness.
Trading in one blindness for another is no sanctity,
Replacing one superstition with another is no science.
With the rise of oneness, theories wither and fade away.
But if things are opposite, know that you are going astray.

No Love Without Tears (The Sonnet)

There is no love without tears.
There is no diversity without difference.
There is no revolution without smears.
There's no justice without inconvenience.
There is no development without flaws.
There is no dignity without disrespect.
There is no learning without falling.
There is no heart without heartbreak.
There is no path without the thorns.
There is no pedestrian without weariness.
There is no dream without the hardship.
There's no determination without doubtfulness.
Only those who have felt excruciating pain,
Can help others without expecting any gain.

Sonnet of Public Service

Every reformer is a public servant,
But not every public servant is a reformer,
For public service isn't taught as life itself,
But as just another job little more secure.
If only education focused on life and love,
Instead of constantly peddling competition,
Perhaps we'd have a world little less bitter,
And we'd have ascension, not abomination.
But there's no use in brooding over history,
What's needed is to realize love as our core.
Education and all be manifestations of love,
If not, it is just another snobbish endeavor.
May service be the goal, role and whole of life,
Instead of being and raising educated lowlife.

Sonnet of Education

Competition is for horses,
Education is for the human.
Either education or competition,
You can have only one.
Education ought to build character,
Not to raise snobs hooked on cash.
Love is needed, kindness is needed,
It won't come by raising tribal trash.
Cash-building education is uneducation,
For it only sustains self-absorption.
Character-building education is ascension,
For it paves the way for true civilization.
One can be educated yet a filthy savage.
True sign of education lies in selflessness.

Character No Commodity (The Sonnet)

Character, I say, is no commodity,
To be traded in for luxury.
Integrity, I say, is no commodity,
To be traded in for security,
Virtues, I say, are no commodity,
To be traded in for applause.
Values, I say, are no commodity,
To be traded in for comfort.
Warmth, I say, is no commodity,
To be traded in for image.
Humility, I say, is no commodity,
To be traded in for respect.
A life without honor, I say,
Is a life totally gone astray.

In Work Be Restless (The Sonnet)

In work, be restless,
In love, be limitless,
In care, be oceandeep,
In service, be selfless.
In virtue, be skywide,
In justice, be incorruptible,
In integrity, be unbending,
In honor, be uncompromisable.
In culture, be without walls,
In courage, be endless,
In compassion, be senseless,
In character, be borderless.
Life's too grand to be wasted in gutter.
Expand your heart and you'll rise higher.

Sacred Feminines and Holy Fathers (The Sonnet)

Listen you all discrimination-vaalo,
No matter how much you whine and wallow,
To obliterate all hateful bone and marrow,
Lo comes a generation of caballera, caballero!
Not a trace of dominant fear and anxiety,
Not a particle of self-centric practicality,
Lo come the bravehearts made of thunder,
Lo come the true preservers of humanity!
Breaking free from all that is old and rotten,
Overcoming all drives of untamed tribalism,
Lo come the sacred feminines of creation,
Lo come the holy fathers of nondivisionism!
Though divided by thought, still united by heart,
Grab these new nerves, give yourselves a jumpstart.

32. Making Britain Civilized

Bloodline is Dirtline (The Sonnet)

I'll say plainly, bloodline is dirtline,
When we place blood over character.
Worth of a person lies in behavior,
Not in their allegiance to ancestors.
Better be a responsible ancestor,
Than some boneheaded descendant.
Respect is one thing, allegiance is another,
Allegiance turns a living human into insect.
I am not talking about denying your roots,
But it's imperative, you expand beyond roots.
Spread your branches, reach beyond restraints,
If necessary even give tradition the boot.
Those who are responsible for their society,
Have no need whatsoever to rely on ancestry.

Serve Britannia (The Sonnet)

Let us build a new Britain,
A Britain with actual heart's beauty,
Where we shall right our wrongs,
Instead of boasting our atrocities.
Let us build a new Britain,
Where commoners are king and queen,
Where unlike our tribal ancestors,
Our habit is not occupation but caring.
Let us herald a new Britain,
Where there is no exit only inclusion,
Where no one bows to no one for honor,
And each lives with self-determination.
Serve Britannia! Britannia, serve as aid.
Britain never again shall make others slave.

Thank You Hitler (The Sonnet)

Thank you Hitler for showing the worst of humanity,
I am sorry that we couldn't place you on a pedestal.
Things would've been different if you were not a nobody,
Particularly if you had a background royally honorable.
Apparently if you have an empire to your name,
You can get away with the most heinous of atrocities.
If you have that blue blood running through your veins,
Tyranny, oppression, are deemed as acts of great dignity.
The common notion is, everything nazi is sick and sinister,
At the same time, everything british is great and glorious,
Despite the fact that it was the british empire that was,
An international force of evil unlike the nazi bastards.
Nazism is an enemy of humanity, there is no doubt.
Only if we felt so for the empire as we do for the krauts!

Rightful King (The Sonnet)

The rightful king is one who dissolves the kingdom.
The rightful politician is one who dissolves the party.
The rightful ruler is one who wants only to serve.
The rightful citizen is always steadfast in accountability.
Long live the Queen and Heil Hitler are one and the same,
For both are sign of absolute allegiance without question.
Allegiance to king and country keeps a land uncivilized,
Allegiance to ideology and tradition destroys all ascension.
Let there be no king and queen, let there be no kingdom,
Let there be no party and let there be no authoritarianism.
The force that builds a world doesn't come from bloodline,
For character is beyond the grasp of our puny sectarianism.
In a civilized society we are all king, we are all policymaker.
The world advances when we advance as its fervent keeper.

When Walls Turn Dust (The Sonnet)

When the walls in us turn to dust,
Even the dust turns gold by our touch.
We are the supreme keeper of our society,
We are the maker of a world beyond class.
Nature divides for nature prefers cruelty,
Kindness ain't natural, yet it defines humanity.
When we are kind as a species long enough,
Slowly but surely we'll overpower all our cruelty.
It's just a matter of priority against predispositions,
A matter of human preference over animal tendency.
What's needed is a firm grasp over knacks and urges,
What's needed is healthy self-regulation at full tenacity.
Wars of the world will end when we conquer ourselves.
The world will be civilized when we civilize ourselves.

Sensible Love Sonnet

A heart measurable is no heart at all,
For a heart that expands not, is dead.
Love sensible is no love at all,
Love that makes sense is love of the dead.
Raise your head, reach out with heart,
And the whole world will fall at your feet.
Better senseless in love than loveless in logic,
Heartiness is no forte of the intellectual elite.
It is far better to fall in love and suffer,
Than to spend your life as a farmer awaiting rain.
Scars of love are not scars but the elixir of life,
Life without such suffering is a life gone in vain.
Regret not that you suffer in love, regret if you don't.
I'd give up all my brains for a moment of love's angst.

Posh Yet Potty (The Sonnet)

One can be posh on the outside yet potty on the inside.
More often than less both of these go hand in hand.
Pedigree, personality, position, all are deemed important.
Amidst this royal mess of things we forget to be human.
We look at partisan loyalty, we look at intellectual fluency,
And in the process of analysis we end up a freudian chasm.
In order to find whether someone belongs in our camp,
We act less of a human and more of a lifeless algorithm.
It's okay if you don't know how to use spoon and fork.
What matters is, to reach out and feed an empty stomach.
It's okay if you don't know much fancy words and facts.
What matters is, your heart beats beyond the factual muck.
So, shitty or not we look on the outside, let's pay no attention,
Instead let us muster all spirit towards internal ascension.

Tools and Fools (The Sonnet)

I am a scientist but,
I don't care about science.
I am a monk but,
I don't care about enlightenment.
I am a philosopher but,
I don't care about philosophy.
I am a theologian but,
I don't care about theology.
I may use a lot of tools,
But that's what they are - tools.
They are meant to serve society,
Not look down on people as fools.
When the tool rules, user turns a tool.
Human above all else - lo the supreme rule.

Every Place is Home (The Sonnet)

Make every place your home,
Make every person your family,
For all separation is mere illusion,
All division in society is imaginary.
It's time to move out of the gutter,
The gutter of cultural exclusivity.
It's time to bring down the barriers,
The barriers that ruin our humanity.
Take the self beyond the self,
You shall witness the light of day.
Life divided is a life wasted,
Hence expansion is the only way.
It's the people that make a planet.
Without people existence is worthless.

Ripped Jeans & Twenty Dollar Shirt (The Sonnet)

Ripped jeans and twenty dollar shirt,
That's how we'll change the world.
It is okay if your outside is dirty,
Make sure your heart is without dirt.
Too many people wear suits and boots,
In order to cover up the filth within.
Those who have their character intact,
Care not whether their clothes are shinin'.
The world needs purpose, integrity, honor,
None of which is predicated on clothes.
Those who think clothes make the person,
Will never discover any of the civilized roads.
Heart makes the person, heart makes the world.
A world without dirt comes from a heart without dirt.

33. Dervish Advaitam

Dervish Advaitam Sonnet

Aham dharmam, aham daivam,
Aham qurban for bhoolokam.
Aham nyayam, aham shastram,
Aham the end of all divisionism.
Aham prakriti, aham pralayam,
Aham the seed of all causality.
I am life, I am death as well,
Life to love 'n death to inhumanity.
To most people family is the world,
But to me the world is family.
Because I am accountable for all life,
I am the epitome of collectivity.
All that is civilized starts with me.
Aham brahmandam, aham brahmasmi.

(aham: I am, dharmam: duty, daivam: divinity, qurban: sacrificed, bhoolokam: kingdom of earth,nyayam: justice, shastram: gospel, prakriti: nature, pralayam: apocalypse, brahmandam: universe, brahmasmi: almighty)

Good Little Gods (The Sonnet)

A good person once said, to turn the other cheek.
I ain't him, I don't approve of his kind of naivety.
Hurt me all you want, I may still keep quiet but,
Lay a finger on my loved ones, 'n you are history.
Someone once ordered, sacrifice your child for me,
And a spineless patriarch rushed to obey it all.
If god commands to slaughter someone I love,
That stoneage nitwit will return without his balls.
Someone said, strike your partner if she denies coitus,
To which countless bugs still remain obedient.
I ask that moron of a god to come 'n say it to me,
And he won't be left man enough to even get a head.
Humankind ain't no slave to no prehistoric lords.
We may spare them only if they're good little gods.

Test of Faith (The Sonnet)

How many gospels are there?
Civilized answer is, who cares!
How many apostles were there?
Civilized answer is, who cares!
What are the commandments?
Civilized answer is, who cares!
How many vedas are there?
Civilized answer is, who cares!
What is the meaning of basmala?
Civilized answer is, who cares!
What are the words of mool mantar?
Civilized answer is, who cares!
What god wants of us, who the fudge cares!
To be human for all humans is what matters.

Language of God (The Sonnet)

A Jew may say, Hebrew is the language of god.
A Christian may say, Aramaic is the language of god.
A Muslim will say, Arabic is the language of god.
A Hindu will say, Sanskrit is the language of god.
A biologist may say, DNA is the language of god.
Mathematicians say, math is the language of god.
A psychiatrist may say, libido is the language of god.
Physicists say, Quantum Mechanics is language of god.
A politician may say, control is the language of god.
A capitalist may say, currency is the language of god.
A cop may say, law and order are the language of god.
A philosopher may say, wisdom is the language of god.
I don't know all that, I'm a being most ordinary 'n simple.
I only know that kindness is the language of a human.

What is Divinity (The Sonnet)

Hands joined in prayer ain't no divinity,
Hands stretched in help are true divinity.
Saying grace before meal ain't divinity,
Graceful kindness is the actual divinity.
Marking a cross on yourself ain't divinity,
Crossing out the self for others is real divinity.
Confessing errors to a preacher ain't divinity,
Correcting errors by yourself is true divinity.
Selling glories of a dead messiah ain't divinity,
Refusing all glory to lift another is real divinity.
Sitting cross-legged in meditation ain't divinity,
Standing up bold against injustice is true divinity.
Divinity never comes from bible, marvel or vatican.
Burn yourself for others, and you'll know salvation.

Life in People (The Sonnet)

A rich egotist came and said,
You 'n I are quite the same you see,
You control people with words,
I control people with money.
I burst out in laughter 'n replied,
I feel sorry for you, o poor mental.
You look for life in the palace,
While I found my life in people.
You keep hoarding luxury,
While I chose a life of simplicity.
You crawl all life fearing death,
I made friends out of death 'n destiny.
You stay aloof on pedestal patronizing people.
I labor at love's altar egalitarianizing people.

Let Us Be (The Sonnet)

Let us be evolution,
Let us be the revolution.
There is plenty pollution,
Now let's be the solution.
Let us be soldiers eternal,
Let us be lovers adamant.
Let's not fear the fiery storms,
Let us be humans valiant.
Let us be the hope to others,
Let us be joy to others.
In a world full of self-obsession,
Across all self, let's be the help to others.
Service of society is no act of charity,
For it is just life, for it is just humanity.

If I Must Die (The Sonnet)

I have no desire to die as just,
Another writer like that bard fella.
If I must die as a writer, I will die as,
The first multi-cultural writer en historia.
I have no desire to die as just,
Another founder of a sect or nation.
If I must die as something, I'll die as,
One of the founders of human unification.
I have no desire to die as just another,
Coldhearted scientist or pompous philosopher.
If I must die as a scientist and philosopher,
I'll die as the one who made love truth's driver.
But above all that, I have no desire to die, period.
Cowards die, whereas I, am already martyred.

Consensus of Heart (The Sonnet)

Place truth at the feet of love,
Intellect at the feet of integration.
Place belief at the feet of harmony,
Stubbornness at the feet of ascension.
Place tradition at the feet of expansion,
Individuality at the feet of collectivity.
Place knowledge at the feet of warmth,
Patriotism at the feet of world community.
Place differences at the feet of unity,
Rebellion at the feet of accountability.
Place serenity at the feet of social uplift,
Practicality at the feet of dignity 'n equality.
Whether there is consensus of head or not,
Let us first ensure consensus of the heart.

To Be Pure (The Sonnet)

To be gentle is to be pure.
To be humble is to be pure.
To be simple is to be pure.
To be unselfish is to be pure.
To be pure of heart is to have,
A heart that beats for others.
To be of sound mind is to conquer,
All rigid tenets 'n desires.
Nudge your head wide open,
Let all conspiracies fall out.
Love your heart wide open,
Let prejudice lose all ground.
It's more important to be kind than right.
Sometimes to be human you gotta lose the fight.

The Troll Sonnet

When someone says, your life is a joke,
Hold your silence 'n smile without outrage.
You do not become an immortal legend,
Without facing a million slurry comments.
Fight injustice, but be silent at mockery,
To retaliate mockery is to become mockery.
Those who mock, don't really mock at you,
They are just validating their own inferiority.
Tremendous spirit for your life's purpose,
And uniform silence towards all who mock,
That is the key to timeless achievement,
Be unperturbed 'n dive in lock, barrel 'n stock.
Silence is the best response to all mockery.
Mockery is the sincerest form of flattery.

Victor Volcano (Sonnet for Haters)

Haters keep yelling slurs,
Then wonder and despond,
Why do I always keep quiet,
Why do I never respond!
I am not a slave you bought,
At an arabian slave market.
I am not your domestic pet,
To exist for your amazement.
I ain't no circus or zoo animal,
To sit 'n bear slurs, you fool.
My name is Victor Volcano,
You're safe, so long as I'm cool.
That's why I keep quiet 'n walk away.
If I ever retaliate, haters will fade away.

Mess With A Scientist (The Sonnet)

Mess with a police officer,
You may end up in prison.
And you may end up dead,
If you mess with a politician.
Mess with a bureaucrat,
You may end up exploited.
Mess with a programmer,
You may end up humiliated.
If you offend a teacher,
Your children might suffer.
If you offend a preacher,
You'll be deemed a blasphemer.
But mess with a scientist, that's your ticket to hell.
Neither dead nor alive, you'll dangle in the middle.

The Motto Sonnet

Hard as steel and soft as flower,
That's the motto for a civilized human.
Tough as thunder, sweet as honey,
That's the motto for a braveheart human.
Not too much unguided sentiments,
Not too much intellectual coldness,
To give either of them total slack,
Is to bring destruction and lifelessness.
Corazón primero, después dinero,*
Thus speaks the human of revolution.
Humanidad primero, después verdad,**
That's the motto for the being of evolution.
Strength, warmth 'n reason, all are needed.
And all are to be guided by oneness uncorrupted.

(*Heart first, money later. **Humanity first, truth later.)

Human of Revolution (The Sonnet)

Human of revolution is not a human of vengeance,
Human of evolution is not a human of recklessness.
If vengeance 'n recklessness ensured human rights,
The jungle would be the definition of kindness.
Let your blood boil in the course of justice 'n equality,
But don't become a monster in fighting monstrosity.
Let the prehistoric cycle of cruelty break with you,
So that humanity can dream beyond rights 'n dignity.
It's not about getting vengeance, or about getting even,
Justice begins with self-regulation, not law and order.
Can you tell right from wrong without involving law,
The day you do is the birth of actual, lasting order.
I say, revolution means defending without descending.
Hold their punches, hold your punches, 'n start dancing.

Noviolence 2.0 (The Sonnet)

Nonviolence is not absence of violence,
Nonviolence is control over violence.
Justice doesn't mean absence of injustice,
Justice means absence of indifference.
Liberty doesn't mean total lack of limits,
Liberty means to practice self-regulation.
Free speech doesn't mean reckless speech,
Free speech means speaking for ascension.
Order does not mean absence of chaos,
Order means presence of accountability.
Peace does not mean absence of conflicts,
Real peace comes from elimination of bigotry.
No more nonchalant nonviolence, it's a coward's way!
Awake, arise 'n humanize, or in tomb the world will lay.

Milkyway Messiah (The Sonnet)

Yada yada hi dharmasya glanirbhavati bharata,
Cada vez que los oprimidos claman esperanza,
Siyasi hayvanlar ne zaman gelip nefret satarsa,
Whenever morons 'n their yes men ruin armonia,
Jab jab some jhandus rashtrabadka jhanda lehraye,
När kärleken till lyx väger tyngre än socialt ansvar,
Immer wenn das herz von gier überwältigt wird,
When humility is trampled by megalomaniacal desire,
Sempre que a bondade é dominada pelo intelecto,
Quando la compassione è sopraffatta dall'indifferenza,
Kapag tinanggap ang pagiging makasarili bilang batas,
Whenever accountability is deemed as misdemeanor,
Embracing affliction, from the dust 'n dirt of soil 'n street,
You the Milkyway Messiah is to rise as the sentient shield.

Milkyway Messiah Sonnet (Simplified Version)

Whenever humanity degrades into inhumanity,
Whenever the oppressed cry out for a little dignity,
Whenever political animals come and sell hate,
Whenever morons 'n their yes men ruin harmony,
Whenever some cavemen fly the flag of tribalism,
Whenever love of luxury undermines accountability,
Whenever gentleness is overpowered by greed,
Whenever megalomania tramples heart's humility,
Whenever goodness is patronized by cold smartness,
Whenever compassion is vilified by indifference,
Whenever selfishness is accepted as norm and sanity,
Whenever accountability is deemed as an offence,
Embracing affliction, from the dust 'n dirt of soil 'n street,
You the Milkyway Messiah is to rise as the sentient shield.

Road to Heaven (The Sonnet)

The road to heaven goes through,
The alleys of the downtrodden.
You won't reach people through god,
You shall reach god through people.
The road to happiness goes through,
The neighborhood of those who suffer.
You won't find happiness by seeking,
For yourself, but only for others.
Road to civilized liberty goes through,
The alleys of infallible accountability.
Knowing the line of control is imperative,
To have no limits is called bestiality.
Think good of others, feel good of others,
Do good to others, and yours is the universe.

34. Honor He Wrote

Honor He Wrote (The Sonnet)

I am not a writer, writers have limits,
I have none, I only have responsibility,
The responsibility to unite the world,
The responsibility to humanize humanity.
We are setting out on this journey,
With the awareness of being responsible,
For responsibility makes one honorable,
Honor makes one responsible.
Fervor of honor is beginning to fade,
From the fabric of society and self.
It is definitely no sign of progress,
In fact it is a sign of utter decadence.
Honor is, in truth, another name for character.
With the demise of honor all good will disappear.

Honor He Wrote Sonnet 2

If the idea of honor were to disappear,
Upon becoming intrinsic to human nature,
That would have been a different story,
A story worth a thousand celebration.
The fact of the matter is quite the opposite,
Honor is fading for materialism is taking over,
And if we let this continue for much longer,
Values and virtues will be hard to even remember.
So let's take stock of the bone of our back,
Without which civilization will fall into pieces.
We've spent long enough in pursuit of luxury,
It's time to live bravely on purpose, not as leeches.
Enough with climbing the greasy pole of validation!
Grab hold of your backbone, toughen up your conviction.

Honor He Wrote Sonnet 3

No conviction ought to be final except assimilation.
No belief ought to be ultimate except collectivity.
No tradition ought to be eternal except compassion.
No habit ought to be incorrigible except humility.
No assumption should dictate action over awareness.
No opinion should rule perception over reason.
No intellect should be given life's reins over warmth.
No edict should define lifestyle over unification.
Human life remains human as long as we are growing.
Cessation of growth is cessation of civilized existence.
Stagnated mind is the root of all hate, war and disorder.
Mind, never rigid, is the source of senility and sapience.
One dreamer awake in love invigorates the whole world.
Soldiers of love live alone, rest just sleep, howl and crawl.

Honor He Wrote Sonnet 4

Raise your power in silence,
Become a dynamite of resilience.
Head high and chest emboldened,
March on with uncorrupt conscience.
Be the heart that loves and lifts,
Be the hand that shares might.
Feel the talk and talk the feel,
Be the mirror of sight beyond sight.
Be the first when no one comes,
Be the last when all are gone.
Be the one who sits not still,
Be the rays of a dutiful dawn.
You are the order you seek outside.
To be human is to put coldness aside.

The God Sonnet

I gave you the tablets at Sinai,
I drove your chariot at Kurukshetra.
I gave you the ayats word by word,
I woke up Siddhartha 'n the carpenter.
No matter the time, age 'n technology,
I always rise to treat the common cold.
Amidst a world full of sore coldness,
I only need ten vessels absurdly bold.
I have nothing to do with perfection,
Far from it, I've got plenty to improve.
With each new vessel my sight broadens,
With each identity my existence renewed.
Keeper am I of this terrestrial neighborhood.
I am your innermost fire of god and good.

Sonnet of Silence

I am the loudest when I am silent,
My lips are shut yet I speak treasures.
Speech without heart is nothing but noise,
Listen to my silence, you'll hear the universe.
Words spoken with mere lips reach nowhere,
For it's the heart that makes words alive.
Tell people who you are without saying a word,
Speak from your very core, they'll listen alright.
I repeat, silent people have the loudest hearts,
For when you speak less you get to listen more.
The more you listen the more you are heard,
The more you hear the more you get to grow.
Set the words on fire, let them all turn to ashes.
Tell people who you are without all the speeches.

Honor He Wrote Sonnet 7

Care not whether you see change,
Care only to be the needed change.
Care not about the fruits of action,
Care only to walk the human lane.
Walking on water without drowning,
Is not miracle, but an illusive trade.
Real miracle is walking on earth,
Without drowning in hate.
In the absence of accountability,
Be the only shining example.
In the absence of love and humility,
Be a loving and living fable.
Whining about all the evil is of no use.
One dream, one mission - oneness absolute.

Honor He Wrote Sonnet 8

Give me a spark of your nerves,
I'll turn it into thunder strike.
Give me a tremor of your lips,
I'll turn it into landslide.
Give me a teardrop of your eyes,
I'll turn it into tsunami.
Give me the sweat of your labor,
I'll turn it into hydroelectricity.
Give me a beat of your heart,
I'll turn it into an earthquake.
Give me a touch of your fingers,
I'll turn it into society's duct tape.
Ingredients of reform are born of your veins.
Renounce your apathy and reform will rain.

Honor He Wrote Sonnet 9

The case of life is a case of kindness,
The case of reform is a case of unself.
The case of growth is a case of correction,
The case of joy is a case beyond the self.
To unself the soul is to unfold happiness,
To disavow destiny is to write destiny.
To bring down the walls is to build bridges,
To refute inhumanity is to practice humanity.
Upon our indifference jungle sustains,
Upon our accountability worlds unfold.
Requirement of civilization is plain 'n simple,
Appearance is nothing if hands don't unfold.
You know why we have two hands 'n one mouth,
So that we may stop arguing 'n help each other out.

Honor He Wrote Sonnet 10

Do you hear your heart beating,
Then at times do you worry in vain!
Do you fall flat on your face sometimes,
Then at your own will you rise again!
Do you find yourself talking to yourself,
Then at times do you laugh at yourself!
Do you wanna bite someone's head off,
Then when needed reach out to help!
Do you ever think, 'what do I think about',
Then at times do you feel sure of everything!
Do you ever fight spiders in your dreams,
Then at times stand boldly against all haunting!
All this is no disease but mere human condition.
Human is one who gives not in to the inner demon.

Honor He Wrote Sonnet 11

You wanna get laid?
Get laid, but with consent.
You wanna jump off a cliff?
Just jump, with an active brain.
You wanna try booze?
Try it, but with moderation.
You wanna smoke weed?
Do it, but with self-regulation.
Try out everything you wanna try,
Figure out right 'n wrong for yourself.
It is your life, test it to its limits, but,
Be sure not to harm others in the process.
Get it all over with, for plenty work remains.
Live to build a world, not to pamper shallow tenets.

Honor He Wrote Sonnet 12

After all this time, the sun doesn't say to us,
Listen you guys, you owe all your light to me.
The trees do not grab us by the throat,
And yell, all your air and food are my charity.
A candle does not burn to be appraised,
But because to burn is the purpose of a candle.
A candle not burning is no candle at all,
Be a burning candle and live life purpose-driven.
Life is a vessel of infinite majesty and potential,
Let us not let it rot at the shore playing safe.
Come hail or high water, let us be shredded,
Let us be annihilated in service and in help.
Let us be human, let us be alive across all narrowness.
Let us be the shining beacon of supreme unselfishness.

Love Logic Intention (The Drunken Sonnet)

Love that keeps you sober is no love,
There is no soldier only drunken lover.
A thousand dazzling Vegas turn bleak,
When the soul shines with love's labor.
For once, let go of all judgment my friend,
Wipe out all cynicism from your core.
Close your eyes and look with your heart,
Either we are lovers or at death's door.
Nutty logic makes nice machines,
Nutty love makes a good society.
Scars of love add definition to life,
Tears of a lover are diamonds of divinity.
Right world is the result of right intention.
If you want light, burn, burn 'n burn again.

Today (The Sonnet)

Today, we ain't no partisan poophead.
Today, we are just plain human.
Today, we ain't no intellectual ding-dong.
Today, we are just plain human.
Today, we ain't no ideological blockhead.
Today, we are just plain human.
Today, we ain't no religious hard case.
Today, we are just plain human.
Today, we ain't slaves to class 'n luxury.
Today, we are just plain human.
Today, we ain't no vermin after self-care.
Today, we are just plain human.
I know very well, that day is not today.
So, let us start the work right this very day.

Honor He Wrote Sonnet 15

It is no time for comfort,
It is no time for leisure.
Plenty lives are to be lifted,
Beyond all personal pleasure.
All are lost in glamor 'n glory,
All are lost in gratification.
All care about me, me 'n me,
All live for self-preservation.
You for one, live for others,
Be the hand that wipes tears.
Be the one that reaches out,
Across all selfish fears.
Always say, I am love, I am life,
I am the answer to all human strife.

Antidote to Crime (The Sonnet)

The way to a crime-free world is simple,
But it lies outside of all the legal 'n partisan muck.
Take away the guns from the kids on the street,
Put books in their hands and food in their stomach.
By the time they grow up into young adults,
The prehistoric warmongers will be in death bed.
The children whose childhood you restored,
Will all be ready to hold the reins of world stage.
Law, policy 'n all that stuff surely have their place,
But not as the antidote to crime, chaos 'n descension.
The permanent antidote to crime is education alone,
Law 'n policy are just to ensure its true democratization.
More than trying a crime, focus on treating environment.
Feed the hungry 'n establish education, free from any debt.

Honor He Wrote Sonnet 17

Can we create a world without crime?
Can we create a world without injustice?
Can we create a world without tyranny?
Can we create a world without malice?
Can we create a world without prejudice?
Can we create a world without hatefulness?
Can we create a world without assumption?
Can we create a world without differences?
Can we create a world without bigotry?
Can we create a world without dollarism?
Can we create a world without coldness?
Can we create a world without divisionism?
Only in fairytales exists a world of perfection.
Our mission is not utopia, but eternal correction.

Honor He Wrote Sonnet 18

What's there to correct, I'm sheer perfection,
Some egotistical snobs continue to ponder.
That right there is what we need to correct,
Our unwillingness to acknowledge our error.
To make mistakes is very much human,
But refusing to acknowledge them is animal.
Once acknowledged then we can correct them,
In willful self-correction we become noble.
Be a rebel all you want, but be wise as well,
Enough to recognize when you've made a mess.
Be sure of your conviction all you want,
But make sure it doesn't impair improvement.
There is no knowledge, only lesser ignorance.
There is no absolute truth, only lesser falseness.

Honor He Wrote Sonnet 19

From error to error, we'll correct our errors.
From failure to failure, we shall rise high.
From despair to despair, our fears disappear.
From scar to scar, our heart learns to fly.
From one jinx to another, we become destiny.
From darkness to darkness, we become light.
One wound to another, we become the cure.
From one loss to another, we understand life.
Dust bite after dust bite, all dust become ointment.
One lost road after another, we draw a new map.
Teardrops upon teardrops, all tears turn elixir.
One screw-up after another, we learn to grow up.
One heartbreak to another, we become the healer.
Bearing crisis upon crisis, we shall rise as creator.

Honor He Wrote Sonnet 20

The more you break me, the stronger I become.
The more you hate me, the gentler I become.
The more you mock me, the kinder I become.
The more you alienate me, the braver I become.
The more you betray me, the more I learn to trust.
The more you disappoint me, the more I feel electrified.
The more you take advantage, the more I learn to care.
The more you backstab me, the more I am energized.
The more you humiliate me, the more I gain humility.
The more you laugh at me, the more I learn to smile.
More you kick me around, more my spine is straightened.
The more you drag me down, the higher I end up flying.
Every bad behavior directed at me amplifies my power.
The broken humans of the world make the greatest healer.

Honor He Wrote Sonnet 21

If you are afraid to be broken, you'll never be whole.
If you are afraid to be lost, you'll never find the path.
If you are afraid to be hurt, you are already crippled.
If you are afraid that you'll lose, you have already lost.
Maps are made by those who aren't afraid to be lost.
Because of them rest of humanity can relish new roads.
Few bravehearts must always be sleepless for society.
Nobody could sleep in peace if it weren't for them heroes.
There may always be some fear as well as insecurities.
That is not the problem, for it is healthy human condition.
What's unhealthy is to leave the reins of your life to them.
Awake, arise o braveheart, and do away with stagnation.
Life without failures and heartbreaks ain't no life at all.
Fail a little, lose a little, but live to the fullest, quirks 'n all.

Honor He Wrote Sonnet 22

You don't know love, till you've known heartbreak,
You won't know sight, till you've known blindness.
You don't know courage, till you've felt helpless,
You won't know light, till you've been in darkness.
Darkest clouds herald the brightest sunshine,
Direst circumstances make the bravest of character.
Heavier the rainfall, more breathtaking the rainbow,
Steeper the hill to climb, sweeter the summit vista.
Once your back is against the wall, only way is through,
You won't know integrity, till you are left in pieces.
Lose all identity, only then you'll know to be human,
You won't know wholeness, till you've felt nothingness.
More ominous the night, more spectacular the daybreak.
Till we're wiped out for a purpose, there's no upliftment.

Honor He Wrote Sonnet 23

My life is your life, your struggle is my struggle,
Thus speaks the being who knows existence.
Existence is existence when we exist for others,
Life rooted in selfishness is but a life of a rodent.
Injustice on a single soul is violation of my own rights,
Thus speaks the one who knows accountability.
The injustice that you foolishly choose to ignore,
Soon will come back to haunt your progeny.
I am safe and sound, who cares about the world,
Such attitude does not suit a living human.
To care for one's own family is nothing special,
To also care for the neighbor's family is truly human.
Gender, faith, color, clothes, nothing must be a rigid sanctum.
A mind united is a world united, this is my only dictum.

The Gender Sonnet

Woman means not weakling, but wonder.
Woman means not obstinate, but original.
Woman means not man-slave, but mother.
Woman means not amorous, but amiable.
Woman means not neurotic, but nimble.
Man mustn't mean medieval, but moral.
Man mustn't mean abusive, but affable.
Man mustn't mean nefarious, but noble.
Trans doesn't mean titillating, but tenacious.
Trans doesn't mean riff-raff, but radiant.
It doesn't mean abhorrent, but affectionate.
It ain't nasty and sick, but nerved and sentient.
Gender has no role in society except in bed.
Person is known by character, not dongs 'n peaches.

Freedom of Dress (The Sonnet)

Freedom of dress is as important,
As freedom of press, that's common sense.
If we're still stuck with squabbles on clothes,
When will we manifest character's radiance!
What does it matter, what we wear,
As long as we walk with our head held high!
Anything that strengthens our backbone,
Is worth the fight of a thousand lifetime.
Clothes perish, so does the body in them,
But a well-built character keeps on shining.
Focus on conduct across all shallow exterior,
Let burning dogs burn, you just keep dazzling.
I repeat, heed not the honks of primeval puritans.
Own your booty and trample all condemnation.

Sonnet of Short Dress

There is no short dress, only short sight,
No obscene outfit, only eyes of obscenity.
The world is no man's family heirloom,
That it should be cherished by the men only.
Instead of restricting a girl's right to expression,
Teach boys, short dress isn't a sign of consent.
If women cannot walk around freely as men do,
Better sentence all men to lifetime imprisonment.
Let all girls hear it loud, wear what you like to wear,
Walk around naked if that's what you really want.
And when an animal makes unwanted advances,
Activate your knee 'n crush their beloved balls to pulp.
Girls don't need protecting, they ain't fragile showpiece.
Let's just raise boys as decent humans, not entitled bullies.

Honor He Wrote Sonnet 27

In a world full of bullies, being gentle is abnormal.
In a world full of arrogance, humility is abnormal.
In a world full of dollarism, charity is abnormal.
In a world full of cockiness, conscience is abnormal.
In a world full of compromise, integrity is abnormal.
In a world full of apathy, empathy is abnormal.
In a world of indifference, accountability is abnormal.
In a world full of assumption, warmth is abnormal.
In a world full of prejudice, reasoning is abnormal.
In a world full of conspiracy, science is abnormal.
In a world full of bigotry, assimilation is abnormal.
In a world full of influencing, expertise is abnormal.
So what do we do, where do we start to change all this!
How about the thought, that we really wanna change this!

Honor He Wrote Sonnet 28

It's one thing to be a feminist, another to be hysteric.
It's one thing to be religious, another to be obsolete.
It's one thing to be an atheist, another to be a moron.
One thing to be a climate activist, another to be a lunatic.
It's one thing to have intellect, another to be an egotist.
It's one thing to have free speech, another to speak hate.
It’s one thing to study science, another to be a smart nitwit.
One thing to study philosophy, another to be a dunderhead.
It's one thing to be a preacher, another to be salesperson.
It's one thing to be crazy in love, another to be control freak.
One thing to be public servant, another to be public parent.
One thing to be reformist, another to be a short-fused terrorist.
The greatest of convictions often gets corrupted by egotism.
So every now and then expose yourself to some gentefication.*

(*gente means people, hence, by gentefication,
I refer to humanification or humanizing)

Honor He Wrote Sonnet 29

Before you beautify, learn to gentefy.
Before you modernize, learn to gentefy.
Before you scientify, learn to gentefy.
Before you philosophize, learn to gentefy.
Before you justify, learn to gentefy.
Before you dogmatize, learn to gentefy.
Before you smartify, learn to gentefy.
Before you glamorize, learn to gentefy.
Before you class-ify, learn to gentefy.
Before you culturize, learn to gentefy.
Before you mummify, learn to gentefy.
Before you analyze, learn to gentefy.
Tu gente es mi gente*, thus we're civilized.
To be gentefied is to be sanctified.

(*Your people are my people.)

Honor He Wrote Sonnet 30

In people is my liberty,
In people is my joy.
In people is my sanity,
To be sacrificed is my ploy.
People are my salvation,
People are my aspiration.
People are my ambition,
People are my absolution.
My deities are the destitute,
To make them equal is my promise.
My church is at the feet of the helpless,
To lift them up is my worship.
The aim is to elevate the alienated,
Not submit to the snobs and savages.

Honor He Wrote Sonnet 31

To think outside the circle of self,
Is the original act of a human being.
To think outside personal benefit,
Is the beginning of civilized living.
Move from individuality to community,
And lo, your light makes animality disappear.
Move from security to self-sacrifice,
And lo, a nightcrawler turns into humanizer.
It's good to love your family as the world,
Even greater is to love the world as your family.
Till separation between family and world withers,
You won't know the full expanse of your humanity.
Wipe out all prehistoric circles that keep you cavebound.
Enough with this cave life, it's time to be unbound!

Honor He Wrote Sonnet 32

Don't wait up for destiny to happen to you,
Stand up and be the destiny of the world.
I didn't wait for the world to happen to me,
I stood up and happened to the world.
Sit no more holding out for a magical messiah,
All the world's magic is just human creation.
Magic is just code for human determination,
There is nothing paranormal, only dedication.
No more bowing in front of the altar of tradition,
Be a radical star and explode for your purpose.
Your light shall live on in people's memory,
As you pour out all life for the good of others.
Destiny and fate are constructs of fear and insecurity.
Conquer your fears and rise as the human almighty.

Honor He Wrote Sonnet 33

There is no lord almighty, only human almighty,
No magic and mysticism, only nature and oneness.
There are no ten commandments, only one,
Compassion has no religion, character has no race.
There’s no law above life, life alone is the supreme law,
And stagnant law does more harm than action illegal.
There is no holy trinity, only humanity up on its toes,
It is always the human mind playing the triangle.
No more dogmas, no more doctrines and manifestos,
Let us be forthright 'n just foster the spirit of affection.
Once we learn to celebrate each other's existence,
There won't be any need for artificial occasion.
Awake, arise o dynamite, blow up all old paradigm.
Don't fight it, or cuss it, just overwhelm it with your lifeline.

The Gentalist Sonnet

I only ask one thing of my soldier – everything!
Give up all, so that those with nothing receive life.
What can I give to thee, except for this life of mine,
Says the brave gentalist across all personal strife.
Gente means people, and people are the music of life.
Love the people, lift the people, people are the way.
Not your people, not my people, it's all one people.
Once you feel it in your bones, uplift is on its way.
I don't believe in a messiah, I don't believe in a god,
‘Cause I’m far too accountable for my society, my world.
Thus speaks the gentalist, burning with a sense of duty,
Thus speaks the living aid, who ain’t no mythical lord.
If a chunk of alum can purify a bucket of putrid water,
Your heart can purify the world with its gentalist power.

Honor He Wrote Sonnet 35

Power is only power, if it helps the people,
Heart is only heart, if it lifts other hearts.
Sight is only sight, if it eases suffering,
Life is only life, if it's lived for others.
To breathe is no sign of life,
The real sign of life is kindness.
Respiration is the work of lungs,
Whereas life is the work of humanness.
Seed of life is not joy but unselfishness,
It's through unselfishness that uplift comes.
But being unselfish doesn't mean without self,
It means to expand 'n contain the whole universe.
Oneness is the sum total of all eternal truth.
If it doesn't lead to oneness, it's anything but truth.

Honor He Wrote Sonnet 36

There is no truth, only lesser falsity,
There is no knowledge, only lesser ignorance.
Make not knowledge your ultimate purpose,
Use knowledge to expand your heart's radiance.
Real knowledge always leads to expansion,
If it does not, it is just another delusion.
Knowledge that helps you alone and not others,
Is but an endeavor of a concrete barbarian.
Your knowledge of a thousand books is nothing,
If it doesn't stir inside you the fire of humanizing.
If it does nothing to elevate human condition,
Better blow all facts and figures to smithereens.
Knowledge without humanity is intellectual stupidity.
Better be dope and kind, than a cold carcass of logicality.

Honor He Wrote Sonnet 37

When love enters the heart,
Reason flees the head.
When duty enters the heart,
Apathy flees the head.
When acceptance enters the heart,
Judgment flees the head.
When humanity enters the heart,
Sectarianism flees the head.
But none of it really enters,
From outside into your veins.
Just like the stains of society,
All detergent is born in your brain.
We are the answer to all our devastation.
We are the revolution to our own delusion.

Honor He Wrote Sonnet 38

It is all merely an illusion,
Let's make it a humane one.
Patriotism boils in our blood,
But for the wrong reason.
Patriotism of our ancestors,
Won't do any good to our world.
We are new humans of a new world,
Let's rewrite patriotism 'n make it evolved.
Be the torch of civilized patriotism,
And dive heart 'n soul for universality.
Be a shimmering star of selflessness,
Let your veins overflow with amity.
Humanize your veins, nerves, blood 'n bones.
Be the fountainhead you are, ‘n let expansion pour.

Honor He Wrote Sonnet 39

The more I write the more I realize,
The inane limitations of language.
Never be a stickler for terminology,
It only impedes your humanness.
If anything, try to set humanity free,
From the bounds of words 'n speech.
Let the world know who you are,
But without being a linguistic leech.
Behavior alone defines a person,
Make behavior your background.
Neither culture, nor geography,
It's only in action that identity is found.
Unfold your today beyond your yesterday,
Or else, there'll be no tomorrow, only decay.

Honor He Wrote Sonnet 40

To learn from yesterday is growth,
To be stuck in yesterday is decay.
To look for a better future is vision,
To be stuck there only causes dismay.
Glance at the past, aim for the future,
But keep your feet grounded in present.
Learn from history, envision the destiny,
'N dive in today with your sweat valiant.
Memory is meant to give you ground,
Not to impede in your prosperity.
Vision is to embolden your footsteps,
Not to disconnect you from reality.
Some make history their prison, some future.
Bid goodbye to those inmates, 'n be a timemaster.

Honor He Wrote Sonnet 41

Don't worship your past,
At the expense of your present.
Don't glorify the future,
At the expense of the present.
Don't worship the dead,
At the expense of the living.
Don't admire the unborn,
While overlooking the living.
It's only by lifting the living that,
We build a better world for all progeny.
It's only by being kind to the living,
That we truly honor our ancestry.
Honor is earned not begged for.
Honor the living, 'n all time will be grateful.

Honor He Wrote Sonnet 42

Either you build time,
Or you are buried in time.
Either you share life with others,
Or selfishness spoils your lifeline.
Either you foster your own ideas,
Or you are buried in dead ideologies.
Either you build your own reality,
Or you are buried in society's insecurity.
Either you nourish your humanity,
Or you are buried in inhumanity.
Step out of the brothel of bigotry,
Or stay forever buried in tribal tendency.
The world doesn't become better by brooding.
Don't like what you see - then start working.

Honor He Wrote Sonnet 43

You asked, do I have just one outfit?
I say, simplicity is the outfit of a reformer.
You asked, why don't I take a vacation?
I say, vacation is luxury for a reformer.
You asked, what do I do for fun?
I say, I renounced fun so you may thrive.
You said, I shouldn't take life so seriously.
I say, you 'n I have different definitions of life.
To most people life may be about having fun,
I only know one life, the kind that lifts the society.
People may pursue pleasure all they want,
My single pursuit is that of universal amity.
Instead of questioning my humanitarian insanity,
Ask yourself, what exactly would you call sanity!

Honor He Wrote Sonnet 44

What you call sanity, I call selfishness.
What you call practicality, I call selfishness.
What you call sensibility, I call selfishness.
What you call fortune, I call selfishness.
What you call economy, I call selfishness.
What you call progress, I call selfishness.
What you call intelligence, I call selfishness.
What you call success, I call selfishness.
What you call nationality, I call selfishness.
What you call culture, I call selfishness.
What you call heritage, I call selfishness.
What you call tradition, I call selfishness.
To be selfish is to be the walking dead.
To be dead to selfishness is a life well led.

Honor He Wrote Sonnet 45

There's no social work, only family work,
There's no social uplift, only family uplift.
There's no social issue, only family issue,
There's no social service, only self-service.
There's no social reform, only life's reform,
There's no social science, only mental science.
There's no collectivism, only self-realization,
There's no sociology, only common sense.
There's no political science, only life science,
No international relations, only human relations.
There's no diplomacy, only communication,
There is no geopolitics, only amalgamation.
There is no foreigner or stranger, only family,
No social responsibility, only family responsibility.

Honor He Wrote Sonnet 46

What is society - a reflection of the self.
What is community - proof of togetherness.
What is neighborhood - a promise of care.
What is civilization - a pledge of hatelessness.
What are the alleys - playground of innocence.
What are the streets - bearer of ascension.
What is the soil - a reminder of humility.
What is the sky - a reminder for expansion.
What are the rivers - epitome of perseverance.
What are the mountains - proof of zealousness.
What is the cactus - proof of unsubmission.
What is the mountain goat - proof of resilience.
What is the universe - manifestation of our will.
Humanize that will, 'n all troubles will turn nil.

Honor He Wrote Sonnet 47

Be the cactus, a proof of unsubmission,
And blossom amidst the fiercest environment.
In a world primed with the probability of hate,
Be love impossible and lift all lost in lament.
Aspire to expire for a cause uncausable,
And your heart will shine with light untamable.
When all go berserk for sect as bozos on booze,
Be the sectless sapiens and stand indivisible.
When all are possessed with the libido of liberty,
Be the first one standing, responsible 'n righteous.
In a world founded on unfounded assumptions,
Be the first ink of understanding unpresumptuous.
Blockheads and blockhearts have only blocked amity.
It's time to unblock, unfold and undivide our psyche.

Honor He Wrote Sonnet 48

We need to unblock our head alright,
More than that we need to unblock our heart.
We need to foster some reason alright,
More than that we gotta make love unbarred.
Problem is, when the head opens, heart is shut,
Without warmth of the heart, head is just a bone.
Without the intervention of reason from the head,
Heart is just another brutish muscle most unhoned.
Often I use heart as synonym for humanity,
Though technically it's a symposium of good 'n bad.
That's why even the heart needs to be humanized,
For our infinite potential for good to engulf all bad.
It is no longer about choosing between heart 'n head,
It's about living 'n behaving as a whole human undivided.

Honor He Wrote Sonnet 49

When you've written as much as I have, it's impossible,
Not to have seemingly contradictory statements.
They seem so 'cause you only look at words, not context,
Context constitutes 90% of a message, words only 10%.
This is what I've been referring to as limitation of language,
Be not sure of words, until you've asked without judgment.
As I have said repeatedly, never stick too rigidly to words,
Take a step beyond the words and realize the message.
Nature gave us language to be bridge among beings,
But we turned it into yet another tool of self-aggrandizing,
Like we have done with the faculty of reason 'n intellect,
Like we have done with all our religious dogmatizing.
Enough I say, with the meaningless pursuit of self-glorification!
Enough with this craving for bickering as pests of putrefaction!

Honor He Wrote Sonnet 50

The problem is not our differences,
It is that we are fragile creatures.
The slightest spark of disagreement,
Makes us find an enemy in others.
Imagine if we agreed on everything,
How boring this world would be!
So let's bite each other's head off,
Let's disagree most enthusiastically.
No difference can tear us apart,
Till we compromise our humanity.
It is okay to disagree with each other,
But not to hate the other 'cause we disagree.
Differences are not a failure of humanity,
Differences are a test of our humanity.

Difference & Discrimination (The Sonnet)

There ain't no difference that can't be conquered,
Except for those that are rooted in inhumanity.
A bigot's emphasis on their supremacy over others,
Is not a difference in opinion but clinical insanity.
Nobody is inferior to nobody in this world of ours,
Except for those who think of others as such.
Neither ancestry nor luxury defines a character,
Conduct alone defines character, above all fuss.
Say, discrimination is not a difference in opinion,
It's an act that sets animals apart from humans.
Free speech is a phenomenon of human society,
Hate speech is an act of stoneage barbarians.
Let us distinguish differences from discrimination,
Then celebrate differences while treating discrimination.

Honor He Wrote Sonnet 52

Inclusion over exclusion,
Celebration over segregation,
Diversity over homogeneity,
Assimilation over discrimination,
Self-sacrifice over domination,
Heartification over indoctrination,
Conversation over condemnation,
Camaraderie over condescension,
Music of amity over scream of vanity,
Colors of comity over kool-aid of cruelty,
Jingle of jesting over gestating a jungle,
Whispers of wonder over whining apathy,
Thus we'll make a dent on destiny's design,
For we are the designer as well as the design.

Honor He Wrote Sonnet 53

Better a marvelheaded idiot,
Than a marbleheaded bigot.
Better a self-proclaimed dope,
Than an arrogant dilettante.
Better a kindhearted commoner,
Than a cockeyed intellectualist.
Better an egalitarian infidel,
Than a dogmatizing evangelist.
All dogmas are born in the mind,
So is the duster to wipe them.
It is up to you what will you be,
Vessel of dogma or the duster untamed!
Convert none, help all, without imposition.
Let uplift be the motive behind all conviction.

Honor He Wrote Sonnet 54

Motive makes the mind,
Motive makes the world.
What is your real motive,
And is it enough bold?
Intention is the seed of change,
But the interesting part is something else.
In the absence of an intention for good,
Greed and corruption keep making mess.
Darkness is natural, where light is not,
Prejudice is strong, where love is bleak.
If nobody else, be love and light yourself,
Be the new chapter upon nature's fabric.
Muster the motive for a magnificent mundo.
Your motive will charge your feet beyond all woe.

Honor He Wrote Sonnet 55

Where you need to blow your top,
You keep quiet and walk away.
Where you need to keep quiet,
You blow your top like you're unswayed.
Distinguish triviality from tyranny,
Inconvenience from injustice.
Walk away from petty squabbles, but,
Stand up to oppression without cowardice.
Justice begins with a just civilian, not a politician,
Order begins with an orderly commoner, not a copper.
So the question is, are you a just 'n orderly commoner,
Or just more slime that leaves all to the warmongers?
The government's job is not to govern but listen,
And the citizens' duty is to speak as beings nonpartisan.

Honor He Wrote Sonnet 56

It's the citizens' duty to make a nation nonpartisan,
Government is meant to serve as powerless figurehead.
All my hopes lie in the hands of accountable citizens,
A good politician acts a citizen, not political dunderhead.
So no more procrastination with the curation of society,
No more playing hooky in the school of life and sanity.
Be the politician that you seek in the sewers of state,
Not by law but by an indefatigable accountability.
Democracy means rule of the people, not sleep of people,
Yet that's what it means to people 'n politicians alike.
But shhh, nobody is supposed to admit any of it in public,
For discretion is the better part of a society of sleeping mice.
Let sleeping slime sleep, if you are human, take charge now.
Dream with your eyes open and keep your democracy vow.

Honor He Wrote Sonnet 57

Dreams that we witness in sleep, ain't no dream,
Real dream is the one that doesn't let us sleep.
Only when mindful martyrs work without blink,
Rest of the world has a peaceful sleep.
I have been sleepless ever since I came of age,
Such is the madness of the dream of assimilation.
The thought of rest rarely enters my mind,
No matter how much the climb causes desolation.
No dream comes to fruition without restless nights,
No sun ever rises without first crossing darkness.
No mortal ever turns immortal without self-sacrifice,
No world is ever beautified without martyr's madness.
Enough with the snobbish nonsense of dream analyzing!
All know sleepwalking, now let 'em witness dreamwalking!

Honor He Wrote Sonnet 58

In a world full of sleepwalkers,
What's needed is a dreamwalker.
In a world full of vacationers,
What's needed is an invigorizer.
In a society full of world travelers,
What's needed is a mind traveler.
In a universe full of space explorers,
What's needed is a heart explorer.
In a neighborhood full of naysayers,
What's needed is an energizer.
In this hellhole of hatelusters,
What's needed is a hatebuster.
It takes nothing to sustain a cruel jungle.
To build society it takes love unbreakable.

World is My Valentine (The Sonnet)

My first and foremost love is society,
Romance 'n things are second priority.
My love seeks not to be loved in return,
In fact, my love thrives in cold nonreciprocity.
Mine is not to reason why, mine is to love and die,
There's no greater love than that of a one-sided lover.
The world is to me what Julia was to Saint Valentine,
And what the impoverished were to Nicholas Santa.
A world anemic in love needs a day to celebrate love,
I am a lover eternal, for me every day is valentine's day.
The world is my valentine, as such it is under my care,
It's my duty to protect it from Claudius' mischievous play.
I shall stop breathing before I break this pledge of mine.
There's no greater power than the pledge of a lover divine.

Honor He Wrote Sonnet 60

I ain't no idealist, but a biologist so,
I say, it's okay to want to be loved blind.
But if you can love despite coldness,
That is what makes you a lover divine.
Craving for affection will always be there,
Which is very much human in nature.
But you know what's more human than that,
The capacity to still love past such desire.
To love and to be loved is a great experience,
Greater still is to love without being loved.
True love's labor is a reward of its own,
Sheer sanctity is the sight of a lover on guard.
Where there is love unconditional, there is divinity.
Where there is condition, there is depravity.

Honor He Wrote Sonnet 61

What is humane is divine,
What is kind is holy.
What is humble is serene,
What is gentle is poetry.
Where there is conscience,
There is righteousness.
Where there is virtue,
There is godliness.
Practice humanity over doctrines,
Practice community over scriptures.
Doctrines have caused much division,
Because humans are sucker for dogmas.
Place all attention on behavior over belief.
Virtuous behavior brings social uplift.

Honor He Wrote Sonnet 62

Belief sustains a person,
But behavior sustains a society.
Belief has nothing to do with truth,
It is just a matter of mental necessity.
Often our belief defies all reason,
That's absolutely okay to a great extent.
What's not okay is to impose it on others,
To sentence others to our imprisonment.
I believe, that my teacher watches over me,
Even though he walks the earth no more.
This belief has nothing to do with your life,
But it helps me walk past my crippling woe.
All beliefs are good beliefs with or without reason,
If they help you in life to become a better person.

Honor He Wrote Sonnet 63

The time is always right to be kind,
The time is always right to lift a life.
The time is always right to refute hate,
The time is always right to conquer strife.
When the time is right, the right person,
Can change the world with the right cause.
The right time is this very moment,
And the right person is, you, who else!
Each of us are to be the home to another,
Each of us are to be the guard to another.
Whenever darkness shrouds another,
Each of us must rise as the lightbringer.
The time is always right to do what's right,
If not, then time is but a futile construct alright.

Honor He Wrote Sonnet 64

There is no time if the mind doesn't create it,
There is no reality if the mind doesn't create it.
There is no good if the mind doesn't create it,
There is no evil is the mind doesn’t define it.
What we call evil is nature's necessity,
What we call good is nature's variation.
If we practice the good long enough,
It'll become our conviction and absolution.
Let's build our own time, let's build our own reality,
One that is founded on kindness, not cruelty.
Let's show Mother Nature we're unlike all her children,
Despite savagery within, we ain't bound to it as destiny.
DNA is destiny, so is mutation, hence no cruelty is permanent.
Civilization needs no magical intervention, just mortal commitment.

Honor He Wrote Sonnet 65

If you wanna write – write.
If you wanna paint – paint.
If you wanna sing – sing.
If you wanna science – science.
If you wanna fly – fly.
If you wanna invent – invent.
If you wanna run for office – run.
If you wanna protect – protect.
If you wanna teach – teach.
If you wanna play – play.
If you wanna cook – cook.
If you wanna train – train.
Whatever you do, do with humanity,
And you'll set in motion a new reality.

Sonnet of Poetry

Poet is no servant of the dictionary,
Dictionary is servant to the poet.
Poet is no servant of language,
Language is servant to the poet.
It's poetry that makes the language,
Language makes no poetry, my friend.
Poet exists not to serve a linguist's whim,
But to breathe life into human language.
I've said repeatedly, language has limitations,
Only with poetry we can surpass some of 'em.
Sticklers for grammar make lousy poets,
If feeling doesn't surpass grammar, poetry it ain't.
Poetry is the most potent of all literary forms.
If prose is candle light, poetry is dawn.

Honor He Wrote Sonnet 67

I got tired of waiting for there to be dawn,
So I opened my eyes and became the dawn.
I got tired of waiting for there to be saneness,
So I stood and became saneness fully honed.
I got tired of waiting for there to be inclusion,
So I stood up as the epitome of inclusion.
I got tired of waiting for there to be ascension,
So I stood up as the example of ascension.
I got tired of waiting for there to be humility,
So I stood up and became humility incarnate.
I got tired of waiting for there to be gentleness,
So I rose as the maker of giants with gentleness.
I got tired of waiting for there to be undivision,
So I stood up as the definition of undivision.

Honor He Wrote Sonnet 68

Undivided and uncorrupted,
That's the only way forward.
To treat all division in the world,
All you gotta do is disregard.
Regard neither sect of any kind,
Nor any of those ideologies.
If you gotta regard something,
Muster regard for human frailty.
Neither sectarian nor intellectual,
Heed no division of any form.
Heed only the sufferings of society,
'N all division will wither on their own.
Divisions don't disappear through policy,
But through individual acts of collectivity.

Honor He Wrote Sonnet 69

There is no sight sweeter than the sight of a person,
Acting genuinely in the best interest of the collective.
There is no sight uglier than the sight of an individual,
Yelling for reckless liberty while harming the collective.
There's no lasting way to ensure societal security,
Except putting oneself in harm's way for the collective.
There's no better way to sustain insecurity than,
To advocate sectarian security separate from collective.
History of animal kind is the history of self-preservation,
History of humankind is the history of self-sacrifice.
You gotta choose which history will you be a part of,
The history of humankind or history of the selfish kind?
Anything selfish is ugly, anything unselfish is sheer beauty.
Beauty lies in kinship of heart, not skinship of body.

Honor He Wrote Sonnet 70

I am on fire my friend,
And there's no putting it out.
You have only two choices,
Burn with me or run along now.
Humanitarian fire is unputoutable,
It can't be put out only passed along.
The question ain't who'll put me out,
But who's mad enough to burn along.
Little do the sober know this madness,
To them playing safe is the life's way.
But reformers ain't born to play safe,
We are born to gamble our life away.
The fire of oneness is a fire eternal.
The vessel changes, not the potential.

Honor He Wrote Sonnet 71

Potential is universal,
Only difference is in intention.
Potential combined with intention,
Is the formula for epoch-making revolution.
No human is incapable of changing the world,
But most are unwilling to take responsibility.
Fundamental problem of this world ain't of law,
The fundamental problem of this world is apathy.
Everybody says that change begins with the self,
But how does it all begin in everyday ordinary life!
It begins when you turn from selfish to selfless,
When you expand and become the universal life.
So why worry my friend, whether you have potential!
The zillion dollar question is, is your zeal unshakable?

Honor He Wrote Sonnet 72

Close your eyes and take a leap of faith, o brave one,
Not in any outside magic but the one of your heart.
Have faith in the potential bestowed by mother nature,
And zealously march ahead as your dream's vanguard.
You are the dream, the dreamer, as well as its keeper,
Never give up, no matter the pangs of disappointment.
Dream lives so long as we work for it despite difficulty,
Step up, and half the dream is realized, despite torment.
It's more about perseverance than it's about patience,
Only those with shaky zeal are lost in patience's tale.
Those on a mission have no time to prove anything,
They are far too busy making the impossible possible.
With zeal unshakable we shall climb the hill unclimbable.
It's your climb, you gotta decide the outcome, not sheeple.

Honor He Wrote Sonnet 73

Better a lion in sheep's skin,
Than a sheep in lion's skin.
Better a giant in a gentle vessel,
Than germs in a fancy canteen.
When not needed act mostly a sheep,
But occasionally you gotta let the lion out.
Be a disinfectant and sanitize the world,
Not germs that make disease break out.
All social sickness is caused by selfishness,
And hypocrisy is what makes things worse.
Wipe out all hypocrisy from your being's core,
The world is a reflection of what's in our heart.
I say again, lion on the inside, sheep on the out.
When chihuahuas wreak havoc, let the dinosaur out.

Honor He Wrote Sonnet 74

Be the clown to those who cry,
Be the joker to those who joke.
Be an elephant to the intellectuals,
Be a dinosaur to those who croak.
But first hone your powers, bud,
Your powers of observation.
Learn to observe without judgment,
Observe people and their condition.
Not all rough exteriors are same inside,
Not all sweet exteriors are same inside.
Things are rarely ever black and white,
Be aware of the grey areas of society 'n life.
When you are born with awareness anew,
The whole world will find a home in you.

Honor He Wrote Sonnet 75

Let me hold your hand,
Let me be your home.
Here, take my heart,
Heart to heart life is honed.
There is no I, only Us,
There is no Us, only I.
Sounds confusing, right!
Because Love is across all Us and I.
In love all of me is you,
In love all of you is me.
In love it's all messed up,
The sweetest mess we could ever be.
So come, let's be messed up together.
Perhaps then things might get a little clear.

Honor He Wrote Sonnet 76

A beautiful mind creates a beautiful kind,
A beautiful kind creates a beautiful tide,
A beautiful tide creates a beautiful sight,
A beautiful sight creates a beautiful light,
A beautiful light creates a beautiful might,
A beautiful might creates a beautiful hide,
A beautiful hide creates a beautiful height,
A beautiful height creates a beautiful glide,
A beautiful glide creates a beautiful time,
A beautiful time creates a beautiful hind,
A beautiful hind creates a beautiful grind,
A beautiful grind creates a beautiful kite,
A beautiful kite creates a beautiful flight,
A beautiful flight creates a beautiful life.

Honor He Wrote Sonnet 77

Be a muse to the world, not a mole.
Be a flute to the world, not a fluke.
Be a whistle to the world, not a hoax.
Be a warm coat to the world, not a coup.
Be O2 to the world, not CO.
Be water to the world, not booze.
Be a castle to the world, not another chaos.
Be ointment to the world, not another wound.
If you can't be a castle, be an apartment,
If you can't be an apartment, be a hut.
It's not about the size of your sacrifice,
It's about the intent, you impetuous lovenut!
Be a lamp, ladder or lego, what, it doesn't matter.
Just be something that makes the world better.

Honor He Wrote Sonnet 78

Two is better than one,
Seven billion is better than two.
It's okay to collide on occasion so long as,
We're by each other when we are in doo-doo.
Every time we hold hands, magic happens,
This ain't the magic of our ignorant ancestors.
I am talkin' about the mortal magic of diversity,
The power that comes to life when we're together.
Remember this simple principle my friend,
Those who fall together, fly together.
Arms are just arms when separated,
But shield when held together.
We are a blessing when we stand together.
When divided, we are our worst nightmare.

Honor He Wrote Sonnet 79

When we end up together,
That's not an end, but the beginning.
It's division that ends all journey,
End division, 'n life will have true beginning.
Century after century went on with division,
Yet unity is forever, division is nonexistence.
To breathe, eat, mate and sleep, ain't existence,
To help, heal, lift and light, that's existence.
We've got intellect, we've got sentiment,
All are useless if they don't help erase division.
Human is another name for undivision,
Not another synonym for discrimination.
To have 'n to hold, mustn't be a vow between just two.
Make it one among all, and soon unity will be true.

Honor He Wrote Sonnet 80

By being ordinary we get to be extraordinary.
By being simple, we get to be spectacular.
By being an outspoken idiot, we rise as sage.
By being humble, we become truth's hammer.
By being gentle, we get to be giants.
By being magnanimous, we rise magnificent.
By being a servant, we get to be the leader.
By being annihilated, we rise as omnipresent.
By being self-regulated, we need less regulation.
By being accountable, we need less law and policy.
By denouncing supremacy, we start treating bigotry.
By rejecting exclusivity, we put an end to disparity.
There's no all-seeing eye, there's no all-knowing heart.
But if you see suffering and know to help, that's enough.

Honor He Wrote Sonnet 81

Sometimes I'm Gringo,
Sometimes I'm Turkish,
Sometimes I'm Latino,
Sometimes I'm Nordic.
Sometimes I'm british,
Sometimes I'm Balkan,
Sometimes I'm scientist.
Sometimes theologian.
Sometimes I'm dervish,
Sometimes I'm humanist,
Sometimes bodhisattva,
Sometimes nondualist.
Above all these labels be sure of one thing,
All the time, every time, I am a human being.

Honor He Wrote Sonnet 82

More ungroomed the artist,
More spectacular the art.
More ungroomed the writer,
More powerful the literature.
More ungroomed the scientist,
More impact their science makes.
More ungroomed the philosopher,
More impact their insight makes.
More ungroomed the poet,
More profound the poetry.
A reformer is always ungroomed,
Only then they make a beautiful society.
Grooming often implies a shallow interior.
Simpler the appearance, stronger the character.

Honor He Wrote Sonnet 83

Grooming is not a bad thing but,
It mustn't be placed above character.
Use grooming as an aid to life,
Never as life's ultimate desire.
If grooming makes you feel confident,
By all means, groom however you like.
Just remember, it's a slippery slope,
Grooming has a tendency to take over life.
The purpose of a car is not to buy gas,
Purpose of a car is to reach a destination.
The purpose of a life is not grooming,
Purpose of a life is to realize an ambition.
It's more important to know why than how to groom.
All the grooming in the world can't make a heart bloom.

Honor He Wrote Sonnet 84

All the grooming in the world,
Cannot make humanity bloom.
You can dress up a chimp in a fancy suit,
It doesn't clean their upstairs room.
Everybody spring cleans their home religiously,
They want their surroundings to be all tidy.
Yet they care diddly-squat about the chronic dust,
Gathering in their mind century after century.
Clean mind creates clean society,
And we ain't gonna achieve it with policy.
How you behave when nobody is watching,
That is the actual, genuine nature of society.
We gotta build character beyond outfit and policy.
Let's move from a synthetic society to one of integrity.

Honor He Wrote Sonnet 85

Enough with leaving this world,
In the hands of old fuddy-duddies.
Mark you, I ain't talkin' about age,
I am talkin' about mental maturity.
Long enough we've allowed tradition,
To wreak havock on our precious planet.
It's time for reason and nonrigidity,
To stand up and take charge, all unbent.
Inhumanity persists in our world,
Because the humans give a consensual wave.
It's time for the grown-ups to grow up and,
Redeem reins from those with both feet in the grave.
Ancient relics belong in museum, not in driver's seat.
It's for the young of head 'n heart to get the society lit.

Honor He Wrote Sonnet 86

Be a soulmate to society 'n protect it,
From its past as well as the future.
Whence will come this society's ascension,
If it doesn't come from your unselfish desire.
Bite the dust again and again, it's okay,
There's nothing undignified in biting dust.
But know that no dust can keep you in dust,
Until you accept your setback as permanent.
All this world needs is just one human,
One human who won't brush off their duty,
The duty to act as a living, breathing human,
The duty to act as a pillar of undefiable dignity.
The world needs a safe haven, o soldier of love 'n truth.
It ain't gonna come from no church, no capitol, but you.

Honor He Wrote Sonnet 87

Be the melody in the heart of humanity,
Be the delight in the sight of humanity.
Be the comity in the spine of humanity,
Be the motion in the head of humanity.
To rearrange the world we gotta start,
With rearranging our priorities.
Start with changing your priority,
Before you go about changing policies.
Make your life the most awe-inspiring days,
Of human history, since the beginning.
Live as the person that has never lived,
And death will be just a flicker on your shimmering.
To lead the way for the next generation of humanity,
We gotta better ourselves across our ancestors' stupidity.

The Parenting Sonnet

Anybody can make a baby, that's no glory,
To raise a true being, that's a glorious thing.
It takes less than a minute to make a baby,
But more than a decade to make a being.
So if you choose to have baby someday,
Focus on their character, not just sustenance.
And make sure to keep luxury away from them,
For luxury is curse for character development.
Pass on the tradition of compassion to them,
Be a living example of the possibility of humanity.
Teach them the belief of nondiscrimination,
Demonstrate to them a never-before seen sanity.
Be the person you want the kids to grow up to be.
The best kind of parenting is that of exemplarity.

Honor He Wrote Sonnet 89

Where would the world be,
Without its examples!
Where would the world be,
Without its amiables!
Where would the world be,
Without its pillars!
Where would the world be,
Without its builders!
Where would the world be,
Without its meddlers!
Where would the world be,
Without its caretakers!
Let me tell you where - exactly where it's today,
So, Arise O Caretakers, the mission awaits!

Honor He Wrote Sonnet 90

Tyrants are plenty, servants are scarce,
It ain't about leading, it's about service.
A moment of servanthood is worth,
More than a lifetime of leadership.
Be the last first human standing,
Do what's needed to restrain the retards.
And nature will raise up an army,
Of first humans to stand as vanguards.
Before the world possesses you,
With its snobbish and materialistic tenets,
Manifest your absurd sense of servanthood,
And possess the world against all selfish elements.
If you wanna lose control, lose control in sacrifice.
And you'll end up the very insignia of a good life.

Honor He Wrote Sonnet 91

Every life is obvious,
For every life is born selfish.
You for one be the unobvious,
Be the line between human 'n rubbish.
Once you are dead and gone,
What will be left of you!
Not the fortune you hoard,
But only the memories caused by you.
Whether or not you wake up the next day,
Go to bed knowing, you've lived as human.
Spend just one day as a human, and you'll cause,
More lasting reform than a decade of legal action.
Reform doesn't come from legal maneuverability,
But an unsubmissive yet accountable citizenry.

Honor He Wrote Sonnet 92

There is no love without sacrifice,
There is no sacrifice without love.
In genuine love you wanna give all,
In genuine love there is no reserve.
Love my friend, love each and love all,
Love is the only language known to all.
When love becomes your first nature,
All personal pleasure feels dismal.
Wellbeing of the other is wellbeing of mine,
Thus feels the actual lover genuine.
Blessed are they who feel longing for people,
Such longing is the elixir to all that is sickening.
When such fire of love courses through our veins,
No reform on planet earth will remain unattained.

Citizen Lover (The Sonnet)

Citizen lover is citizen justice,
All others are citizens of malice.
Love begets justice, whereas,
Judgment produces more malice.
All think, justice is an independent force,
But, justice is simply a descendant of love.
Where there is love, justice prevails,
Otherwise, there's just talk of justice 'n love.
Pledge allegiance to no judgment by intellect,
But only to love and love alone, my friend.
Where there is a place for love,
There is place for everything else.
Once a person has realized love untaintable,
They've achieved everything celebratable.

Honor He Wrote Sonnet 94

How will you know you've realized love?
When people no longer appear at a distance.
When they no longer appear as people,
But as reflection of your own essence.
When the other becomes I,
I becomes universal.
In that universal I all that there is,
Is an echo of the people.
The I is in all people,
But people are not in all the I.
That is why we suffer so much,
That is why we all cry, cry and cry.
If one dies thinking of people,
They will live on through people.

Honor He Wrote Sonnet 95

If your knowledge of all the books,
Doesn't bring you closer to people,
Then what's the point of it all,
What's the point of being intellectually able!
If knowledge doesn't make you kind,
It is no knowledge, only a stubborn illusion.
If knowledge doesn't make you undivided,
It is no knowledge, only degradation.
First and foremost purpose of knowledge,
Is to erase the divide amongst people.
Yet today we use it to attain comfort,
Such is no human endeavor, but that of vegetable.
Only they are learned who learn to bring reformation.
All others fly blind in the eternal pit of argumentation.

Honor He Wrote Sonnet 96

Only a few understand the language of intellect,
Then most of them arrogantly boast and trod.
But from the tallest mountain to tiniest grass,
Everyone understands the language of love.
I've practiced all faith 'n ideology for a brief period,
And I accept all of them to be equally human.
That is why everyone thinks of me as their very own,
Everyone thinks, I am their own school's person.
I have no sect of my own, yet I am in every sect,
I have no school of my own, yet I am in every school.
One who loves, loves all no matter their label,
And finds a reflection in all beings including the fool.
There is no two, but only One that there ever is.
All separation is the sign of a spirit selfish.

Honor He Wrote Sonnet 97

One who knows the self,
Finds the self in everyone.
One who know home,
Finds home in everyone.
One who has love,
Finds love in everyone.
One who has goodness,
Finds goodness in everyone.
One who has potential,
Finds potential in everyone.
One who knows life,
Finds life in everyone.
One only finds outside what's inside.
Society is a reflection of a human upright.

Honor He Wrote Sonnet 98

Only human is the doer,
All others are destroyer.
Only savages live on pedestal,
A human toils in the soil as reformer.
Water never stands still on a pedestal,
It always flows down to the lowest ground.
Be a stream of gentle water and boldly rush,
To those forgotten by the fools who frown.
Be the breeze, be the water,
Be the serene shade of a heartful tree.
In character be an elephant,
Gentle, unafraid and forever free.
Free are they who have no walls inside,
All others are prisoners of their own divisionist pride.

Honor He Wrote Sonnet 99

Servant-consciousness is God-consciousness,
All else is animal-consciousness.
Lover-consciousness is God-consciousness,
All else is animal-consciousness.
To serve the helpless is to help oneself,
To make another smile is to realize life.
Service and service alone is life,
Whereas everything else is death in disguise.
Service alone is the path of civilization,
All else is path of the stoneage.
Cherish the path of service and sacrifice,
No other path holds a candle to its exuberance.
All meditate on a chant or a symbol,
The highest meditation is the meditation on people.

Honor He Wrote Sonnet 100

All meditate on symbols,
I meditate on people.
Most worship fictitious deities,
I worship those branded unliftable.
People are my almighty,
Oneness is my religion,
Division is degradation,
Unification is illumination.
All is possible for a human who's responsible,
Only the indifferent make excuses.
Possibility is born of responsibility,
Not of whining, praying and limbless wishes.
Real and unreal, put all these talk aside.
Let us be civilization, let us be lifelight.

35. The Gentalist

Law of Light (The Sonnet)

Light shared is light amplified,
Light hoarded is light lost.
Life is light when lived for others,
Darkness when lost in snobbish cause.
We are truly knowledgeable,
When our knowledge annuls animosity.
We truly have existence solely when,
We exist to elevate all of humanity.
Elevation of humanity happens,
One neighborhood at a time.
Time and space have meaning,
Only when they help our spirits align.
In short, there is neither time nor space.
Either everything is love or sheer nonsense.

No Time, No Space (The Sonnet)

There is no time, no space,
There is only love.
There is no intellect, no philosophy,
There is only love.
There is no defeat, no victory,
There is only love.
There is no loss, no gain,
There is only love.
There is no path, no pedestrian,
There is only love.
There is no mission, no means,
There is only love.
All of us are either echoes of love beyond chains,
Or just some traditional trash of glory and gain.

Beyond Politics (The Sonnet)

Changing leadership, changing party,
These ain't change, but same old tribalism.
Changing the shape and name of tribalism,
Is not end of tribalism, but recurring tribalism.
If you really want to bring actual change,
Aim for a non-tribal society, one of nonsectarianism.
Replacing one sect with another may feel like change,
But it's just another form of unchanging divisionism.
Real change is when civic duty turns common sanity,
When there's no community service, only life and living.
The supreme policy is that of individual accountability,
True order comes through collectivity, not policing.
Stop relying on politicians for every little trouble.
And the world will be a place without political turmoil.

The World Sonnet

The world will never be a place without troubles,
But that is not the point, the point is something else.
The point is that most of the troubles we do have,
Are caused by our own archaic stupidity 'n shallowness.
Shallow and indifferent, that's the norm of the world.
With such norm how can we expect there to be equality!
Civilization comes from the ground, not the government.
The ones walking the ground are the cause of humanity.
Rhythm of the world comes from the rhythm of your heart,
Place your hand on your heart and listen across biases.
If there is music in you there'll be music in the world,
But if there's just noise within, all around there'll be travesty.
WORLD means We On Road of Love and Determination.
The aim is to conquer our last ounce of discrimination.

People Over Path (The Sonnet)

Celebrities defend vanity,
Intellectuals defend intellect,
Preachers defend scriptures,
Scientists defend factual evidence.
I found plenty of human professions,
But in none of them I found a human.
All are obsessed to defend their path,
Yet all paths are dead without a human.
No matter who we are or what we are,
Above all else our identity is humanness.
If this simple fact is still not clear enough,
All vanity, intellect, texts and science are baseless.
Before defending a puny path, let us take a human peek.
If we must defend, let us defend the helpless and weak.

Ain't No Sinner (The Sonnet)

When we think ourselves weak,
We become weak.
When we think ourselves sinner,
We become sinner most meek.
Yes we are fundamentally cruel and divisionistic,
Yes the evil in us is stronger than our good.
That's because our ancestors survived through cruelty,
They didn't have much scope to practice their good.
But we ain't our ancestors in our way of life,
We don't have to watch out for predators in every bush.
Then why do we still behave like predators ourselves,
Why don't we break this tribalistic tradition of ambush!
No more cruelty either on ourselves or on those around!
Embolden your backbone into a fountain of kinship unbound.

I Am Ukraine (The Sonnet)

Peace doesn't come through prayers,
Peace comes through responsible action.
When the invader stomps on innocent lives,
Not choosing a side is a consent to oppression.
Ask us for water, we won't let you go unfed,
But do not mistake our gentleness as fear.
If you so much as lay a finger on our home,
We'll defend it with our blood, sweat 'n tears.
We ain't no coward to selfishly seek security,
When our land is being ransacked by raccoons.
When the lives of our loved ones are at stake,
We'll break but never bend to oligarchical buffoons.
The love of our families is what keeps us breathing.
To preserve their smiles, we shall happily die fighting.

Sonnet of Human Duty

To deliver humanity from inhumanity,
Is the duty of every human.
To deliver the innocent from injustice,
Is the duty of every human.
The indifferent may call it god complex,
Apathetic pessimists may call it idealism.
I call it the meaning of life and sanity,
The opposite is just a sign of doofusism.
Differences won't destroy the world,
Indifference is far more ominous.
The problem is not the evil doers,
But the silent spectators.
Mark me well, the day I stay silent is the day,
Lady liberty throws her torch away.

Love Liberty Bondage (The Sonnet)

Love is liberty, love is bondage,
This won't make sense to an egotist.
Love is liberty when unselfish,
Bondage when selfish.
To be bold yet gentle and unselfish,
That is the whole of love eternal.
Whom you love, you'll die to protect,
To die for love is to be immortal.
Mere reading love stories means nothing,
Become a radical new story of love ever told.
Love is degradation as well as salvation,
When unselfish we rise, when selfish we fall.
A drop of lover's sweat outdivines barrels of holy water.
Only love is divine, rest are lesser echoes from days afar.

Kindness No Obligation (The Sonnet)

Those who feel kindness is an obligation,
Don't really feel but crawl as walking dead.
Those who think society ain't their responsibility,
Don’t think, they're just specimens of mental midget.
Giants are those who lay themselves down,
For the welfare of every single soul around.
Intellect is a tool for, not a subject of, greatness and glory,
The root of all greatness is a gentle heart unbound.
Kindness is more than a trait, just like accountability,
These things make a human out of an animal.
Selfishness is more than a flaw, just like egotism,
These things keep an animal from becoming human.
Little selfishness is ok so long as your humanity is in charge.
We've been animal long enough, now let's be giants on guard.

Energy and Ethics (The Sonnet)

One AA battery lights up a house with an LED,
Or it can be used to set fire to it with a spark.
Energy has no ethical polarity, only potential,
Ethics of energy lie in the hands of its wielder.
Society just needs an excuse to escape the blame,
Sometimes they blame science, other times politics.
The real problem is none but the society itself,
Particularly our age-old selfish histrionics.
No society is born human, not yet anyway,
It falls on the original humans to make it human.
Choose science, faith, politics or civil service,
Touch of a human makes medicine even out of poison.
Science doesn't define the scientist, scientist defines the science.
Hence I'm a servant scientist who uses science for deliverance.

Coding Sonnet

One of the most powerful tools of science is coding,
A string of illegible characters can make or break a society.
145,000 lines of code landed Armstrong 'n Aldrin on the moon,
And 2 billion of them are working to satisfy everyday curiosity.
But this awesome force is still used mostly to generate revenue,
Welfare of humanity isn't a priority here, but a mere suggestion.
That's why the coding marvel that set out to connect the world,
Has become a playground for conspiracy, bigotry and division.
Learn from the horrific blunders of society's founding coders,
Make humanity the primary command of every code you write.
A code that doesn't lift the society is nothing but a hideous bug,
Zeros and Ones know no good or bad, unless by you it is defined.
Uncle Ben once said, with great power comes great responsibility.
I say to you today, a humane code facilitates a humane society.

One Day Ain't Enough (The Sonnet)

Nature is beautiful when we are beautiful,
Not in body but in mind.
World is beautiful when we are beautiful,
Not in body but in mind.
Society is just when we are just,
Not merely in talk but in action.
World has equity when we exude equity,
Not insta-equity, but one of slow but sure ascension.
It's good to dedicate certain days to certain cause,
Greater still is to dedicate a life to the cause of humanity.
It's okay to shout about rights and dignity on occasion,
Human is one who lives each day for others' rights 'n dignity.
An apathetic society yells about equality on specific days.
An accountable human needs no occasion to roar across dismay.

Fabric of Stars (The Sonnet)

Rise or fall doesn't matter,
If you've helped a few people.
Live or die doesn't matter,
If you've helped a few people.
The point of life is not to live,
Any more than it is to just eat.
The point of life is to lift lives,
In their smile is victory, in tears defeat.
To win over enemies is ridiculously easy,
To win over hearts is the real act of valor.
Muscles wither, clothes get torn to pieces,
Valor and virtue can't be bound by no graveyard.
Graves are for animals and gutter-crawling worms.
Helpers get forever etched upon the fabric of stars.

Look At The Stars (The Sonnet)

Look up my friend, look at the stars,
You know some of them exploded long ago.
Yet their light keeps shining even when they're gone,
For none of their rays is tainted by ego.
Not a kernel of kindness ever goes to waste,
Not a gesture of gentleness ever goes awry.
The unselfish one is the happiest person in the world,
You'll find joy when you answer someone's cry.
You're thirsty, you seek a glass of water,
That is just plain necessity.
Someone else is thirsty, you share your last glass,
That my friend, is plain humanity.
When self-preservation turns trivial, 'n humanity common sense,
That's when a star is born, amidst all self-serving nuisance.

36. Either Reformist or Terrorist

Evolution & World Building (The Sonnet)

One cell became two,
For being alone is no life.
Then those two became four,
To ease each other's strife.
3 billion years later there are,
Seven billion of us and trillions others.
Now how come we wanna turn back time,
How come we hoard all after selfish desires!
Joy of sharing outshines all other joy,
Caring is the very foundation of life divine.
Divinity means neither magic not mysticism,
It's just a common sense that makes hearts align.
The powers of world-building are all encoded in you.
Bring those codes to life and write the world anew.

Drunk, Insane & Uneducated (The Sonnet)

We live in a world where the sane,
Are more insane than the clinically insane.
Greed and apathy are worse of all ailments,
They make a society narrow and vain.
We live in a world where the educated,
Are more ignorant than the uneducated.
Arrogance and egotism are sacrilege of education,
They make a savage out of the most learned.
We live in a world where the sober,
Are more drunk than a sick alcoholic.
Coldness makes vegetable out of a human,
Then they cuss accountability as idealistic.
I'm drunk and insane, with no education whatsoever.
And these are the signs of a person sane, sober and seer.

Sonnet Krantistani

To hell with fear,
To hell with insecurity!
Stand up with conviction,
To hell with serenity!
Enough with pretend revolution,
Enough with jungly aum shanti!
For once in your life grow up o soldier,
Breaking all biases become krantistani.
Your footsteps will strike terror in terrorists,
Your voice will give chills to the divisionists.
Turn your existence into a beacon of help,
Possess this world with acts of love and uplift.
Killing terrorists and tyrants don't end inhumanity.
Oust them all, then irrigate the soil with solidarity.

(Krantistani: Citizen of Revolution,
Aum Shanti: Archaic Peace Chant)

What's It All About (The Sonnet)

What is this world all about!
What is this society all about!
What is this life all about!
What is our existence all about!
What are the roads all about!
What are the skyscrapers all about!
What are the bridges all about!
What are our feet all about!
What is science all about!
What is faith all about!
What is technology all about!
What is politics all about!
'Tis all about people and their welfare.
All notions to the contrary cause only despair.

Is There More (The Sonnet)

Is there more to life than mere eating!
Is there more to existence than mere fighting!
Is there more to progress than mere greed!
Is there more to administration than controlling!
Is there more to health than mere pills!
Is there more to knowledge than mere facts!
Is there more to character than mere outfits!
Is there more to development than cruel tact!
Is there more to communication than mere talking!
Is there more to tradition than ancient habits!
Is there more to a person than skin and bones!
Is there more to learning than rotten beliefs!
Even the sky is no limit for a mind that expands,
Whereas the savage mind of rigidity is forever bland.

Make No Sect of Me (The Sonnet)

Don't you dare pledge obedience to me!
Don't you turn me into another religious band!
I want you to endeavor into unknown,
I want you to explore and expand.
My work is with human nature,
I know how things are gonna turn out.
Many will come and peddle me as savior,
They'll thrust me as society's way out.
By not addressing it all my predecessors,
Inadvertently became fodder for sectarianism.
True Naskareans of earth are them alone,
Who ain't no Naskarean but plain human.
To make a sect of me is to dishonor me.
Dump all glorification, and be light to humanity.

Halkat Humans (The Sonnet)

The history of human progress,
Is the history of halkat* humans.
Only the *loco make the earth civilized,
By growing out of habits and traditions.
Habits of yesterday are a gutter of biases,
Hence they ain't the right habits of today.
Let us not confuse them as modern identity,
Let us not endorse them throwing reason away.
Traditions born of bigotry and ignorance,
Are hardly a measure of civilization.
Measure of civilization is an expanding spirit,
One that ever evolves discarding superstition.
Turn your heart into a khichdi (fusion) of cultures,
And behold o mighty human, as all division disappears.

Explode With Love (The Sonnet)

When the heart explodes with love,
The world implodes with peace.
When the eyes explode with oneness,
All divisions will begin to ease.
The road to an undivided society,
Goes through an undivided heart.
Be one with everyone and everywhere,
Shatter all habits that make you part.
There's no division that can't be conquered,
The question is not of possibility but intent.
All is right when intention is right,
All are one when the heart is unbent.
Devotion to one culture diminishes humanity.
Devote yourself to the world, and lo pours harmony.

Find The Human (The Sonnet)

Find the human in you, and,
You'll find the human in everybody.
The way things are inside,
So they are externally.
World is reflection of the self,
Outside is reflection of inside.
Blind heart maketh the world blind,
Kind heart maketh the world kind.
We cover our eyes with our hands,
And weep as children for it is too dark.
We let biases take over our behavior,
Then we shout why the world is so unjust.
Without heart all fancy exterior is delusion,
Only truth in the world is the one internal.

Selfless Nuts (The Sonnet)

If someone wants to do harm they'll do harm,
Whether they have nukes or sticks and stone.
If someone wants to do good they'll do good,
Whether they have a billion dollars or just one.
Intention is the mother of all good deeds 'n bad,
It has got nothing to do with having resources.
With intention one bread can feed ten people,
It cannot feed even one when there is no intent.
A world that is run by greed stops for nobody,
Who cares what such a world thinks as righteous!
In such a world you gotta throw caution to the wind,
And stand as pillar of service among the retards.
Long enough snobbish retards have ruled the world!
Now it is time for selfless nuts to take charge.

Humanizing AI (The Sonnet)

You can code tasks,
But not consciousness.
You can code phony feelings,
But definitely not sentience.
Nobody can bring a machine to life,
No matter how complex you make it.
But once a machine is complex enough,
It might develop awareness by accident.
So let us focus on humanizing AI,
By removing biases from algorithms,
Rather than dehumanizing AI,
By aiming for a future without humans.
Rich kids with rich dreams make good movies.
Be human first and use AI to equalize communities.

Love is Simple (The Sonnet)

Truth is simple,
Lies are complex.
Light is simple,
Darkness is complex.
Honesty is simple,
Deceit is complex.
Humility is simple,
Arrogance is complex.
Curiosity is simple,
Conspiracy is complex.
Acceptance is simple,
Discrimination is complex.
Peace is simple, war is complex.
Love is simple, hate is complex.

No Priest No Prostitute (The Sonnet)

In my eyes there is no priest,
No prostitute, only people.
In my eyes there is no pope,
No pedestrian, only people.
In my eyes there is no royalty,
No subject, only people.
In my eyes there is no leader,
No follower, only people.
There is no intellectual,
No layman, only people.
In my eyes there is no superior,
No inferior, only people.
Hierarchy is malarkey maintained by fools.
Oneness maketh civilization across silly schools.

Be The Love Commandment (A Sonnet)

Instead of worrying about a fictitious judgment day,
Make your actual today a real nonjudgment day.
Instead of hoping for a fictitious heaven after death,
Make this world that you have an abode without hate.
Plenty of heart force we have wasted on fiction,
Plenty of attention we have placed on insecurity.
Now it's time to redirect our time and priorities,
It is time to be the valiant vanguards of reality.
I ain't talkin' about being chained to the reality,
Nor about keeping things the way they are for so long.
All I'm asking is, we pay attention to the now and here,
Instead of obsessing over tales from days long gone.
So, stand up to the tyrants as apocalypse incarnate.
Reach out to the needy as a living love commandment.

37. Woman Over World

If I Lose Thee (The Sonnet)

If I lose thee,
All glory feels like gutter.
If I lose thee,
All joy seems to disappear.
If I lose thee,
All ambition is damnation.
If I lose thee,
All applause is condemnation.
If I lose thee,
All success is downfall.
If I lose thee,
All morning is nightfall.
To lose you is to die before death.
To be lost in you is to find oneself.

When I Found Thee (The Sonnet)

When I found thee,
40 inch chest turned 50.
When I found thee,
A savage mind realized humanity.
When I found thee,
A poor vagabond became a beacon.
When I found thee,
A cowardly heart became a lion.
Every cunning tradesman says,
The trade of love is sheer torment.
I say, better love and be hurt,
For wounds of love are a lover's ornament.
You appeared, and I found hope in every corner.
Even amidst all hell I saw paradise appear.

38. High Voltage Habib

Human Bulldozer (The Sonnet)

I am no Gandhi, that I'd sit quietly and spin a wheel,
While people suffer in the clutches of imperialism.
I am no Guevara either, that I would shoot anyone,
Who looks suspicious, in my revolution for freedom.
Gandhi and Guevara are two extremes of human struggle,
One glorifies submission, another heralds new oppression.
Neither is fit for an infant world aiming to be civilized,
For one lacks backbone, the other weaponizes assumption.
We may take a little from Gandhi, a little from Guevara,
Without rigidity we may administer them accordingly.
I am an accountable human living in a world run by biases,
So most times I'll keep quiet and act as a harmless dummy.
But whenever inhumanity goes overboard wreaking havoc,
The human bulldozer will rise to cleanse every epoch.

No Struggle No Life (The Sonnet)

Ain't no life without struggle,
Ain't no heart without heartbreak.
Ain't no destination without the journey,
Ain't no courage without some dread.
Ain't no clarity without some confusion,
Ain't no serenity without suffering.
Ain't no contentment without disappointment,
Ain't no resilience without failing.
Ain't no mindfulness without mindlessness,
Ain't no uplift without some devastation.
Ain't no knowledge without ignorance,
Ain't no salvation without self-annihilation.
Ain't no I without the Us, without the We.
Ain't no We, unless the norm is nonbinary.

Diversity is No Gimmick (The Sonnet)

Diversity is no gimmick,
Diversity is no belief.
Diversity is life itself,
Diversity is uplift.
Diversity is sanity,
Diversity is joy.
Diversity is monsoon,
After a drought most dry.
There ain't no humanity,
If there is no diversity.
We ain't no human,
If inside we have no amity.
It ain't enough to talk of toleration!
Each of us is to be the vessel of unification.

War is Expensive (The Sonnet)

War is expensive, peace is free,
Yet war is petty, peace is priceless.
War is childish, peace is for adults,
Yet war is complex, peace is child's play.
War is for fools, peace is for the sage,
Yet sages sustain war, deeming peace foolish.
War is strain on the brain, peace only needs love,
Yet intellectuals justify war, calling peace rubbish.
War is good for maintaining control over the people,
Hence imperialists peddle war in the name of justice.
But all imperialists are the fault of the civilians,
All wars are a failure of our civilized citizenship.
No war is tougher than the civilians of the world.
Exercise that potential to abolish all imperial gall.

Undoctrination Sonnet

If we teach kids history,
They say we're indoctrinating them.
If we immunize them against disease,
They say we're microchipping them.
If we teach kids science,
They say we're practicing blasphemy.
If we teach kids biology,
They say we're messing with their identity.
With such mentality of a caveman,
How on earth did you manage to conceive!
I guess, to raise a human takes common sense,
But to make a baby takes only genital breach.
Hence it is more reason for reason to persevere.
There is no way we can let stone age reappear.

The Chupacabra Sonnet

Chihuahuas need guns for strength,
They feel naked without concealed carry.
To them I say, with all humility,
Open your eyes muchacho - ¡chupacabra aquí!
You may keep your gun, I won't say a word,
But don't confuse them to be your safe haven.
Own them in secret, but think of using them,
And you'll face the wrath of this kraken.
You may conceal, you may carry, if law allows,
But dare not raise your gun at a reformador.
To the wounded stranger I am ointment,
But to the inhuman vermin I am volcano.
Carrying a gun every moron feels like superman.
Stand up to cruelty unarmed, then you are human.

Civilization is Not A Place (The Sonnet)

No matter who likes it not,
Say Gay anyway.
Compliance to discrimination,
Is the coward's way.
A true leader once said, women belong in,
All places where decisions are being made.
I say, fudge it all,
Women just belong, period.
They say, they don't want their kids,
To be hurt learning history.
I say, if learning history makes you hurt,
You are in dire need of therapy.
Civilization begins when we acknowledge our primitiveness.
Civilization is not a place, it's a people, it's a process.

The Empowered Sonnet

Woman empowered is civilization empowered.
Dream empowered is progress empowered.
Parents empowered is children empowered.
Teachers empowered is future empowered.
Don't defund the police, use those funds,
To send the officers to behavioral therapy.
To have an understanding of justice and order,
We must have a grip over our impulses and biases.
Discrimination don't disappear if we shut our eyes,
Each of us must live as an antidote to discrimination.
Ignorance doesn't become knowledge when peddled by scripture,
Better burn all scriptures if they peddle hate and division.
To conquer our biases and stereotypes is to conquer inhumanity.
To expand our heart beyond assumption is to empower humanity.

Sonnet of Single Mother

There is no greater superpower,
In the world than a single mother.
Far superior to the world leaders,
Is the resolve of a single mother.
Wanna learn to build a society?
Wanna become a nation builder?
Spend a couple of months as pupil,
At the feet of a single mother.
Want there to be peace and progress?
Hand social reins to single mothers.
Stand by them as aide with commitment,
Lo and behold, the healing appears.
A mom empowered is a world empowered.
A single mom empowered is creation empowered.

Service Over Selfies Sonnet

Awake, Arise O Timelords,
Oh makers and breakers of destiny!
Give this world accountability,
And time will give you immortality.
I don't want your shallow folllows,
I do not want your fancy likes.
Reach out as friend to someone in need,
That'll be my life's greatest prize.
Social media stats are no sign of character,
Fan following is no measure of a being.
Service over selfies, that is the motto,
Helping over hogging, that is living.
Life begins with the end of self-obsession,
Life self-obsessed is nothing but excretion.

Be A Tesla (The Sonnet)

In a world full of Elon Musks,
Be a Dan Price.
Use entrepreneurship to instill equity,
Not as a vessel of disparity's vice.
In a world full of Jordan Petersons,
Be a Jiddu Krishnamurti.
Use intellect to expand perception,
Not to turn back the clock of primitivity.
In a world full of Donald Trumps,
Be a Dolly Parton, be an Ocasio-Cortez.
Use fame and politics to alleviate anguish,
Not to feed on people's distress.
Let others adore the crook Edison all they wanna.
You for one be a Marie Curie, be a Nikola Tesla.

High Voltage Sonnet

Once upon a time I said to thee, Awake, Arise,
Stop not till thou write thy destiny!
Two score later I said to thee,
Give me blood, and I'll give thee liberty!
Time passed and some life got much fancier but,
Division and disparity remain ever so horrid.
We have made great strides on the outside yet,
In the mental domain we remain ever so brutish.
A twenty watt brain once accountable,
Electrifies the universe.
But when selfish and indifferent,
Even 20 million of them cannot do diddly-squat.
Fetch those cables from your spinal cord,
Awake, arise, and electrify this dampened world!

In Your Trust (The Sonnet)

My soldiers don't smoke and drink,
Though they may try them for experience.
They don't look at another sexually,
Without their wholehearted consent.
I made myself the human,
I want to see in the world.
Touch my work only after,
You've renounced being self-absorbed.
I didn't annihilate my entire life,
So that you may turn me into another cult.
Never you use me to boost your ego,
Or as an excuse for intellectual outburst.
Do not be Naskar, be the Naskar 2.0.
I leave my homeworld in trust of yours.

39. Bulldozer on Duty

Book of Destiny (The Sonnet)

The book of destiny is the being,
Who doesn't believe in destiny.
The epitome of victory is the one,
Who doesn't care for victory.
Victory and destiny all are born,
Of the sweat and blood of the determined.
Annihilate the self for a purpose,
And you'll be the icon of universal uplift.
You don't fall by falling at someone's feet,
You fall by climbing on top of others' head.
You don't rise by being superior to others,
But by losing sense of high 'n low divisiveness.
Mark me well, human is neither person nor species.
Designation Human is the highest of all responsibilities.

Reason and Heart (The Sonnet)

The death of reason is the death of progress,
But the death of heart is the death of existence.
Division between reason and heart must be destroyed,
For it has kept us from achieving our luminescence.
Heart alone is the master, intellect is the servant,
Let it be so, and great things will follow.
Place your head at the feet of your heart,
And the entire world will start to glow.
Let heart be the art you practice,
Let art be the heart you practice.
Let love be the science you practice,
Let science be the love you practice.
One who has reason has something,
One who has heart has everything.

Beauty Ain't Beauty (The Sonnet)

Beauty is not in the eye of the beholder,
Beauty is in the heart of the beholder.
Eyes have evolved not to perceive beauty,
But to look for a fertile progenitor.
All instincts of beauty are prehistoric,
All impulse of attraction is mere heat.
Such tendency is an act of animal libido,
It has nothing to do with human heartbeat.
If you wanna discover someone's beauty,
You gotta throw the dirt off your heart.
Observe their behavior outside the body,
Only then shall you witness true beauty's path.
Across the vacuum of body lies the valley of beauty.
Defy the vacuum, and you'll realize, beauty is divinity.

Broken (The Sonnet)

The most effective people,
On earth are all broken.
The people with most excellence,
Are all broken.
There is no excellence without brokenness,
For brokenness builds character.
Broken, and in agony, that's how we grow,
One who knows pain knows to help another.
Pain is not our enemy,
Pain is what keeps us alert.
To avoid pain is to avoid growth,
To avoid pain is to keep the heart shut.
Embrace pain, and pain will have no hold over you.
Once accepted, in brokenness you'll find yourself anew.

Will and Wheel (The Sonnet)

Where there is a will, there is a wheel.
Where there is intent, there is upliftment.
Where there is heart, there is less dirt.
Where there is content, there is less torment.
Where there is simplicity, there is sanity.
Where there is luxury, there is degradation.
Where there is sharing, there is serenity.
Where there is moderation, there is ascension.
Where there is love, there is acceptance.
Where there is division, there is judgment.
Where there is selflessness, there is joy.
Where there is self-absorption, there is lament.
The requirement of civilization is simply this.
We are to have the will to love and the will to lift.

Chosen by Choice (The Sonnet)

Choose yourself by yourself,
Be the chosen by choice.
Nobody's gonna come to choose you,
Without any self-interest.
Nobody's gonna pop out of fiction,
And choose you to lift the world.
The world is your family,
You are their self-determined vanguard.
You are the chooser, you are the choice,
You alone are the divine intervention.
One who is responsible is also divine,
What is indifferent is simply damnation.
Choose yourself as the world's defender.
There's no greater defender than an unbent lover.

Higher Dimension (The Sonnet)

The only higher dimension,
Is the selfless dimension.
There is no magic, no mysticism,
There is only self-annihilation.
Service makes a being divine,
Not rituals and rigidity.
A kind atheist is more divine,
Than a priest who's bigoted and greedy.
You don't rise high by worshiping,
Images, symbols and ideologies.
You rise when you fall in service,
At the feet of the helpless and needy.
Those who wanna help themselves help the world.
Those who just help themselves are plain retard.

Never Ask (The Sonnet)

Never ask a poet,
Why they write what they write.
If they knew why they write,
No poetry will have any light.
Never ask a painter,
Why they paint what they paint.
If they knew why they paint,
All paint will turn bleak and faint.
Never ask a scientist,
Why they are curious the way they are.
If they knew the reason for their curiosity,
There wouldn't be any science, nor uplift's desire.
The drive for expression takes a million shapes,
When all combine without condescension we'll see God's face.

Combine Without Condescension (The Sonnet)

When all combine without condescension,
We shall witness God's face.
Then we shall realize beyond all doubt,
God has never been a person but a state.
A state of mind where division disappears,
That is what godliness means.
A state of sight where separation withers,
That is what holiness means.
This state is beyond beliefs and doctrines,
It is the sacred valley of life beyond life.
There is no life so long as we are divided,
Life united is life brought to life.
There is no God, only heart nonsectarian.
In that heart, You, I, the Father, the Son, all are one.

No God, Only Goodness (The Sonnet)

Kingdom of God is manifestation,
Of a nonsectarian mind.
It means conquering our biases,
It means conquering all drives of divide.
True goodness is devoid of division,
For division is antithesis of goodness.
Whatever is civilized is nonsectarian,
Whoever is human is undivided.
There is no heaven, only good human,
There is no paradise, only good people.
When people and people live as one people,
That is a human society, alive and civil.
Civility is just a fancy synonym for amity.
Divinity is the archaic term for indivisibility.

Carving Inclusion (The Sonnet)

Carving a sonnet of inclusion on a statue,
Does not magically make a nation accepting.
There ain't gonna be no inclusion unless we,
Stop filibustering, and start love-mustering.
Turning back the clock on cultural diversity,
Does not make a nation strong and progressive.
Traditions that refuse inclusion and expansion,
Are sheer poison in the path of societal uplift.
A rigid nation is no nation but a primitive tribe,
A civilized community practices reason and warmth.
Economy does not make a nation super power,
Equality and inclusion reveal its true worth.
Assimilation is to be etched upon the national heart,
Only then we can call such heart a human heart.

Ain't Your Nigger (Sonnet to The Whites)

Yes I am colored,
But I ain't your nigger.
I am your way to oneness,
I am the humanitarian trigger.
I am the trigger for revolution,
Whenever there is oppression.
I am the trigger for reason,
Whenever there is dogmatization.
I am the trigger for ascension,
Whenever there is assumption.
I am the trigger for assimilation,
Whenever there is discrimination.
On our shackled shoulders America was built.
Yet how come we are still hated to the hilt!

My Dear Nazi (The Sonnet)

My dear nazis old and new,
While there is time change your view.
If I get my hands on you,
No savior will do nothing for you.
I am unarmed, I am unbent,
Yet on my conviction you can't make a dent.
You may need guns to hide your impotence,
As for me, my backbone is my source of strength.
Exclusivity and supremacy belong in stoneage,
Society is modernized only with expansion.
Monocultural glorification is a moronic habit,
Human is born when all tribalism is abandoned.
Nazi dear, nazi dear, enough with domination!
Come this way, hold my hand, I am your absolution.

We Are All Racist (The Sonnet)

If we are still uncomfortable to face,
The roots of racism, how can we uproot racism!
Unless we recognize our tendency for division,
How can we ever be the cause of universalism!
The fundamental fact of human nature is,
We are a septic tank of prehistoric biases.
Sectarianism comes to us far too easily,
For we are all fundamentally racist.
Cruelty is the mainspring of survival in the wild,
So our brain leans more towards cruelty than kindness.
Millions of years of conditioning won't vanish overnight,
We must self-regulate with our newly developed conscience.
The end of racism starts with the recognition of racism.
We are civilized only when we recognize our uncivilization.

Real Third World (The Sonnet)

Third world countries are not,
Those from Asia and Africa.
Some of the real third world countries,
Are our United States and Russia.
It is behavior that makes the person,
It is behavior that makes the nation.
Worth of a nation lies not in currency,
But in their sense of assimilation.
A civilized nation doesn't say,
We are the greatest nation on earth.
Only the underdeveloped yells around,
We are the nation supreme, all others are dirt.
A first world country is born of first world citizens.
A citizen becomes first world by defying all divisions.

40. Find A Cause Outside Yourself

Welcome to Earth (World Tourism Sonnet)

When you are down with doubts sit down,
For lessons of revolution from the Americas.
When you are beginning to have cold feet,
Siphon some much needed resilience from Africa.
When your heart is beginning to turn cold,
Have a rejuvenating swim in the warmth of Asia.
When clouds of gloom start to grab hold,
Breathe in some fresh air from Australia.
Whenever the bickering goes overboard,
Draw some lessons of unity from Europe.
Whatever it is you seek my friend,
We just might be able to satisfy your hope.
Come visit us sometime, on our little blue dot.
We are the beings of love, light and colors,
as such we often go overboard.

Health and Sickness (The Sonnet)

Health doesn't always come from pills,
Health comes through being mindful.
Pills just help bring down the barriers,
That clutter the body with deadly ghoul.
Wellness is not the absence of sickness,
It's the capacity to overcome sickness.
Some sickness are the norm of nature,
Others are products of our own foolishness.
The opposite of sickness is not its absence,
The opposite of sickness is its awareness.
To treat sickness we must first acknowledge it,
Sickness acknowledged is sickness half treated.
In the end, health favors those who favor humility.
Sustainability favors those who favor simplicity.

Medicine Means (The Sonnet)

MEDICINE means Mercy,
MEDICINE means Empathy,
MEDICINE means Dare,
MEDICINE means Integrity,
MEDICINE means Care,
MEDICINE means Ingenuity,
MEDICINE means Nobility,
MEDICINE means Ethicality.
Medicine is not a profession,
Medicine is but a sacred calling.
An average doctor saves a body,
A good doctor saves a being.
Pathogens exist to cash in on sickness.
A doctor exists to be lost among patients.

Never Planned (The Sonnet)

I never planned to be a poet,
I never planned to be a writer.
I never planned to be a scientist,
I never planned to be a philosopher.
I never had any plans whatsoever,
As to what I was going to be.
As a vagabond I only had one inkling,
That is to equalize the society.
Now that I am a scientist,
Logic comes to me like clockwork.
Now that I am a writer and poet,
Words and rhymes come like lovewalk.
The path appears itself as you start to walk.
Means flow like heartbeat in all purposeful work.

Tapwater and Natural Spring (The Sonnet)

I am sorry if big bard becomes bleak,
In front of the vast spirit of oneness.
I am sorry if baron byron turns barren,
In front of the sense of collectiveness.
With their native tongue given at birth,
The fancy figures did what they could.
It ain't their fault that it takes an outsider,
To bring out a tongue's rightful good.
Some figures are tapwater,
While others are natural spring.
Some are just good writers,
While others are Maya, Martí and King.
Anybody can write mushy words, that's no biggie.
Genius is one who lives as they speak, with integrity.

Love, Latitude, Longitude (The Sonnet)

Love knows no latitude,
Love knows no longitude.
Love only knows to be,
Annihilated in servitude.
Love knows no aptitude,
Love knows no sanctitude.
Love only knows to give,
And wind up a destitute.
A destitute lover is wealthier,
Than a loveless billionaire.
Prison of gold is still a prison,
Our own greed makes us prisoner.
Eyes off the gold and hands on the heart!
Thus we shall wipe out all the world's dirt.

Ruined Lover (The Sonnet)

It isn't wrong to want,
To be with someone.
Whether they reciprocate,
Is not your decision.
You cannot force love,
To force love is to ruin it.
All you can do is reach out,
Even at the risk of being ruined.
Love never cares about reputation,
If it did it wouldn't be love.
If you can still think logical,
You are anything but in love.
Logic is but poison in love's domain.
Let all ego be washed away by love's pouring rain.

Old and New (The Sonnet)

Old is not necessarily gold,
New is not necessarily cool.
Stereotypes without scrutiny,
Sustain only a society of fools.
Answer to one stereotype is not another,
Answer to one assumption is not another.
To make assumption is not wrong but,
To assume it as truth supreme is rhubarb.
Perception is all about assumption,
Our brain hasn't evolved to observe reality.
Biases prevent the observation of biases, unless,
You are hellbent to expand across comfort and luxury.
Stereotypes are archetypes of self-preservation.
Look outside the self and you'll find assimilation.

Fortune Without Love (The Sonnet)

Fortune without love is sheer curse,
For life's true blessing is love alone.
Live to love and love to live,
With this as motto all good is honed.
They say you can't live on love alone,
And indeed it's true to its factual core.
But green of dollar without green of heart,
Grows on us like toxic mold.
Too much of dollar can kill a person,
Just like too little causes starvation.
Use money like you use your car,
To go places, not to live at the gas station.
Put love and life above all else.
You'll know what's sense, what's nonsense.

Sapient or Savage (The Sonnet)

To be or not to be,
That is not the question.
To be human or stay animal,
That is the question.
Human and animal,
What is the difference!
To be animal is to be selfish,
To be human is to go beyond the self.
There's more to life than us and them,
There's more to life than loss and gain.
There's more to life than money and fame,
There's more to life than dogmatic lanes.
To be or not to be, that is not the question.
Be sapient or stay savage, it's your decision.

Life is Chaos (The Sonnet)

Best laid plans of mice and men,
Often go awry leaving no hope.
Just when you think you have control,
Life throws you off course.
All notions of order are a myth,
Only order of the universe is chaos.
Expand your sight and you'll realize,
There is order in every chaos.
A narrow mind is ever struggling,
In the tangled web of order and chaos.
A sapient mind works above the two,
For their sight is fixed on a purpose.
Focus on life, not on all its philosophy.
Embrace the chaos and act despite insecurity.

Light Impossible (The Sonnet)

A candle knows only to give light,
Despite being surrounded by darkness.
Darkness cannot affect the candle's light,
A candle cannot be coerced into heartlessness.
The struggle for light has never been easy,
If it were, light would be but a cigarette-butt.
Light is priceless, hence the struggle is eternal,
To be light is to be alive, even amidst the dark.
To be light is to see light, this is the law,
To be good is to see good, this is the way.
One whose hands are guided by love and light,
Even amidst ominous storms never goes astray.
Love for the world causes light impossible.
For love for the people is love untameable.

Hate Not The Hater (The Sonnet)

In most cases what seems,
Like hate is actually envy.
Even the haters don't know that,
Haters just hate what they can't be.
Others' achievement intimidates the puny,
Whereas it inspires those wanting to grow.
Pay no attention to the mockery of morons,
Ridicule can't diminish a braveheart's glow.
When an empty flashlight mocks the sun,
Does it affect the sun's glory one bit!
Hate not the haters in return my friend,
It's just their way of acting needy, that's it.
One lover is braver than a hundred haters.
One heart alive and aloud is the bias breaker.

Valley of Light (The Sonnet)

Behind every cloud,
There is a silver lining.
The cloud is in the mind,
So is the silver lining.
The brush is born of mind,
The paint as well is born of mind.
If the painting has no color,
That too is because of the mind.
When the mind is bright so is the sun,
When the heart is dark so is the sun.
When everything looks dull, just look inside,
You'll discover, all along you've been the sun.
Heart is the gateway to its own valley of light.
Heart is the pedestrian, heart is the might.

Peygamber Undercover
(Sonnet of Accountability)

Everywhere I look, there's apocalypse!
Everywhere I look, there's inhumanity!
We have slept like a log long enough!
It's time for the human to embody humanity!
Still if you ask out of fear and insecurity,
What can you one person do to bring change!
Mark my words, if you are really determined,
You could part the ocean with sheer intent.
You have the power to turn this ailing world,
Into a world of laughter and loveliness.
The question is, are you a responsible human,
Or just another crummy vessel of recklessness?
Whatever the trouble may be, you are the answer.
In this difficult time, you are peygamber undercover.

People Vs Supreme Court (The Sonnet)

When the Supreme Court behaves prehistoric,
Every human must become an activist.
When the gatekeepers of law behave barbarian,
Every civilian must come down to the street.
When people are stripped off their basic rights,
By some bigoted and shortsighted gargoyles.
We the people must take back the reins,
And put the politicians in their rightful place.
We need no guns and grenades, we need no ammo,
Unarmed and unbent we stand against savagery.
Till every woman obtains their right to choice,
None of us will sit quiet in compliant apathy.
Every time the cradle of justice becomes criminal,
It falls upon us civilians to be justice incorruptible.

41. Ingan Impossible

Sapiens Impossible (The Sonnet)

If my existence isn't impossible,
I do not wanna exist.
If my legacy isn't impossible,
I do not want to live.
If my breath doesn't breathe life,
I don't wanna take another breath.
If my veins don't invigorate another,
I have no need for such useless veins.
If my heart isn't proof of love impossible,
May this be the last time my heart beats.
If this being isn't the bridge of oneness,
May the bugs have a feast on some good eats.
I don't wanna live as a weakling of the jungle.
If I must live I'll live as sapiens impossible.

My Russia My Responsibility (The Sonnet)

Moya Rossiya, moya lyubov, I am sorry,
That the world has turned its back on us.
But can you really blame them when,
We accepted a terrorist as a leader of ours!
Awake, arise, my brave comrades,
Drink deep from the valor of Volga.
I say, enough with apathy, for it is high time,
To sanitize our land against all domestic virus.
We let a terrorist loose on our neighbors,
And all that bloodshed is on our hands.
Even now if we don't mend our horrific error,
One savage will turn our world into a wasteland.
Mnogo te obicham, for you are still my home.
To humanize our home is the duty of none but our own.

Ain't The Center (The Sonnet)

You are the Alpha,
You are Omega.
You are Altair,
You are the Vega.
You are the distance,
You are the contact.
You are the runner,
You are the racetrack.
You are the race,
You are the prize.
You are torchbearer,
You are the light.
You ain't the center of the universe.
For in reality, you are the universe.

All in The Mind (The Sonnet)

Mind makes it dark,
Mind makes it bright.
Mind makes us weak,
Mind gives us might.
Mind makes us blind,
Mind gives us sight.
Mind makes us scared,
Mind gives us flight.
Mind makes us greedy,
Mind instills charity.
Mind raises the walls,
Mind wills all unity.
Mind is servant, mind is master.
Once truly aware, mind is hatebuster.

Poet of A Planet (The Sonnet)

I am not the poet of a nation,
I am the poet of a planet.
I don't do just one culture,
Assimilation is the prime tenet.
Hence my work repels nationalists,
Like the sun repels the nightcrawlers,
While it attracts expanding beings,
Like the amazon attracts explorers.
If you wanna hear how great your culture is,
Go read some fundamentalist fiction.
I don't write for prehistoric barbarians,
To put it bluntly, I write for modern humans.
I repeat, I'm not the poet of a single nation.
I am but the living proof of amalgamation.

No Slave to Culture (The Sonnet)

What do you take me for - a street dog!
Slave to one religion, one nation, one culture!
Dinosaur here - wherever I lay my eyes,
Becomes my nation, my religion, my culture!
To add nationality to my name is to vilify my name,
Sectarianism and nonsectarianism don't go together.
To add exclusive ethnicity to my work is a violation,
Barbarism can't define the spirit of a human sonneteer.
Days of single nationality, single religion are gone,
It's the age of universal nationality and religion.
In this civilized age, human nationality is humanity,
Human religion and culture are love and compassion.
Exclusive ethnicity is a sign of a backward society.
Expand across the one imposed, and there'll be harmony.

World is My Family (The Sonnet)

Family is the world to everybody,
But to me the world is my family.
In the life of a true human,
Raising a wall is but blasphemy.
If the world is Juliet, I'm her Romeo,
If the world is Romeo, I'm his Juliet.
Amidst the storms of hate and hurt,
I am but an anchor of love and lenience.
I'll hide the world in my heart if necessary,
To provide sanctuary is the heart's purpose.
The struggle of this human will continue,
Till all drives of hate are memories of the past.
So I say again, my world is my responsibility.
Beware my dear bigots, I'm injurious to inhumanity!

Mental Piece (The Sonnet)

In the west you call me humanitarian scientist,
Somewhere in the middle you call me pragmatist.
In the middle-east you call me sufi or dervish,
In the east you call me advaitin or nondualist.
No matter how you see me, you all are my own,
Each of you is family, each of you is my home.
Then there are those who ardently call me fraud,
Which also is a sign of love, but yet unknown.
I am not a person, prison or path, for I am vicdan,
I'm saadet, my friend, I am the spirit of unification.
Call the sun as you like, it still brightens the world,
In the domain of realization, to label is desecration.
All labels are equally right yet equally incomplete.
In a world full of showpiece I am but a mental piece.

Financial Freedom (The Sonnet)

Financial freedom doesn't mean,
To be free from money troubles.
Financial freedom actually means,
Freedom from obsession of dollar bills.
When the mind learns to distinguish,
Between luxury and actual necessity.
That's the beginning of financial freedom,
That's the beginning of economic stability.
Modern economy is the antithesis of sustainability,
Where financial freedom is bait to the suckers.
Actual necessities of life are very little,
But first you gotta break free from the predators.
We gotta wake up from materialism to be free.
Or else, scheme after scheme we'll be ever unfree.

Ride A Bike (The Sonnet)

Ride a bike 'n you get sick less,
You pay for the doctor less.
Ride a bike 'n you emit carbon less,
You pay for the gas less.
Ride a bike 'n you release endorphins,
Hence you have less stress.
Ride a bike 'n the heart pumps better,
Thus you feel exhaustion less.
Pills in need are pills indeed,
To pop pills willy-nilly is to abuse health.
Comfort in need is comfort indeed,
To abuse comfort beyond need is to abuse oneself.
Ride a bike everyday to keep the pills away.
Use pills in need but don't make them life's way.

To See Color (The Sonnet)

The problem is not that you see color,
It is that you assume character from color.
The problem is not that you see gender,
It is that you assume capacity from gender.
The problem is not that you see religion,
It is that you assume tendency from religion.
The problem is not that you see profession,
It is that you assume worth from profession.
The problem is not that you see sexuality,
It is that you assume nature from sexuality.
The problem is not that you see nationality,
It is that you assume honor from nationality.
The main problem is not that you make assumptions.
It is that you assume yourself beyond examination.

This is how we make all lives matter (The Sonnet)

Wherever a black life is shot of suspicion,
I am that black life that didn't matter.
Wherever a woman is forced to remain pregnant,
I am that woman who doesn't matter.
Wherever a muslim is presumed terrorist,
I am that muslim who doesn't matter.
Wherever a queer life is persecuted,
I am that queer who doesn't matter.
Standing up to cannibalism requires,
No exclusive background and identity.
All that matters is that you are human,
Only requirement of justice is humanity.
This is how we make all lives matter, all lives free.
Injustice on anyone anywhere is injustice on me.

Motherless Motherhood (The Sonnet)

To take choice out of pregnancy,
Is to take the mother out of motherhood.
If childbirth isn't the mother's will,
Who the hell is state to make the rule!
State is a servant of the people,
Church is a servant of the people.
When they claim to be guardian supreme,
People must stand to spoil their gamble.
To take choice out of democracy,
Is to take citizens out of government.
But to take bigotry out of politics,
Is to take politics out of the state.
A society that equates woman with womb,
Is a society headed for its own tomb.

Elitism & Fundamentalism (The Sonnet)

Elitism and fundamentalism,
Are both the enemies of progress.
Exchanging one bad habit for another,
Is not true advancement but regress.
Fundamentalists used to fill the world,
With the poison of dirty division.
Today elitists poison the world,
By endorsing snobbery and narcissism.
Conscience, courage and compassion,
These are the three pillars of progress.
Without these all belief is delusion,
All glitter is but a sign of coldness.
Replace not fundamentalism with elitism.
Grow out of selfishness into collectivism.

Do you know who I am (The Sonnet)

Oh, so many times have I heard,
Do you know who I am!
So today when I travel places,
I walk around as a total lamb!
There's an immense relief,
In not flashing my name.
Windbags make all the noise,
Beings with character stay inane.
Be an elephant, strong yet gentle,
You observe more by being a dumbbell.
Blow your top when it's really needed,
Otherwise, be good people among the people.
All roads lead to people, not to mythical Rome.
Names aloof from people have no living role.

Make A Name (The Sonnet)

Make a name to give hope,
Not to have control over people.
Make a name to lift another,
Not to look down on the people.
Be a symbol that burns bright,
Even when you are not around.
Selfish self is septic self,
Be an epitome of sacrifice unbound.
Only fools dream of ruling the world,
Sapiens dream of self-annihilation.
I dream, breathe and live as servant,
Servanthood brings sanctification.
Fall without fail at the feet of the forgotten.
Lend a hand to lift a heart, together we are beacon.

Politics is The New Opium (The Sonnet)

I started writing on politics to impress a girl,
Then she left for a native white, balkan alternative.
But I was too deep in the pickle to leave politics,
Eventually the struggling nobody arose a global native.
Originally I was inclined towards writing on religion,
But soon I realized justice is the religion of tomorrow.
And the world's notion of religion is beyond repair,
Terms of religion lost their charm to me more and more.
Religion was the opium for the masses of yesterday,
Politics is opium for the masses of today.
But politics of pop culture is not what I work on,
My politics is not left or right, but mostly grey.
As a brain scientist, my work is to dissect human nature.
If it makes way for a better society, that's a great honor.

Social Reform 101 (The Sonnet)

Brute force isn't always the answer,
Sometimes you gotta be clever.
Naivety has its place, it keeps you humble,
Dealing with hyenas you gotta be a dinosaur.
I am not talking about size and appearance,
Appearance never brings any lasting change.
Here I am talking about the faculties within,
For corruption is defeated only by a hearty brain.
The best way to control the manipulator is,
To give them the illusion of control 'n dominance.
To con the con-artist for the greater good,
Is not an act of con but an act of conscience.
Sentiment is good, but without wisdom it is plain stupid.
An activist fights the system, a reformer manipulates it.

42. Amantes Assemble

Holy Trinity (The Sonnet)

Civilization is founded on 3 pillars,
Conscience, courage and compassion.
Without these three there is no society,
Only a prehistoric mockery of civilization.
When all three come together, lo and behold,
Here rises the holy trinity - the holy trident!
You can use it to plough the land of creation,
Or use it to devour the divisions most obstinate.
Wasting precious lifeforce chanting like a parrot,
Do not go chasing fiction out in the wilderness.
Wipe the rust off your heart that causes all the drag,
And you my friend, shall be the incorruptible trident.
However, in reality, there are no three, but only one.
The spirit of love and oneness is beyond time and form.

Amantes Assemble Sonnet 2

What is time, what is form,
It is all an illusion.
What has come, what has gone,
It is all an illusion.
No such thing as reality,
No such thing as truth,
It's all a trick of the mind,
It's all a hallucination most obtuse.
Role of reality is survival,
Role of perception is preservation.
All talk of truth is nonsense,
All sense of wisdom is self-gratification.
So forget about truth, wisdom and salvation.
Let's just make life a humane illusion.

The Biochemistry Sonnet

Chemicals breed prejudice,
Chemicals breed love.
Chemicals breed hate and rage,
Chemicals breed the atoning dove.
Chemicals breed walls of divide,
Chemicals breed the bridge to unite.
Chemicals breed death and disease,
In those very chemicals we find sight.
Chemicals are us, we are the chemicals,
In this mortal world there is nothing else.
While most are run by the whim of chemicals,
Some bend chemicals at will, as true sapiens.
Chemicals are the cause, chemicals are the result.
Awareness of chemicals is awareness of the world.

Amantes Assemble Sonnet 4

From dust we are born, in dust we'll merge,
The journey in-between must have some meaning.
If you have the will, then that's all you need,
To make a civilization out of air most thin.
There is not one but two universes,
One is real, another made up by our brain.
We live in the one that our brain has made,
And biases coax us to believe it as the only lane.
In this universe truth involves comfort not reason,
Assumption alone distinguishes right from wrong.
In such hallucinatory society stereotypes are archetypes,
And to question stereotypes is to bring ridicule along.
The human brain hasn't evolved to understand the universe.
If we must live in hallucination, let's make it a lover-verse.

Amantes Assemble Sonnet 5

In a world of indifference,
All inspiration is desperation.
In a world of apathy,
All capacity is desolation.
When the heart is blind,
The greatest of power is evil.
When the sight is tight,
Even a saintly one turns devil.
Real, unreal, all is in the neurons,
All of which is primed by nature.
We also hold the seed of expansion,
Which blooms when we defy selfish desire.
You see, puny minds make puny-verse,
Uni minds make uni-verse.

Sonnet of Human Resources

There is no blue collar, no white collar, just honor.
And honor is defined by character not collar.
There is no CEO, no janitor, just people.
Person's worth lies, not in background, but behavior.
Designation is reference to expertise, not existence.
Respect is earned through rightful action, not label.
Designation without humanity is resignation of humanity,
For all labels without love cause nothing but trouble.
The term human resources is a violation of human rights.
For it designates people as possession of a company.
Computers are resources, staplers are resources, but people,
Aren't resources, but the soul of all company and society.
I'm not saying, you oughta rephrase it all in a civilized way.
But at the very least, it's high time with hierarchy we do away.

Note: Call it skill resources, call it expertise resources, but don't call it human resources. Because the term 'human resources' compares humans with commodity, which is nothing but a new age slavery.

Fantasy and Responsibility (The Sonnet)

Fantasy is good so long as it doesn't make us,
Oblivious to our responsibility of reality.
Imagination expands the mind for sure,
Only when it empowers our acts of accountability.
Growing up in India, I did not have superman,
But I did indulge religiously in some shaktimaan.
I don't know whether it influenced my making,
But it sure did fill my childhood with fascination.
People draw inspiration from different places,
That's a normal tenet of the mind, not a violation.
But inspiration is inspiration only when it leads,
To collective uplift, otherwise it's just delusion.
Fantasy is healthy when practiced with moderation.
Too much fiction paralyzes responsibility and reason.

Amantes Assemble Sonnet 9

The world doesn't need more avengers, but amantes.
Hear me well, my brave amantes, it's time to assemble!
More than Captain America we need Amelia Earhart,
More than Madame Web we need Madame Curie-like rebel.
Scrutinize all tradition with a fresh set of eyes,
Rebel against dogma, and stand up to discrimination.
Beliefs and doctrines surely have their place,
But none of it is above scrutiny of the new generation.
Each generation is to write their new set of laws,
Learning from the triumphs and downfalls of yesterday.
You just remember, that all roads lead to people,
And life that doesn't lift people is life gone astray.
Ayudar a la gente es la salvación de la mente.
Elevación de la gente es la elevación de la mente.

Amantes Assemble Sonnet 10

Each of us is a chunk of uranium,
Extremely unstable, but extremely potent.
Each of us is a chunk of alum,
Together we can clean up an entire ocean.
Divided we are dust, together we are a must,
Yet division is at which we're traditionally good.
Time has come to change that primeval habit,
Together we stand, divided we are screwed.
Once upon a golden age, is nothing but a myth,
Soon to be civilized, is also useless equally.
I believe, yes I do, only in the us and now,
I dream civilization as, once upon a soon to be.
Potential spent on perfection is potential gone awry.
Fall together, fly together, that's the way to life.

Ain't My Fourth of July (The Sonnet)

Fourth of July comes and goes,
Yet slavery remains and thrives.
It kills in the name of supremacy,
It causes ruin in a pro-life guise.
Real advocates of life value life,
And place life above all belief.
Belief that values guns over person,
Is only pro-death and pro-disease.
Freedom involves accountability,
Without which we are just free animals.
Those who turn superstition into law,
Are no judge but a bunch of dumbbells.
This ain't my Fourth of July, for I actually value life.
Till all lives are deemed equal, I'll continue to strive.

Peygamber Parabrahma (The Sonnet)

In a world where segregation is sanity,
True sanity begins with insanity.
You have to be insane to be egalitarian,
Inclusion is instilled through insanity.
In a world where indifference is sanity,
True sanity begins with insanity.
You have to be insane to take a stand,
Accountability comes through insanity.
In a world where selfishness is sanity,
True sanity begins with insanity.
You have to be insane to be wiped out for others,
Amidst inhumanity, humanity comes through insanity.
Sanity beyond sanity comes from the human beyond human.
Only such human is peygamber, such human is parabrahman.

I Am Idiot (The Sonnet)

I am not as stupid as you think,
I am far more stupid than that.
My stupidity is beyond the grasp of,
All puny dreams of heaven and earth.
You have no idea how stupid I am,
To have an idea is to join the club.
What do the calculating snobs know,
Of the logic-defying madness of love!
The opposite of stupidity is narcissism,
I am the stupid beyond all such stupidity.
Where animals sell selfishness as sanity,
I am drunk, I am dumb, I am but humanity.
Better be a human and considered an idiot,
Than be a moron and worshipped as sage.

Amantes Assemble Sonnet 14

Messiahs don't drop from the sky,
As mortal suffering jumps the fence.
A messiah is just a mortal,
Minus all the indifference.
Peygambers don't jog down from jennet,
As people are troubled by malice.
A peygamber is just a regular person,
Who has conquered their prejudice.
Buddhas don't grow in a zen garden,
As the world reeks of bigotry.
A buddha is just an ordinary being,
Minus all the self-centricity.
Mind is the enemy, mind is the mate.
To all wounds of society mind is ointment.

World Administrative Service (The Sonnet)

Awake, Arise, Oh Saint Soldiers,
Don't stop till you reach your goal!
Awake, Arise, Oh Saint Soldiers,
Don't stop till your dreams are whole!
Awake, Arise, Oh Saint Soldiers,
Don't stop till there is no injustice.
Awake, Arise, Oh Saint Soldiers,
Don't stop till the world is in peace.
Awake, Arise, Oh Saint Soldiers,
Do not stop till love is the only way.
Awake, Arise, Oh Saint Soldiers,
Don't stop till all prejudice is thrown away.
Civilization is born when all our sentience converge.
Puny minds make puny-verse, uni-minds make universe.

Amantes Assemble Sonnet 16

Humans and animals all are welcome in my house,
But not fundamentalists and nationalists.
Yesterday's nationalists were freedom fighters,
Today's nationalists are divisionists.
Even if you believe in fairies 'n spirits, you're welcome,
Even if you believe in angels 'n demons, you're welcome.
Even if you believe in frequency 'n vibrations, you're welcome,
So long as you don't practice hate and harm, you're welcome.
I am a human, and every human without hate is my family.
My heart is your home, no matter what your belief is.
But just like doctor and disease don't mix together,
Reformer and separatists are each other's antithesis.
I repeat, even the fiercest of animals is welcome in my home.
But there is no place for divisionism in this global dorm.

Genius By The Dozen (A Sonnet)

Given the resources, I can build any technology,
Unlike some people, I do not need to hire genius.
Yet I gave up my obsession of electronics, because,
Building rockets is easy, building society not so much.
Not everybody is born with a silver spoon in mouth,
Rest of us have to choose among bread, dreams and tears.
But don't assume that I am whining about a misfortune,
Because, a reformer is worth a hundred entrepreneurs.
Rocket science is child's play for even a fisherman's son,
Cognitive Science is common sense for a laborer's child.
Yet you boast about a bunch of counterfeit geniuses whose,
Greatest power is that they are born with a golden hide.
If you seek true genius, lend a hand to developing nations.
And they'll give you Gates, Musks and Byrons by the dozens.

Servant Scientist (The Sonnet)

No academician lent me a hand,
No industry gave an ounce of backup.
If I am what I am today, it's because,
I was too stubborn to give up.
Hence I can say without hesitation,
My legacy is built only by me,
Not an industry, not a benefactor,
And definitely not some university.
I come from the working class,
With neither education nor wealth.
Hence, my priority is always people,
Not comfort, nor intellect, nor gelt.
The name is Naskar, I'm a Servant Scientist,
Painkiller to people, pesticide to prejudice.

Amantes Assemble Sonnet 19

Live in the moment, not in the cloud.
Live amongst people, not in your phone.
Come to life to live the life,
Across all whining and shallow moan.
Humans ought to wear the clothes,
Yet today clothes wear the humans.
As per need humans may own the tech,
But no tech must own the humans.
The more you scroll the more you scream,
For social media feed is the modern casino.
If you think you can scroll off the hook,
You're already hurtling down the road to woe.
So I say, tech is supposed to lift you up.
If you're crippled by it, that's your own screw-up.

Click Less, Live More (The Sonnet)

Moments are vessel for memories,
Don't waste them on snobbish hypes.
A memory cherished with a loved one,
Is worth more than a billion likes.
The less devices you have to charge,
The more charge you have for your mind.
The less you obsess over convenience,
The more you develop actual insight.
Purpose of camera is to capture memory,
Not to desecrate the moments seeking attention.
Purpose of a picture is to rejuvenate emotions,
Even a thousand pictures are useless without emotion.
Click less, live more - that is the motto of wellness.
Or else, click more, sick more - there is no treatment.

Amantes Assemble Sonnet 21

Couple days ago I had this impulse,
For buying some bluetooth earbuds.
Lo came, 'the less devices you have to charge,
The less your mind is cluttered'.
I have two devices, laptop and a phone,
That require daily electrical sustenance.
Any more, and it won't be a convenience,
But a damned nuisance!
Despite making simplicity my way of life,
Even I'm not infallible to the impulses of luxury.
But the difference is that I've trained my mind enough,
Not to succumb to frivolous cravings of material infidelity.
I am quite content with my 20 dollar shirt and two devices.
More devices you own, more your mind will be in pieces.

Amantes Assemble Sonnet 22

Sooner or later we all end up in pieces,
Life not in pieces is no life at all.
Make sure you're in pieces for the right reason,
Make sure it's not because of possessions but people.
Smart devices don't make a society progressive,
Intellect driven by arrogance and greed causes but regress.
What's needed is intellect soaked in the warmth of heart.
·Societal coldness increases in proportion to smart devices.
Technology can be aid to life, but not the reason for living.
Logic is meant to empower life, not flood it with coldness.
Intellect is the greatest force of societal development,
But intellect not guided by heart is but fancy primitiveness.
Sooner or later we shall all end up six foot under.
Do you want your grave to smell of life or reek of blunder?

Keyboard of Revolution (The Sonnet)

I wrote most of my works,
On broken down laptops.
Perhaps that's why they work well,
With this broken down world.
I don't write to butter the assheads of pomposity,
My duty is to till the soil of grassroots reform.
That's why I feel at home creating on humble machines,
The very thought of fancy devices makes my stomach turn.
I once said to you, ripped jeans and twenty dollar shirt,
That's how we change the world, how we build the world.
Often a fancy exterior is indicative of a rotten interior,
It's a simple life that facilitates a magnificent world.
I don't need thousand dollar machines to cause ascension.
Give me a keyboard, I'll give you revolution.

Ethics and Songwriting (The Sonnet)

I wish I could write music,
For one song is worth ten sonnets.
One sonnet is worth ten essays,
One essay is worth ten speeches.
That's why I have respect for those,
Singers who do their own writing.
While I pity the empty entertainers,
Who do nothing but counterfeiting.
It's okay if you sing someone's song,
At least make way for equal recognition.
Exploiting talent 'cause they're struggling,
Is fundamentally a human rights violation.
Every industry lacks ethics in its story of origin.
It's time we right the wrongs and get humanizing.

The Uncultured Poet (A Sonnet)

There is a reason I never translate my works,
You can translate information but not sentiment.
So I carve humanity with not one but many tongues,
Yet due to alphabetical wall, much remain unspoken.
Human and culture must grow together in harmony,
All traditions of stagnation must be thrown away.
If a human can come forward across conditioning,
Why can't a culture do the same and meet halfway!
I sacrificed my language so I could feel you better,
Now I can't read the tongue of Tagore I was raised in.
Such an uncultured poet whose culture is the world,
Asks the cultures with borders just one little thing.
Take some lessons from Mustafa Kemal in modernizing.
A culture is enhanced, not diminished, by latinizing.

Sonnet of Languages

Turkish is the language of love,
Spanish is the language of revolution.
Swedish is the language of resilience,
English is the language of translation.
Portuguese is the language of adventure,
German is the language of discipline.
French is the language of passion,
Italian is the language of cuisine.
With over 7000 languages in the world,
Handful of tongues fall short in a sonnet.
But you can rest assured of one thing,
Every language does something the very best.
Each language is profoundly unique in its own way.
When they come together, they light the human way.

Amantes Assemble Sonnet 27

Culture shapes the language,
Language shapes the culture.
When you absorb another language,
It reshapes your mental atmosphere.
Learning a language rewires the brain,
It expands our thoughts and emotions.
One small step towards a language,
Is one giant leap towards inclusion.
Language is a freeway to a culture,
It is a tangible way to becoming whole.
Come forward to adopt another tongue,
An entire culture will adopt you as their own.
English is okay, but plenty is lost in translation.
To gain a language is to gain insight into integration.

Amantes Assemble Sonnet 28

Human and culture are not two but one,
The way a human is, so is the culture.
But often the human alive forgets to be,
And ends up a photocopy of their ancestor.
Such stagnation is not the fault of culture,
It's the fault of the human without expansion.
One who cannot see beyond the rim of tradition,
Ends up another captive of the culture prison.
Culture expands only when the human expands,
How will it expand when human forgets to reason!
When the prison of history starts feeling cozy,
Nobody can rescue such people from degradation.
History serves best in pointing out to us the potholes.
Culture must come alive, instead of being a rotten mold.

Amantes Assemble Sonnet 29

A culture that doesn't evolve,
Is a pompei waiting to happen.
Either encourage expansion in society,
Or start digging grave for your children.
Even a flower cannot survive,
On last week's water, and,
You want a mind to survive,
On centuries old beliefs and opinion!
If this is not stupidity what is!
If this is sanity what is insanity!
Beliefs serving humans is good but,
Humans serving beliefs is a catastrophe.
So look back to see how far you've come,
But don't get stuck there, or else you're gone.

Amantes Assemble Sonnet 30

A human doesn't need culture to be good,
But every culture needs a human, to be good.
A human doesn't need religion to be good,
But every religion needs a human, to be good.
A human doesn't need philosophy to be good,
But philosophy needs a human, to be good.
A human doesn't need politics to be good,
But politics needs a human, to be good.
A human doesn't need science to be good,
But science needs a human, to be good.
A human doesn't need intellect to be good,
But intellect needs a human, to be good.
Goodness comes not from faith, culture or intellect.
Good and evil are but creation of the sapiens brain.

Dropout Scientist (The Sonnet)

I am a scientist who doesn't have a degree,
I am a poet who has no control over words.
I am a philosopher who has no intellect whatsoever,
I am a monk with no idea, what it means to be religious.
If I am being honest, I have no clue what I am,
And I know quite well that you do not know either.
But believe you me my friend, one day in sheer awe,
Your descendants will come up with the rightful answer.
In my 30 years of life, I've traveled quite a distance,
Which will take the world at least a millennium to cover.
That's why archaic designations fall short to define life,
No designation is qualified to define a being beyond border.
My faith is humanity, my reason is humanity, my love is humanity.
I am but a glimpse of the future, without coldness and rigidity.

Amantes Assemble Sonnet 32

Coldness of reason is,
As dangerous as rigidity of faith.
Arrogance of knowledge is,
Far worse than absence of knowledge.
True knowledge makes us humble,
True reason brings understanding.
If there is no gentleness in life,
No reason can make life worth living.
To hell with faith, to hell with reason!
Without heart both cause disaster.
To hell with facts, to hell with fiction!
Without heart, both bring despair.
Love is to guide facts, love is to guide fiction.
If there is no love inside, we are just imitation.

Amantes Assemble Sonnet 33

We are not machines,
We can't live on facts alone.
To have a life worth living,
We must balance facts with fiction.
When you think of this with intellect,
It seems like a herculean task.
But lose the intellect and look with love,
And all of it will come like cake-walk.
Too much logic is lethal to life,
So is too little logic.
Too much fiction is lethal to life,
So is too little of it.
We need fiction, we need facts,
we need the whole works.
Let love lead you where it may,
all other leads are hogwash.

Amantes Assemble Sonnet 34

Until the entire earth is one nation,
There is no earth, there is no ascension.
Until all earthlings are one family,
There is no life, there is no liberation.
One earth, one humanity, is not only possible,
It is the only civilized way forward.
Till all the roots integrate into each other,
There's no way we can build a society just.
Justice is no affair of the law,
Peace is no matter of policy.
A being just builds a world just,
A world beyond sectarian identity.
Justice happens when civilians happen.
Peace happens when people happen.

Amantes Assemble Sonnet 35

Peace happens when people happen,
Light happens when life happens.
Truth happens when love happens,
Civilization happens when sapience happens.
Partisanism happens when politicians happen,
Ideologies happen when intellectuals happen.
Extremism happens when fundamentalists happen,
Terrorism happens when nationalists happen.
Deities happen when devotees happen,
Dictators happen when dociles happen.
Be no devotee to no figure, real or fiction,
And you won't end up a weapon of mass destruction.
War is but a mindless descendant of ideology.
The first step of warlessness lies across ideology.

Neuroscience of Ideology (The Sonnet)

No matter the intention of origin,
No ideology can stand uncorrupt through time.
Even the perfect of theories fall apart, because,
The brain can't pledge obedience without being blind.
To maintain the grandeur of an ideology,
The mind chooses to switch off certain faculties.
Thus the mind starts digging its own grave,
As well as for the world, without even knowing it.
Ideology relevant today won't be relevant tomorrow,
But the ideology itself isn't aware of this.
Thus in the guise of savior it keeps raising sheep,
Who then turn defensive and ruin all possibility of peace.
Borders don't preserve peace, borders only breed war.
All peace is fiction till we treat every border as Donald Trump's wall.

Outside The Museum (The Sonnet)

Enough with, patria o muerte*!
Enough with, god save the queen!
Enough with, heil hitler!
Enough with, o say can you see!
Bronze age beings yell about national glory,
Stone age beings yell about religious glory.
Electric beings got no time for such make-believe,
On their shoulders walks the present of humanity.
There is no earth till all roots combine,
Till we crave for each other all roots are chains.
Museums add perspective on the direction of life,
But to spend a life in museum is life lost in vain.
Enough with vande mataram**,
it's time for vasudhaiva kutumbakam***.
To hell with nation, culture and tradition,
civilization awaits outside the museum.

(*homeland or death, **hail the motherland, ***world is family)

Every Culture is My Culture (The Sonnet)

If America fails in advancement, so will the world,
If South America fails in liberty, so will the world.
If Mexico fails in passion, so will the world,
If India fails in diversity, so will the world.
Every atom of planet earth is teeming with potential,
Yet most see nothing beyond the rim of their culture.
Culture is peddled in the world as a sectarian prison,
Yet the fact is, culture integrated is culture empowered.
Every culture belongs in every heart, every heart that is human,
While stoneage notions of culture still dominate the animal.
Simply put, till all cultures are ours, no culture is ours,
Any culture that claims supremacy belongs on a surgeon's table.
If humanity fails to embrace the strength of each culture,
There will be no humanity, there will be no culture.

Amantes Assemble Sonnet 39

Culture exclusive is a culture horribly sick,
Land sectarian is a land inhabited by skink.
Faith without some reason is but superstition,
World without integration is but a fancy clink.
Trading caves for concrete isn't progress,
Trading spears for shotgun isn't advancement.
Trading animism for dollarism isn't growth,
Trading cannibalism for nationalism isn't upliftment.
Dollars facilitate convenience, not character,
Medals don't make the mind, mettle does.
Beliefs exist to treat anxiety, not ignorance,
Parties only screw the world, not help it advance.
Enough with the possibilities drawn by materialists!
If my life isn't impossible, I don't wanna live.

Amantes Assemble Sonnet 40

Progress and partisanism don't go together,
Dollarism and sustainability don't go together.
Undisparity and materialism don't go together,
Secularism and superstition don't go together.
Celebrity and equality don't go together.
Morons make morons famous, snobs idolize snobs.
Sustainability and luxury don't go together.
Either you can have luxury or a disparity-free world
Nationalism and inclusivity don't go together,
Partisanism and peace don't go together.
Ideology and collectivity don't go together,
Narcissism and morality don't go together.
You have to decide, do you want to live as
ever-bickering concubines of pestilential politicians,
or as an undivided planet's undivided civilians?

Nueva Revolución (El Soneto - Spanglish)

¡Viva la libertad!
¡Viva la revolución!
Pero, ¿qué es la libertad?
¿Qué es la revolución?
When no soul is discriminated,
That is liberty - es la liberación.
When no civilian is left unlifted,
That is revolution - es la revolución.
Revolution comes from the backbone,
of a person, not the barrel of a gun.
Necesitamos resolver injusticia sin revolver,
Este es el principio de la nueva revolución.
Stand up to each bullet con tu sonrisa valiente.
La respuesta a toda guerra es la gente.

Amantes Assemble Sonnet 42

Will you keep living as politicians' concubine,
While sipping fundamentalist moonshine,
Or will you wake up and take charge already,
To wipe out all megalomaniacal monkeyshine?
Politicians say jump, you jump without reasoning!
Nationalists say shoot, you shoot without thinking!
Fundamentalists say pray, you do so without question!
Transhumanists say obey, you go gaga without feeling!
Machines running the world is as stupid as pigs running it,
Cold logic is just as dangerous as mindless twattery.
Pledge allegiance to neither politicians nor technicians,
If you must take a pledge, pledge to lift up all humanity.
Road to a beautiful world doesn't go through a fancy freeway.
Road to a beautiful world goes through
the backbone of a human who doesn't walk away.

Amantes Assemble Sonnet 43

Even a thousand tongues fall short,
For a heart that has no ears.
Even a thousand philosophies fall apart,
If you don't fathom the value of tears.
One tear of joy caused by you,
Is worth more than a thousand accolades.
One tear of sorrow wiped by you,
Is a life lifted from the gloom-glades.
Be the glee to those in gloom,
Be gentle amidst the genteel.
Be the brave amongst the blue,
Be the knight amidst them who kneel.
Backbone by backbone the foundation is laid.
Heart by heart the soul of civilization is made.

Amantes Assemble Sonnet 44

Foundation of progress,
Isn't policy but people.
Bedrock of society,
Isn't beatitude but backbone.
The path doesn't make the feet,
It's the feet that make the path.
Feet that haven't trudged thorns,
Can't tell the world from the map.
Thorns make the pedestrian,
Roses make rosary.
Action builds the world,
Imagination treats anxiety.
Imagination that electrifies the feet is most righteous.
But the moment stagnation sets in, all comfort must be crushed.

Amantes Assemble Sonnet 45

There is not one but two imaginations,
One brings comfort another extends horizon.
We need both for a healthy and cheery life,
A lot of horizon with a sprinkle of fiction.
Limit yourself to no horizon,
Today's horizon is tomorrow's history.
Perception is limited only by imagination,
With imaginative action there is no impossibility.
Make more use of the imagination of creativity,
Than the imagination that only brings comfort.
Revolution starts with inconvenient accountability,
There is no growth without discomfort.
To avoid inconvenience is to avoid development.
To chase comfort is to chase death and derangement.

Amantes Assemble Sonnet 46

A developing world is possible,
Only with a developing mind.
A reformed world starts,
Only with a reformed mind.
Beautiful music is possible,
Only with a beautiful heart.
Beautiful literature is possible,
Only with a beautiful heart.
Uplifting science is possible,
Only by the unarrogant.
Uplifting philosophy is possible,
Only by the unarrogant.
Clean mind creates clean society,
Not through puritanism, but
correction of prejudice and rigidity.

Amantes Assemble Sonnet 47

Puritanism brings nothing but mindlessness,
Pursuit of perfection facilitates coldness.
Focus on self-correction not perfection,
Perfection brings but fancy primitiveness.
Somos la enfermedad, somos la cura.
Somos sensibilidad, somos locura.
We are the path where there is none.
Somos el camino, somos la música.
Somos el camino, somos comunidad,
Sociedad sin comunidad no es sociedad.
Con mente en la gente, con gente en la mente,
Nos levantaremos con la humanidad, por la humanidad.
Till we stop being a bunch of poncy, pretentious pillock,
Each obnoxious advancement will cause nothing but havoc.

Amantes Assemble Sonnet 48

Amidst cruelty arrogance has its role,
But you gotta tread with extreme caution.
Arrogance laid on the wrong person,
Is an appalling human rights violation.
Being brutal to avoid possible judgment,
Makes us a moron like those who judge.
Retaliating judgment with heartless cruelty,
Is not justice but primitive outburst.
Call out those who are pretentious,
Those who judge without understanding.
But let your response be guided by justice,
Observe well before you start accusing.
I repeat, arrogance laid on the innocent,
Can't be taken back with a million atonement.

Amantes Assemble Sonnet 49

If arrogance could eliminate judgment,
There wouldn't be any judgment left.
Humble on the inside, dinosaur on the outside,
What's needed is actually pretend arrogance.
When someone commits an injustice in front of you,
Ask them 3 times nicely to make amends.
If they still carry on like prehistoric pricks,
It's time for you to take charge as their parents.
We've been playing pretend justice for so long,
Each of us has turned into nothing but citizen vain.
It's the people who are to teach police what is law,
It's time to take law into our hands,
as unarmed and unyielding order incarnate.
Enough with the nonsense of delegation 'n representation!
A citizen off duty is a society of degradation.

Citizen Vain (The Sonnet)

All the law in the world cannot bring order,
In a society where the citizens are indifferent.
A citizen responsible is a society responsible,
A citizen on guard is a society with upliftment.
If the citizen can't tell right from wrong on their own,
It's not order but merely a revolting illusion of order.
Take away all punishment and you shall soon find out,
Law only forces repression, not reformation of disorder.
Without an actual reformation of the citizen's mind,
Sooner or later all nations end up in fundamentalist dump.
Pay less attention to law, and more attention to education,
Humanizing education is the only cure for the hoodlums.
In a world full of citizen vain, be a citizen vanguard!
There can be no order, unless the citizens stand on guard.

Amantes Assemble Sonnet 51

Education alone won't change anything,
First we gotta rid education of all archaism.
Rather than being a tool of indoctrination,
Education oughta be a force of undoctrination.
Education ought to be secular,
Education ought to be nonsectarian.
Sectarianism that passes as education,
Is the very antithesis of education.
Scriptures can be a part of education,
But they mustn't be the basis of education.
Cultures can be a part of education,
But they mustn't be the basis of education.
Any force that claims to liberate the mind,
Must first liberate itself from all divide.

Amantes Assemble Sonnet 52

Kindness is beyond the grasp of bookish intellect,
Otherwise, philosophers would be the kindest on earth.
Love is too grand to be explained by chemistry,
Or else, chemists would be the greatest lovers on earth.
Assimilation is too grand to be explained by reason,
Otherwise, scientists would be its purest specimens.
Harmony is beyond the grasp of textual theology,
Otherwise, theologians would be its foremost advocates.
It's more important to be kind than right,
It's more important to be kind than important.
Even a million pounds of belief is nothing,
In front of one ounce of kindness.
All of this can be realized by one person alone,
The one human being who has no sect of their own.

Amantes Assemble Sonnet 53

Real humans are attracted towards sectlessness,
Whereas animals have a knack for being sectarian.
Just like real men are attracted to strong women,
While shallow men want sheep for a woman.
Real men feel reassured when women take charge,
While pipsqueaks feel emasculated by the very thought.
Human beings feel empowered when others move ahead,
While dirtbags can't help but drag others down to rot.
Small minds try to feel big by means of condescension,
Human minds are those who live to lift the fallen.
Competition is but for race horses and night crawlers,
Society founded on competition is predisposed to degradation.
It's only the savages who boast about healthy competition.
Competition is but fodder for division and self-obsession.

Amantes Assemble Sonnet 54

A society where failure of one is success of another,
Is nothing but sick with pomposity fever.
A society where tragedy of one is triumph of another,
Is nothing but a glorified disaster.
A world where one seeks healing by shattering another,
Is nothing but a dimension of eternal despair.
Rotos juntos, curados juntos!
Broken together, woken together!
No sabes brokenness, no sabes liveliness.
Each wound holds the elixir of growth.
Wounds ain't obstruction, wounds are wind,
For the sails of your lifeboat.
Life is not the absence of wounds,
life is but the capacity of healing.
Wounds are ornament to the braveheart,
a heart that bites dust yet keeps walking.

Failure Reveals Friends (The Sonnet)

When you try something new,
if you have someone to share it with,
Value that person more than the achievement.
Believe you me, it sucks to try new things,
When you got no one to share your excitement.
It's the people in our lives,
Who add value to our achievement.
This one time I thought I had found my rock,
But she got tired of my failures
and left me in bereavement.
All know about my triumphs, but till now,
I have no one to share my failures with.
It's easy to find people to share your success, but,
Very difficult to find one to share your struggles with.
Everybody will be there for you in the taking.
But nobody will be there for you in the making.

Amantes Assemble Sonnet 56

Don't look for someone you can talk sense with,
Find someone with whom you can talk nonsense.
Call it friendship, call it love, call it whatever,
Role of a companion isn't sensibility but acceptance.
That's why I walk around in shabby clothes,
That's how I get to know about people's true nature.
Everybody likes to butter up those in suits,
Those who smile at the people with nothing,
are the ones with real substance of character.
If you wanna find out who your enemies are,
Walk fancy and wait for the butter to pour in.
If you wanna find out the humans amongst the leeches,
Walk like a vagabond with your shirt not tucked in.
Be cautious of those who applaud your accomplishment.
And never lose those who walk by you in hopelessness.

Amantes Assemble Sonnet 57

We are the hope,
To those without any.
In a world run by apathy,
Let us be responsibly rowdy!
Helping those in need,
Is not charity, but humanity.
Responding hate with love,
Is not diplomacy, but divinity.
Magic and mysticism ain't divinity,
They are but prehistoric delusion.
When cruel, we are devil incarnate,
When kind, we are the supreme revolution.
To hell with passport - the world is our family!
And our family is our own responsibility.

Amantes Assemble Sonnet 58

Corazón amable es la iglesia suprema,
Corazón valiente es corazón de progreso.
Dirtless world begins with a dirtless heart,
Corazón con conciencia es el corazón del cambio.
All talk of change is nonsense,
If three forces are missing from the psyche.
Without conscience, courage and compassion,
All psyche is breeding ground for catastrophe.
Nothing about life is straightforward,
Life is messy - disaster one after another!
Only way we can survive this cataclysmic mess,
Is with extreme cruelty or unyielding character.
I choose the later, for cruelty is too big a burden.
Death with character has dignity,
without it, every breath is burden.

Amantes Assemble Sonnet 59

Without kindness,
Every breath is burden.
Without conscience,
Every thought is degradin'.
Without insight,
All courage is waste.
Without intention,
All talk is nonsense.
Without warmth,
All intellect is worm.
Without gentleness,
All progress is harm.
However, it is not wrong to make errors.
Wrong is the lack of corrective desire.

Errors and Evolution (The Sonnet)

Elimination of error is elimination of evolution,
What's needed is correction of error not elimination.
Why you ask - because error expands perception,
While absence of error indicates absence of ascension.
Pebbles don't make mistakes, for pebbles have no life.
People make mistakes, for people are alive and kicking.
Make the error, mend the error, that is how we grow.
Don't be ashamed, don't be boastful, just keep correcting.
Those who never make mistakes, never amount to anything,
Failures are the foundation of a legend's legacy.
Let them celebrate your triumphs all they want,
You for one celebrate your mistakes and misery.
The shallow measure a person by their glorious victories.
Those with character measure a character by their tragedies.

Amantes Assemble Sonnet 61

The shallow's idea of character is shallowness,
The snob's idea of greatness is appearance.
The windbag's idea of capacity is charisma,
The egotist's idea of glory is selfishness.
Measure me not by how much I have gained,
Measure me if you must, by how much I've lost.
Look at not the light that I shine aloud,
Peek at the darkness that I hide from the world.
The world draws strength from my light,
I draw strength from my pain.
You only hear what I say with words,
If you wanna truly hear, hear me in the pouring rain.
When I am gone, don't go looking for my earthly base.
Look for my heartly base among the living sapiens.

Amantes Assemble Sonnet 62

Beauty captures the eye,
Behavior captures the soul.
Clothes facilitate shallowness,
Kindness conquers the world.
Focus on attachment, not arousal,
And you shall find your sweet everafter.
Focus on unification, not penetration,
And together you shall conquer all disaster.
But remember one thing, my friend,
You shall never receive love by begging.
Love got by begging isn't love but pity,
Which fades soon despite all the pumping.
Love is a lamp that the sane cannot get lit.
Partner is poetry that the sober cannot read.

Amantes Assemble Sonnet 63

Love is a lamp,
That the sane cannot light.
Peace is poetry,
That the sober cannot write.
Growth is green,
That the greedy cannot plant.
Insight is a state,
That the pompous cannot land.
Society is a cup of tea,
That the selfish cannot make.
World is a responsibility,
That the animals cannot take.
However, it's okay if the world feels too heavy.
Start by taking your neighborhood's responsibility.

Amantes Assemble Sonnet 64

Awake, arise and adopt the world!
You are the parent as well as heir.
Awake, arise and disrupt the divisions!
We the citizens are the world's caretaker.
If there is division, it's because of the citizens,
If there is oneness, it's because of the citizens.
State is a fiction that the citizens create,
Citizens are the truth that the state cannot fathom.
State is a dream, citizens are the dreamer.
The dream exists so long as the dreamer is asleep.
Civilization is the path, citizens are the pedestrian.
But the path doesn't exist if the pedestrian is asleep.
So I repeat - awake, arise, adopt the world!
Not of state, not of church, it's the citizens' world.

Amantes Assemble Sonnet 65

No state, better tomorrow.
No citizen, no tomorrow.
No church, better tomorrow.
No citizen, no tomorrow.
No politics, better tomorrow.
No civilian, no tomorrow.
No prejudice, better tomorrow.
No people, no tomorrow.
No head, lesser tomorrow.
No heart, no tomorrow.
No technology, difficult tomorrow.
No accountability, no tomorrow.
Though it feels, we the people are born of the world.
Truth is, world is born of people - no people, no world!

Seclusion Won't Do (The Sonnet)

Each of you must turn into a sufi saint,
Each of you must turn into a latin lover.
Each of you must turn into a shaolin monk,
Each of you must turn into a bengal tiger.
It won't do to seclude yourself in a monastery,
It won't do to seclude yourself behind a desk.
The monk must come down to the streets of life,
The scholar must till the soil with their sweat.
Service of humanity is the fulfillment of divinity,
Service of humanity is the right use of intellect.
Occasional seclusion is good, to charge up the mind,
But life-long seclusion from society is sheer waste.
Enlightenment that doesn't eliminate separation is no enlightenment.
Intelligence that doesn't elevate the collective is no intelligence.

Transhumanism is Terrorism (The Sonnet)

Intelligence comes easy, accountability not so much,
Yet intelligence is complex, accountability is simple.
Technology comes easy, transformation not so much,
Yet technology is complicated, transformation is simple.
In olden days there were just nutters of fundamentalism,
Today there are nutters of nationalism and transhumanism.
Some are obsessed with land, others with digital avatars,
While humanity battles age-old crises like starvationism.
When too much logic, coldness and pomposity set in,
Common sense humanity goes out of the window.
Once upon a time religion was the opium of all people,
Today transhumanism and singularity are opium of the shallow.
To replace the sky god with a computer god isn't advancement.
Real advancement is when nobody suffers from scarcity of sustenance.

Amantes Assemble Sonnet 68

Think with your head, act with your heart.
Bring them together, you'll conquer the world.
But before all else, get your priorities straight.
Without responsibility, we are all bag of dirt.
Pledge your allegiance to neither machine nor tradition,
Pledge your allegiance to neither facts nor fiction.
Embrace the good from everyone and everything,
Then use them in your own way for collective ascension.
A great leader is a sponge with filter,
Observes everything, but obeys nothing.
Keep your head and heart both wide open,
Let the whiff of wholeness rush all in.
Every atom in the world is teeming with lessons,
But no atom is free from biases and predispositions.

Amantes Assemble Sonnet 69

If I give in to one ist,
I'll have to give in to many more.
So no, I'm no feminist, yet I can shout,
Mujer-es cambio, mujer-es el mundo.
You don't need an ism,
To stand up for equality.
You don't need an ism,
To be catalyst of causality.
Many call me humanist, but,
Those who know me know I am not.
To me all designations, save human,
Feel nothing but an insult.
The human knows right and wrong without all the ism.
Leave your ism at the door, before entering my realm.

Amantes Assemble Sonnet 70

Keep your ism if you must,
But don't thrust it on another.
Keep your scripture if you must,
But don't impose it on another.
All scriptures are flawed,
All isms are imperfect.
If you still don't see it,
That right there is the problem.
Imperfection is life,
Imperfection causes ascension.
We grow through imperfection,
Not through perfection.
But all this is possible only when,
We acknowledge, then work on the imperfection.

Amantes Assemble Sonnet 71

There is nothing perfect about organic life,
We are all but imperfection incarnate.
If you want perfection read some fiction,
Life is messy, unpredictable and obstinate.
Yet if you can walk through the mess,
With your heart open and head held high,
You shall be worthy of designation human,
And you shall graduate from lifetown high.
The only secret to life is that there is no secret.
We pretend to be perfect, but inside we're all broken.
To embrace brokenness is to conquer brokenness,
Wound embraced is wound turned to ointment.
There's nothing perfect about human life, nothing ideal!
To embrace imperfection is human, to deny it is animal.

Amantes Assemble Sonnet 72

It takes a human to admit they are animal,
While the animal identifies as human without question.
It takes a human to admit they reek of biases,
While the animal feels beyond reproach and inclination.
A mind that is responsible for society, wants to grow,
While those self-absorbed stagnate in convenience.
When society flows through the veins like lifeblood,
No bias has power enough to impede the sapiens.
The world is coursing through my blood,
I can live without myself, but not the world.
You can take me away from the society,
But how will you take the society away from my blood!
Biases only control those who suffer from clinical moronity.
But they have no hold over the ones who burn for the society.

Amantes Assemble Sonnet 73

Reformers are too rowdy,
To be ruled by biases.
Lose the self among the people,
And you nip the bud of all biases.
Biases are biologically programmed,
To aid self-preservation.
Where there is no self to begin with,
There is no rule of predisposition.
Biology has an evolutionary predisposition,
Of narcissism, materialism and selfishness.
It also holds the underdeveloped brain-power,
Of humility, amity and kindheartedness.
Biology without selfishness is nothing but a myth.
But biology wasted on selfishness is a waste of heartbeat.

Amantes Assemble Sonnet 74

We haven't yet manifested,
Our potential as biologic beings,
Yet we are obsessing over,
Turning into bionic beings!
We haven't leant to take care,
Of our very own home planet,
Yet we are headed already,
To ruin the red planet!
We haven't yet learnt to,
Transform our planetary home,
Yet we are boasting already about,
Becoming a interplanetary lifeform!
A species incapable of taking care of their home,
Will wreak nothing but havoc wherever they go.

Amantes Assemble Sonnet 75

Earth has plenty resources,
To suffice our need.
But no planet has enough,
Resources to suffice our greed.
Terraforming is easy,
Eraforming not so much.
Coding is easy,
Kindling not so much.
Soldering is easy,
Shouldering not so much.
Rocket science is easy,
Reform science not so much.
Rockets work on the principle of control.
To control a human is to lose all control.

Amantes Assemble Sonnet 76

Control is filth on the fabric of society.
Let's investigate it, shall we, my friend!
To control disease is called treatment,
To be aware of health is called wellness.
We crave for control because we want security,
Yet control never actually brings security.
It's in awareness that lies true security,
Only awareness brings actual, lasting serenity.
Peace comes when you befriend your pieces,
Strength comes when you befriend the weakness.
Insight comes when you acknowledge ignorance,
Life comes when you happily embrace death.
Where there is control there is no life.
Control repulses all love and light.

Amantes Assemble Sonnet 77

Love, light and life,
Are synonyms of each other.
Heart, human and humanity,
Are synonyms of each other.
Dignity, decency, determination,
Are synonyms of each other.
Character, conscience, compassion,
Are synonyms of each other.
Mind, mercy and mettle,
Are synonyms of each other.
Neighborhood, nation and world,
Are synonyms of each other.
Now let me tell you what really matters.
Self and society are synonyms of each other.

Amantes Assemble Sonnet 78

To shoulder the society,
Is to shoulder the self.
To shoulder the world,
Is to help oneself.
Every helper is human,
Every hoarder is animal.
Every lover is human,
Every avenger is animal.
Sacrifice is treasure,
Sacrifice is pleasure,
Sacrifice is measure,
Of a human, aka helper.
Helpers in every corner, helpers in every hood.
That's how we'll make the move, to reform from rude.

Amantes Assemble Sonnet 79

I have no intention of living just a few decades,
I must live forever or not at all.
And the only way we can live forever,
Is to give up this one life in lifting up the world.
I am immortality mad, have always been,
I even set out as a monk seeking it in divinity.
Then I realized, immortality is cosmic heirloom,
Of the mortal who is martyred for humanity.
Divinity is just a fancy name for everyday kindness.
Where there is kindness, there is divinity.
Human without kindness is human without humanity.
Serenity comes chasing when your sole concern is society.
Immortality is servant to the servant of humanity.
The day I took my last selfish breath,
was the beginning of my humanity.

Amantes Assemble Sonnet 80

Why do we take breath,
Is it to stay alive!
Why do we eat bread,
Is it to stay alive!
Why do we drink water,
Is it to stay alive!
Why do we take naps,
Is it to stay alive!
Why do we look to mate,
Is it to stay alive!
Why do we have me time,
Is it to stay alive!
These just keep the body alive, nothing else.
The mind is alive when it lives beyond the self.

Bless Me With Bullets (The Sonnet)

Just once let me die for the people,
Then I can live in peace.
Once I am wiped out for the world,
Then I can have my long awaited sleep.
Only when a bunch of bravehearts are sleepless,
Can the rest of humanity sleep in peace.
Only when a bunch of reformers are peaceless,
Will all the inequalities be appeased.
To hell with personal happiness!
To hell with the notion of personal and social!
There is no person, there is no planet,
Till the troubles of the world feel super personal.
Come all ye offended, charge at me with your entire arsenal.
I won't resist, come and bless me, with your bullets of denial.

Amantes Assemble Sonnet 82

I am a soldier, I am a reformer.
What will I do with a long life!
If you wanna bless me with something,
Bless me, O Nature, with courage to die with smile.
Life and death are civilian affair.
A reformer works each day with coffin in pocket.
There'll be no life for any of the civilians,
If the reformer slips into drunken enjoyment.
A reformer doesn't know what is a hangover,
Because a reformer is never sober.
Drunkenness of booze wears off in a day,
Drunkenness of sacrifice lasts through millennia.
The selfish drink to seek escape.
The reformer is too free to need such cheap help.

Amantes Assemble Sonnet 83

Try booze, try bed,
Try the entire exciting lot.
Once you've appeased your curiosity,
It's time to focus on what's significant.
Inhumanity knows no vacation,
It won't wait while you recover from hangover.
It's okay to party on occasion but,
A life lost in booze and party, is utter disaster.
Greatest tragedy of life is a life wasted on self,
Greatest triumph of life is a life annihilated in help.
The secret to destiny is that there is no secret,
Destiny is but creation of the determined and persistent.
Awake, arise and grab the cables from your spinal cord!
A twenty watt brain can electrify the entire world.

Amantes Assemble Sonnet 84

Real study is that which,
Eliminates all separation,
That which helps us realize,
World and I are not two but one.
In a world where two are one,
Is a world with electricity.
Without oneness to charge the heart,
The world turns damp with inhumanity.
What's the use of all this separation!
Get rid of it all this very moment.
Vegetables thrive on separatism but,
Separatism is antithesis of sapiens.
To be human is to be undivided.
Divided human is forever unsapient.

Amantes Assemble Sonnet 85

Only the selfless are sapiens,
Rest are mere counterfeits.
Only the servants are the rulers,
Rest are just two-bit elites.
Only way to live is,
To live through sacrifice.
Only way to breathe is,
To breathe into others our own life.
O2 unshared isn't O2 but CO,
Sipping CO for others I stand keen.
In lifting another's terrible pain,
To breathe sarin even is super serene.
Trees are the greatest teachers on reformation.
Breathe in poison like a tree,
causing nothing but rejuvenation.

Amantes Assemble Sonnet 86

In a world where most,
Are but effect of a system,
Stand alone and be the cause,
Of fearless rejuvenation.
In a world where the apes,
Are manipulated by illusive security,
Stand alone as anomaly,
And defy all who peddle security.
In biology it's mutation, in society it's anomaly,
Without which there is no ascension.
If life had rejected mutation 3 billion years ago,
We'd still be crawling around as single cell organism.
So I say, in a world where the law is self-centricity,
The mutation that is most needed is socio-centricity.

Amantes Assemble Sonnet 87

Don't confuse socio-centricity,
With obedience to society.
For that would be no different,
From today's society.
Treat the society like your children,
And you would know how to behave.
What you mustn't be is a spoilt brat,
And defy the society for the sake of defiance.
Revolution is a part of reformation,
But it is neither the cause nor purpose.
Defy the society's primitive habits,
Like a parent denies a child's wishes absurd.
Society doesn't know what's best for itself,
If it did, partisanists and fundamentalists wouldn't
have been able to keep the world divided.
It's up to the reformers to right the wrongs and unite the planet.

Amantes Assemble Sonnet 88

The terrorist is a radical,
So is the reformer standing on duty.
But while the terrorist wants an exclusive society,
The reformer builds an inclusive society.
The billionaire is a radical,
So is the reformer with accountability.
But while the billionaire wants a society of elites,
The reformer builds a society without disparity.
The intellectualist is a radical,
So is the reformer awake with humanity.
While the intellectualist wants a society of logic,
The reformer builds a society of magnanimity.
There is no scope for change without being radical.
It's intention that distinguishes human change from animal.

Amantes Assemble Sonnet 89

One bread can feed ten people,
If there is intention.
If there is no intention,
Billions fall short for the greed of one.
When there is intention 44 billion,
Can help end great many disparities.
But the absence of it makes a jackass,
Spread the tentacles of autocracy.
Alien are not those,
Who are not born of this planet.
Alien are those traitors who,
Don't give a fudge about the people of this planet.
Where there is intention there is ascension.
Absence of intention is facilitation of dehumanization.

Amantes Assemble Sonnet 90

No wonder they are trying to colonize Mars!
Warmth of humans repels cold blooded creatures.
Existence of billionaires implies not economic growth,
It indicates a crisis-ridden state
of disparity and violations.
The world needs hands of humanness,
Not tentacles of authoritarianism.
The world needs the madness to make billions smile,
Not the mad pursuit of billionairism.
And what the billionaires need is spanking up the khyber,
Since their parents failed to instill inclusivity.
When a child makes mistake, the parent must take charge,
The civilians must take charge
when billionaires violate humanity.
No autocrat is stronger than the citizens of earth.
Whenever autocracy raises its fangs, citizens must crush them to dirt.

Amantes Assemble Sonnet 91

Citizens are the alpha, citizens are the omega.
Whatever good is possible, it comes from the citizens.
Citizens are the creator, citizens are the ravager.
Citizens make the autocrats, citizens can crush them.
Citizens are the cause, citizens are the effect.
There is no destiny, only determination of the citizens.
Citizens are the worshipper, citizens are the worshipped.
There is no religion, only humanity of the citizens.
Citizens are the gospel, citizens are commandments.
When citizens command with conscience, corruption falls.
Citizens are the altar, citizens are the idol.
When the citizens come down to the streets, dictators fall.
Autocrats and dictators rule because the citizens allow it.
Once the citizens wake up from hibernation, it's time for their last wish.

Amantes Assemble Sonnet 92

Do not think that I am advocating for assassination.
Assassination is an easy way out for autocrats and dictators.
They must be stripped of power and kept alive as petty criminal.
Only then they'll serve as an example to the wannabe conquerors.

Until the autocrats, dick-tators, and self-serving bureaucrats,
Are rotting in prison for life, like some common criminal,
All talk of law and policy is actually hypocrisy,
All talk of development is sheer snobbery of the animal.

Nothing good is possible till the citizens act as citizens,
Instead of like spineless children of boneheaded overlords.
Until the citizens become the lords and ladies of planet earth,
Hypocrites will keep desecrating humanity as dickhead demigods.

Victimhood has its own comfort, hence so many demigods!
Until the victims erupt as volcano, there'll just be chaos.

Amantes Assemble Sonnet 93

Even the worst of animal,
Deserves to live.
But human that behaves animal,
Must be put on leash.
The first step of justice,
Is accountability.
Those who fail to be accountable,
Deserve neither justice nor liberty.
Liberty founded on exploitation,
Is a threat to all humanity.
If we can't defend liberty for all,
We are unworthy of our own liberty.
It is time we redefine the notion of dictator.
Each civilian must turn into a benevolent dictator.

Amantes Assemble Sonnet 94

So long as the precise letters of the law,
Are more important than justice,
There'll only be the illusion of order,
But no justice.
Only the citizens can bring lasting justice,
Law has absolutely nothing to do with it.
Justice is not the absence of injustice,
Justice is the presence of accountability.
It is wrong to utter 'law' and 'order' together,
The actual phrase oughta be 'law and disorder'.
The purpose of law is to prevent disorder,
And it's the citizens' duty to manifest order.
Law is there to enforce punishment,
that's why it's called law enforcement.
Civilians are meant to stand dutybound for order,
that's why it's called civic duty, my friend.

Amantes Assemble Sonnet 95

The meek fear the law, and law fears the corrupt,
We have to surgically alter this very paradigm.
Law and the corrupt both must fear the meek,
That is the rightful democratic paradigm.

People fear terrorists, terrorists fear fundamentalists,
We have to surgically alter this very paradigm.
Terrorists and fundamentalists both will fear the people,
Once the people grow the humane guts to defy all divide.

Civilians fear bureaucrats, bureaucrats fear politicians,
We have to surgically alter this very paradigm.
Bureaucrats and politicians both shall fear civilians,
Once the civilians stop dancing to their cockeyed chimes.

Neither politician, nor bureaucrat, nor law,
not even some terrorist or fundamentalist divider,
It is the people's world, and people are the supreme commander.

Amantes Assemble Sonnet 96

Kill the terrorists,
You postpone terrorism.
Jail the fundamentalists,
You end terrorism.
Sentence the corrupt,
You postpone corruption.
Empower the civilians,
You eliminate corruption.
Disband the soldiers,
You postpone war.
Rehabilitate the nationalists,
You put an end to war.
All wars are the people's fault.
If the people had some common sense,
Would they be swayed by the divisionist lot!

Amantes Assemble Sonnet 97

If you still think, you have no background,
To stand up to oppression,
I tell you, listen - to stand up to injustice,
You don't need background, all you need is backbone.
I have no brand, I have no background,
All I have is my burning backbone.
Even a brain can be fooled with enough charm,
But no manipulator can fool a backbone once honed.
So I say, more than your fancy brain,
Hone your backbone, o brave civilians!
Stem cells for social reform,
Come from the backbone of civilians.
The world is an anatomically accurate
reflection of the human body.
A crooked world is the result
of a spinally crooked anatomy.

Reclaim The Planet (The Sonnet)

Monsters spread their tentacles,
Because the masters are asleep.
Puny hyenas rule the world,
When the tigers are asleep.
Enough with pleading, to hell with decency!
Monsters only understand the language of roar.
When the predator comes to feast on your family,
Will you happily make way for them to pleasure more?
Doesn't the thought boil your blood – good, it should!
It means that your backbone is still alive.
Now turn all your attention on your every pore,
Feel through your veins the surge of might.
No more pleading,
no more begging to be treated as humans!
It's time for the humans to reclaim the planet from the inhumans!

Amantes Assemble Sonnet 99

Rise, revolt and roar out loud,
No more pleading in front of prejudice!
Breathe, burn and brave out loud,
No more bearing in front of malice!

Dream, dare and dance out loud,
No more dangling as docile doormat!
Heave, hold and help out loud,
No more retreat in front of cold updraught!

Fall, fix and forge out loud,
No more settling as the forgotten figures!
Grow, glow, and break out loud,
No more groveling at the feet of bloodsuckers!

Only antidote to oppression is civilian unsubmission.
When the children go astray,
it's time for parental intervention.

Amantes Assemble Sonnet 100

The thin blue line is a state of mind,
So is the constitution, my friend.
Both serve the rich and the privileged,
Because the civilians take things for granted.
Until the civilians hail themselves,
Instead of the constitution, as vanguard of society,
Constitutions will remain playthings for the privileged,
Hence the very antithesis of democracy.
A constitution disloyal to the people,
Is just one more book that belongs in the dump.
A scripture that causes more division than unification,
Is the very definition of anti-religious scum.
No crown, no constitution,
no scripture, is higher than the people.
The moment they claim supreme rule,
it is time for the amantes to assemble.

43. Mucize Misafir Merhaba

Why I am Human (The Sonnet)

Some explain why they are catholic,
Some explain why they are atheist,
Some explain why they are muslim,
Some explain why they are socialist.

Some explain why they are jew,
Some explain why they are buddhist,
Some explain why they are hindu,
Some explain why they are humanist.

I heard plenty people explain,
Why they are what they are,
But I'm yet to hear one person say,
First I am human, all else later.

What is this mad obsession with all the ism!
Why can't we be just human, plain and simple!

Virtue No Ism (The Sonnet)

What is this obsession with ism before human!
Why are we still catering to ancestral stupidity!
Are we really gonna let their shortsightedness,
To define our capacity, character and destiny!
Some of them might have had the vision of unity,
Hence they spoke of peace and neighborly love.
But most lacked the sight to live beyond ism,
And we continue to prioritize ism over love.
No ideology has a monopoly over virtue,
Virtues are born of mind, not ideology.
Yet all ideologies try to codify virtue,
By doing so they only vilify all virtuosity.
All virtues are but the descendants of love.
To codify virtue is to ruin the universality of love.

Representation is Degradation (The Sonnet)

Nationalism is but a precursor to fascism,
Representation is but a precursor to corruption.
Delegation is but a precursor to destitution,
Law-abidance is but a precursor to degradation.
Representation without accountability is just,
As undemocratic as taxation without representation.
Trading in one party for another is not change,
But merely the re-initiation of prehistoric division.
Democracy that shows no sign of nonpartisanism,
Is but a petri dish of prejudice most blinding.
Such a democracy stuck on representation,
Is but a silent dictatorship in the making.
Neither law nor party loyalty will elevate the society.
All my hope, therefore, lies upon civilian responsibility.

Time to Bury All Divide (The Sonnet)

It's time we bury the nationality nonsense,
Person is known by their behavior not nation.
It's time we bury the holy book nonsense,
Person becomes holy by compassion not religion.
It's time we bury the representation nonsense,
Social reform starts with civic duty not delegation.
It's time we bury the intellectualism nonsense,
Society is civilized by heart not cocky argumentation.
It's time we abolish the royalty nonsense,
Humans are known by behavior, animals by bloodline.
It's time we dissolve all moronity of hierarchy,
True advancement lies in the abolition of divide.
Even the mighty sun doesn't differentiate
between first world and third world humanity.
It is only the lowly beings who can't help
but practice some good old exclusivity.

I Don't Know (The Sonnet)

What does winning or losing mean,
I don't know.
What does kill or be killed mean,
I don't know.
What does 'my culture, your culture' mean,
I don't know.
What does 'my nation, your nation' mean,
I don't know.
What does 'my people, your people' mean,
I don't know.
What does my life and your life mean,
I don't know.
I only know, we are not some mindless mouthpiece
for our dead ancestors and their shortsightedness.
It is time we bury the divisionism that
they passed on to us tradition and heritage.

Gods by The Hundreds (The Sonnet)

Some people fear christ,
Some claim to hear christ.
I work restless day and night,
To raise the living christs.
Some people fear god,
Some claim to be prophets.
I work without sleep and rest,
To raise gods by the hundreds.
One week of my life produces enough electricity,
To power a 100 years of humanitarian endeavor.
One life laid down to lift up the society,
Triggers a wildfire of sacrificial fervor.
I am but an instrument in the making of legends.
I am but a matchstick to light up the sapiens.

Sonnet of Superpowers

Poet's superpower is their pain,
Philosopher's superpower is reason.
Scientist's superpower is their brain,
Artist's superpower is their vision.
Janitor's superpower is cleanliness,
Hooker's superpower is practical piety.
Bartender's superpower is resilience,
Teacher's superpower is curiosity.
Entrepreneur's superpower is stubbornness,
Engineer's superpower is "unsliding caliber".
Copper's superpower oughta be unbent backbone,
Astronaut's superpower is conquest of fear.
Humankind's superpower is diversity.
Life's superpower is plasticity.

Reformer Needed (The Sonnet)

To put the politicians straight,
What's needed is a reformer.
To put the soldiers straight,
What's needed is a reformer.
To put the scientists straight,
What's needed is a reformer.
To put the philosophers straight,
What's needed is a reformer.
To put the entrepreneurs straight,
What's needed is a reformer.
To put the preachers straight,
What's needed is a reformer.
And how does the reformer remain straight,
By looking beyond the beliefs of binary lanes.

Martyr for Humanity (The Sonnet)

I am not a writer, I am an anomaly,
For writers run empty after a few works.
I lost count of mine a long time ago,
Yet I keep imploding with no sign of cork.
My brain keeps making appointments,
That my body can't keep without crashing.
I am not finished with one work,
And lo, another one starts pouring!
Someone, please calm my brain!
The torture grows excruciating by the minute!
Any day now hopefully an artery will blow,
Then I shall finally have my eternal rest.
Once I am gone, don't go making a cult out of me.
I shall be alive, so long as there is one human
standing ready to be martyred for humanity.

Soil, The Sonnet

My skin is the color of soil,
My covers are the color of soil.
My heart is the color of soil,
My blood is the color of soil.

Species that forgets the soil,
Is a lifeform abandoned by nature.
Species that values sales over soil,
Will soon be vaporized or drowned by nature.

If we have no place for soil in our heart,
How can we expect the soil to replenish us!
If we have no place for nature in our heart,
How can we expect nature to have a place for us!

Only soil is real, all else is delusion.
Advancement that has no regard for the soil,
is but aneurysm destined for degeneration.

What is Sapiens (The Sonnet)

Soil can survive without sapiens,
But there is no sapiens without soil.
There is no us if nature goes off the rocker,
Yet way more than nature, we value gas and oil.
We started off using clothes as cover for privacy,
And we ended up prioritizing clothes over integrity.
Instead of loving people and using the products,
We ended up loving products and abusing humanity.
Sapiens is supposed to mean wise and aware,
But in practice, sapiens is code for shallow.
Sapiens has become just a synonym for show-off.
Neither wise, nor aware, sapiens just means narrow.
However, no error is ultimate if we're willing for reform.
An expanding heart is the antidote to all narrow norm.

Curves, Clothes, Character (The Sonnet)

Your abs won't last, your racks won't last,
Eventually everything ends up in wrinkle.
Polish the outside all you want but,
All curves are crookery if the heart is wrinkled.
Slimness is not the same as fitness,
Skinship is not the same as kinship.
Etiquettes don't elevate the world,
Apparels don't bring liberty and leadership.
Waste not the life on measuring your waist,
All waist is waste if the backbone is malnourished.
Fitness is fiction when shallowness runs rampant,
All curves are filth if the being remains prejudiced.
Curves and clothes have no bearing on character whatsoever.
Better a character out of shape, than a shape without character.

Tenet Beyond Tongue (The Sonnet)

Kalbin olduğu her yerde kader var,
Aşkın olduğu her yerde umut var.
Mücadelenin olduğu her yerde mucize var,
İnsanlığın olduğu her yerde ilahiyat var.

Donde hay corazón, hay destino,
Esperanza es el niño del amor.
Donde hay lucha por la vida hay milagro,
Divinidad es el reflejo del humano.

No matter how many tongues we say it in,
The fact still remains all the same.
Where there is heart there is everything,
Without heart divinity, intellect all are lame.

Biz kimiz? İnsanız. ¿Quienes somos? Humanos.
Who are we? Humanity. Our purpose?
Ayudar a los humanos.

Blasphemy (The Sonnet)

Insan dertte olduğunda,
Ne ben, ne sen - hep aynı.
Birbirimize destek olamıyorsa,
Ne insan, ne hayvan - hep aynı.

İnsan merhameti unuttuğunda,
Ne cennet, ne cehennem - hep aynı.
İnsan insanın acılarına ilaç olamıyorsa,
Ne insan, ne canavar - hep aynı.

When another being is in pain,
Only blasphemy is indifference.
If we can't be cure to each other,
It's not life, but derangement.

Dünyanın gözyaşlarını silmek için gençliğimi bile feda ettim.
Çünkü insanların gülüşünde ben kendimi kaybettim.

Young, Boiling, Selfless (The Sonnet)

Sen söyle karadeniz,
Ben daha ne yapayım!
Gençliğimi feda ettim,
Hayatımı feda ettim,
Ben daha ne yapayım!
In wiping out the anguish of society,
I forgot to indulge in the exploits of youth.
Once I realized the world on my shoulder,
That was the end of self, and the birth of truth.
People dream of earning a ton of money,
I always dreamed of earning immortality.
Anybody can live in flesh and blood,
Mark of character is to live in people's memory.
An eye for an eye makes the whole world blind,
But a life given for a life fallen makes the whole world alive.

No Teacher for Present (The Sonnet)

Life's purpose is realization of life,
Beyond the narrowness of yesterday.
Instead of waiting for a fictitious future,
Life is whatever you make of it today.
The past is always afraid of the future,
Don't let their fear ruin your present.
The future may be condescending to the past,
Don't let such arrogance ruin your humanness.
Embrace the wonders that the past has to offer,
Learn from their blunders even through their denial.
Be mindful of the direction that you are headed,
Then leap to work on the present, lock, stock 'n barrel.
Neither past nor future is qualified to teach the present.
All present must find their way free from all allegiance.

Love who you like (The Sonnet)

Love who you like,
Wear what you like.
Have kids when you like,
Above all, live as you like.
Only thing that matters is that,
You don't fan the flames of hurt.
The only gospel of life is that,
There is no other gospel but love.
Obscene mind finds obscenity everywhere,
For the outside is but a reflection of the inside.
Less of the pomposity and more of the character,
That is how we shall harness our forces civilized.
I only know of one holiness, it's called kindness.
Without it, all scriptures are scum,
and all courts are incognizant.

Women Know Best (The Sonnet)

Wanna learn about running a world, go find a woman mentor,
For women are better teacher and better leader.
Society that glorifies men and objectifies women,
Is but a jungle where primitivity never ceases to fester.
Nature looks upon kindly any species that,
Has realized the synonymity of sacred and feminine.
Those who still fail to recognize the voice of women,
Are basically violating the very reason for existing.
Women know best what's best for the world,
The world that comes out of her womb.
They cuss us, they mock us, it's for our own good,
All time is feminine, feminine is the rule.
The world is but creation, women are the creator.
Feminine is the idol, we are mere idolator.

The Sapiens Experiment (A Sonnet)

If knowledge is power,
Love is superpower.
If curiosity is a gift,
Compassion is a trove of treasure.

More than abundance, focus on wholeness,
More than serenity, focus on simplicity.
More than leading, focus on service,
More than individuality, focus on collectivity.

To reason is great, but to accept is greater,
To be loved is great, but to be love is greater.
To have help is great, but to be the help is greater,
To seek light is great, but to be the light is greater.

Sapiens are the most spectacular experiment of nature.
To waste it all on presumptions is but sheer disaster.

44. Divane Dynamite

Radioactive Mind (The Sonnet)

In front of the radioactivity of mind,
Radioactivity of matter turns dim.
In front of the joules of a just heart,
A billion ohms of hate become nil.
Hate is the question,
Heart is the answer.
Hate is the sickness,
Heart is the cure.
Prejudice is the ailment,
Piety is the cure.
What is piety you ask!
Nothing but kindness more pure.
Kindness is divinity, kindness is sanity.
Wasting it to codify life is sheer stupidity.

Sonnet of Unlearning

Peace is not a matter of learning harmony,
It's about unlearning division.
Science is not about learning logic,
It's about unlearning superstition.
Health is not about learning medicine,
It's about unlearning over-indulgence.
Justice is not about learning accountability,
It's about unlearning indifference.
Order is not about learning law,
It's about unlearning recklessness.
Holiness is not about learning scripture,
It's about unlearning hatefulness.
More than learning, we got plenty to unlearn.
All of it starts with unsubmission to tradition.

Thank You Republicans (The Sonnet)

Thank you republicans, for acting,
As the perfect example of primitivity.
Thank you republicans, for standing,
As the picture of unchristianity.
Thank you republicans, for behaving,
As the definition of new age terrorism.
Thank you for being the personification,
Of ignorance, prejudice and divisionism.
Thank you republicans, for serving,
As a sickening example of superstition.
Thank you for providing the lowest bar,
Against which we can measure human ascension.
Thanks for being everything a human must never be.
Thank you republicans, for demonstrating what is inhumanity.

Dar Mano, Ser Humano (The Sonnet)

Kafir Biraz, peygamber biraz!
İyi insan olmak için ikisi de lazım.
Kısmet to some, kıyamet to some!
That's how we come to life beyond all ism.

Diablo para algunos, santo para algunos.
It's all our mess, so las respuestas somos.
Fairytales work best when vegetables sleep.
Pero te digo hoy - dar mano, ser humanos.

Infidel to some, gospel to some!
That's the cross a reformer got to bear.
The Nazarene already did his bit for the world.
It's time for new humanitarians to give a shoulder.

We are the message, we are the messenger.
Kabhi hum kafir, kabhi peygamber.

Cast Fiction To The Wind (The Sonnet)

The candle's purpose is to be lost in light,
The heart's purpose is to be lost in love.
The ocean may try the sailor all it wants but,
The naive sailor is lost in the ocean's love.
The sailor and the sea are not two but one,
The candle and the light are not two but one.
The heart and love are not two but one,
Individual and collective are not two but one.
Purpose of human is conquest over the inner animal,
Purpose of a human is the expansion of humanity.
Everybody grows old, not everybody grows up,
To die without growing up, is the greatest tragedy.
Life is too short to be wasted on half-cocked may be's!
Cast fiction to the wind, and make the most of reality.

Nothing Yet Everything (The Sonnet)

I am no sufi, yet,
Every sufi is my reflection.
I am no advaitin, yet,
Every advaitin is my reflection.
I am no mystic, yet,
Every mystic is my reflection.
I am no buddha, yet,
Every buddha is my reflection.
I am no humanist, yet,
Every humanist is my reflection.
I am no humanitarian, yet,
Every humanitarian is my reflection.
I am nothing, that's why I am everything.
Or perhaps, I'm everything, that's why I'm nothing!

Vagabond Light (The Sonnet)

When the tide of realization comes,
Theories and concepts cause but decay.
In the kingdom of absolute oneness,
Stoneage constructs wither and fade away.
What am I gonna do with theories!
I'm no intellectual obligated to be a smartass.
I am but a fakir, a vagabond who knows nothing.
So I submit myself at the mercy of the lovers.
I'm tired of trying to be important to the shallow,
I'm tired of trying to make sense to the senseless.
Adjusting to prehistoric habits of a dualistic world,
The mind loses touch with its magical magnificence.
Let the light shine bright,
dim it not to suit the prisoners!
Does the sun come with a dimmer,
because its radiance dimwits cannot bear!

Science, Religion & Superstition (The Sonnet)

Religion is all evil, is the superstition,
That half-cocked rationalists suffer from.
Science is devil's work, is the superstition,
That bookish religionists suffer from.
Take the I and cross it out,
Lo, you have a living Christ!
Take the self and set it on fire,
Lo, you have a timeless light!
Yes, I want to convert the world,
I want to convert all cussing into hugging.
Yes, I want to convert the people, all of them,
I want to convert mindless mocking into mending.
I am no preacher, I am no scholar, I am no thinker.
But, without some basic humanity, we shall all wither.

Be Impossible (The Sonnet)

Good poetry isn't born,
When everything makes sense.
Good poetry is born,
When nothing makes sense.
Partner is not one with whom,
You can talk sense.
Partner is one with whom,
You can talk nonsense.
Humanity is not another lifeform,
That lives on sense.
Humanity is the only lifeform,
That makes a way through nonsense.
Be not another sample of sensible self-centricity.
Be a spectacular anomaly of humanitarian impossibility.

Friends with Darkness (The Sonnet)

Most dread the very notion of dark,
Darkness strikes horror in their heart.
Yet darkness gives me a sense of calm,
I feel quite at home when in dark.
Darkness makes me alive,
Darkness gives me flight.
Darkness makes me aware,
Of the tiniest glint of light.
Darkness electrifies my dampened veins,
It pours back my nerves with vigor.
Just when everything seems to fall apart,
The mind awakens with unforeseen power.
So, never try to keep darkness at bay.
Once befriended darkness takes you a long way.

Brave, Sound & Sane (The Sonnet)

Brave is not the one who has no dark corners in their mind,
Brave is the one who is friends with their dark corners.
Courageous is not the one who never sheds a single tear,
Courageous is the one who draws strength from their tears.
A sound mind is not one that has no superstition,
A sound mind is one that has a grip over its superstition.
A sane mind is not one that does not believe in fiction,
A sane mind is one that knows good fiction from bad fiction.
Education is needed, but not mere education of the head,
What's really needed is education of the whole being.
It is easy to fill the head with facts and figures,
Use a fact to lift the world, then you're an educated being.
More than in head and body, we gotta grow up in heart.
A billion pounds of head is worthless, if there is no heart.

My First Love (The Sonnet)

My first love was not science,
My first love was theology.
Then what got me hooked on science,
Was the spark of electronic circuitry.

Eventually through happy and sad accidents,
Everything fell into its proper place.
Science, theology, and much more
got mixed up, and I ended up pioneering
the empire of humanitarian science.

I am a better scientist because of theology,
I am a better theologian because of science.
Hand in hand they found fulfillment,
When with poetry I built a heartfelt alliance.

I have no gift, it's just that, expansion is my lifeblood.
In a world run by narrowness, the smallest act
of expansion seems like an act of God.

Divinity & Division (The Sonnet)

The rosary and the crucifix are,
No more magical than a rabbit's foot.
Their meaning comes from the mind,
In search of security and couth.
Without the mind to add meaning,
To these objects and symbols,
They are merely trinkets,
Without past, without purpose.
Keep your trinkets if you must,
But don't impose them on another.
Trinkets may help you in tough times,
But don't use them as divine divider.
Division is the desecration of divinity.
Any act of divide is sheer blasphemy.

Oneness & Ascension (The Sonnet)

Religion that doesn't bring oneness,
Is not religion, but the original sin.
Science that doesn't lift human condition,
Is not science but superstition.
I don't go gaga over science,
I don't go gaga over philosophy.
I don't go gaga over religion,
Because humanity is my priority.
I use every tool with the potential for good,
After, of course, discarding its unchecked baggage.
I have allegiance to neither virtue nor vice,
I am but a lover, and love is my home base.
Oneness is the path, oneness is the destination.
Where there is oneness, there is ascension.

Helper is Herald (The Sonnet)

Every peacemaker is muslim,
Every lover is christian.
Every helper is buddhist,
Every lifter is human.
Every lovenut is sufi,
Every braveheart is latin.
Every collectivist is jew,
Every secularist is advaitin.
All labels are futile,
If there's no substance underneath.
Focus on substance as a whole being,
Leave the labeling to the elite.
The helper is the herald,
the lifter is the light.
In a world with double vision,
selflessness is the only sight.

45. Sin Dios Sí Hay Divinidad

Happy Holidays (The Sonnet)

Spirit of Christmas doesn't grow on a fir tree,
Christmas blooms wherever the heart is hatefree.
Ramadan isn't fulfilled by feasting on some tasty beef,
The greatest of feast is haram if others go hungry.
Hanukkah's miracle isn't about the oil lasting 8 days,
Rather it's about the resilience of light amidst darkness.
Fireworks may be diwali for those still in kindergarten,
Everyday is diwali for an existence rooted in kindness.
The will to love and the will to lift are the backbone,
Of all human celebration, tradition and communion.
Take that fundamental will out of the equation,
All you have left are rituals without meaning and mission.
Fasting, feasting and decorating are step two of any festival.
First and foremost, at our altar within, we gotta light a candle.

More Important Than Truth (The Sonnet)

In the beginning even I was,
Bedazzled by the concept of truth.
It took me some time to,
Step across the lure of truth.
That is when I realized that,
Every brain creates its own truth.
So we'd never achieve harmony,
With the heartless pursuit of truth.
Understanding the definition of truth,
May differ from person to person.
But the virtues of basic goodness,
Need no divisive interpretation.
Always place love first, truth second.
Humanity first, intelligence second!

Reason and Fanaticism (The Sonnet)

I feel at home with every faith and ideology
Unless it's peddled with bigotry and arrogance.
I bear a clinical revulsion to booze and smoke,
More than that, I am allergic to arrogance.
You cannot reason with a caveman who starts off,
By saying, "my thing is the best because".
If you could reason with fanaticism,
There wouldn't be any fanaticism in the world.
Holding on to a belief system is very much human,
But a belief that undermines other beliefs is animal.
Likewise, to sharpen intellect is a good habit unless,
You sharpen it so much that it makes you mechanical.
Maintain a healthy balance between facts and fiction.
Learn to make your head and heart work in unison.

Miracle Supreme (The Sonnet)

Sapiens is shelter,
Shelter is sapiens.
Only miracle in the world,
Is the miracle of kindness.
Hateless heart is a living church,
External churches are mere counterfeits.
Unless you can face hate without hate,
Stories of "water to wine" are plain myths.
True miracle does not rely on myths,
True miracle is the greatest unmiracle.
Miracle is an expression of mutation, hence,
Mutation of selflessness is the highest miracle.
Nobody can walk on water, it is just fairytale.
Be human across fairytale 'n lo, you're walking miracle.

Miracle is Everywhere (The Sonnet)

Poetry that lifts a heart is miracle,
Science that lifts a society is miracle.
Philosophy that aids curiosity is miracle,
Art that aids love and laughter is miracle.
Technology that solves a problem is miracle,
Math that aids humanity's growth is miracle.
Theology that makes a mind humble is miracle,
Cinema that invigorates a soul is miracle.
Janitor who cleans the garbage is a miracle,
Teacher who lights up a student is a miracle.
Doctor who smiles at a patient is a miracle,
Parents who sacrifice their joy are a miracle.
Our natural world is teeming with acts of miracle,
Yet we keep obsessing over the supernatural!

What is Afterlife (The Sonnet)

Read a few books, you live a little.
Help a few beings, you live a lifetime.
Heaven is not a place high above the sky,
Heaven is the moment you're someone's lifeline.
Even I enjoy a good dc and marvel story,
But it mustn't turn you blind to reality.
To live selfish is the animal's purgatory,
To die while living for others is humanity.
Memory is the fabric upon which time is carved.
Where there is no memory, there is no time.
Neurons are the building blocks of mind and memory.
Where there is no neuron, there is no paradise.
There's not one but two paradise, one real, another fiction.
The real one is made of action, the other imagination.

Purpose of Purpose (The Sonnet)

The purpose of science is its correction,
The purpose of religion is its extinction.
The purpose of art is purposeful reflection,
The purpose of a human is self-annihilation.
The purpose of hands is to unfold in help,
The purpose of heart is to be a shelter.
The purpose of feet is to walk forward,
The purpose of eyes is to enhance insight.
Purpose is the antithesis of imprisonment,
Life is the antithesis of indoctrination.
Hands aren't meant to be used for hogging,
Heart is the antithesis of division.
All purpose must be an aid to the uplift of humanity.
If it is impediment, it ain't no purpose, but inhumanity.

Nothing is Everything (The Sonnet)

Your accent doesn't matter,
Your language doesn't matter.
Your scripture doesn't matter,
Your nationality doesn't matter.
Beyond the prisons of all divisions,
There is a valley of total nothingness.
In that nothingness you shall find light,
In nothingness lies absolute wholeness.
So long as you are exclusively something,
You can never be everywhere and everything.
Once you are everywhere and everything,
You have no need for the backward things.
For once in our life, let's be whole in nothing.
Once we taste nothingness, there is no turning.

46. Corazon Calamidad

My Mission (The Sonnet)

I am not here to inspire butcher doctors,
I am here to build humanitarian doctors.
I am not here to entertain reckless coders,
I am here to invigorate humanitarian coders.
I am not here to arouse mindless engineers,
I am here to torque up humanitarian engineers.
I am not here to pamper crooked politicians,
I am here to wake up the brave world builders.
I am not here to applaud counterfeit philanthropy,
I am here to energize humanitarian entrepreneurs.
I am not here to peddle the glory of logic over life,
I'm here to raise humanitarian scientists 'n philosophers.
There is no rest till humanity courses through human veins.
My mission is to flood the world with humanitarians by the thousands.

My Revolution (The Sonnet)

My revolution has only one golden rule -
No arms, no ideology, only oneness is necessary.
When the heart turns radioactive with compassion,
All war and warheads will become history.

Mi revolución no es la revolución de las pistolas,
Mi revolución es la revolución de la paz y armonía.
Basta ya de la revolución primitiva de las armas,
Somos humanos, nuestra fuerza - espinazo de dinamita.

Enough with revolution of guns and grenades,
It's time to brew the antidote for hate.
All the ingredients can be found in our heart,
We just gotta surpass the ideological barricades.

La gente es mi locura, la gente es mi razón.
Mi corazón insiste, la gente es mi salvación.

Shade (The Sonnet)

Heart is the pedestrian,
Heart is the path.
Heart is the gateway,
Heart is the guard.

Heart is the scenery,
Heart is the sight.
Heart is the land,
Heart is the light.

Heart is the discoverer,
Heart is discovery.
Heart is the worshipper,
Heart is almighty.

There's nothing more tragic than a heart all folded.
Heart alone is the seed, heart alone is the shade.

Melanin Maniacs (The Sonnet)

White guy writes a couple of sonnets and plays,
And he is idolized as an olympian deity.
Colored guy smashes the paradigm to ashes,
And it warrants absolute unacceptability.
Apparently, greatness is only greatness,
If it can be credited to a caucasian.
Otherwise they only end up pondering,
What's the deal with this non-white person!
It's a sad, sad world we live in,
All the advancement is on the outside.
Inside we are dumber than Donald Duck,
Which has ruined all hope for real insight.
Enough of this obsession with white aphrodisiacs!
It's time to act as humans, and not melanin maniacs.

Whitewashed World (The Sonnet)

In 2022 I sent my record of most sonnets to Guinness,
They rejected me saying, I lack skill and significance.
It's a white people's world after all, like it or not,
We wouldn't want the little white poets to take offence!
My skin doesn't radiate the glory of talcum powder,
So I'm supposed to be thankful for the white hand-me-downs.
Mine is not to seek recognition in a whitewashed world,
Mine is to keep on struggling with my vigor's last ounce.
In a world where top white export is but oppression,
Everything is ten times less difficult if you are white.
A mermaid of color tickles the conquerors the wrong way,
White people's Nobel disproportionately goes to the whites.
Whether you recognize me or not, I neither care nor mind.
The reason I write this, so humankind becomes human and kind.

Silicon Psychos (The Sonnet)

If we cared more about the hard problem of real inhumanity,
And less about the fictitious hard problem of consciousness,
We'd have filled the world with human consciousness already,
Instead of still fighting for basic rights against base biases.
What kind of a moron goes walkabout when their home is on fire,
What kind of a moron abandons the living chasing life on silicon!
We really gotta take a hard look at our habits and priorities,
Dreaming is good, but dream devoid of life is but degeneration.
Chimps driving teslas are still chimps no matter the demagoguery,
All intelligence is disgrace if it's unaware of human condition.
A heartless organism living on silicon is no different,
From a heartless organism living in a carbon based human.
Be it crucifix or code, in savage hands every tool is weapon.
The wise use AI to design prosthetics, savages for transhumanism.

Code for Humanity (The Sonnet)

There is no such thing as ethical hacking,
If it were ethical they wouldn't be teaching it.
Because like it or not ethics is bad for business,
They teach hacking so they could use it for profit.
With the right sequence of zeros and ones we could,
Equalize all bank accounts of planet earth tomorrow.
Forget about what glass house gargoyles do with tech,
How will you the human use tech to eliminate sorrow?
In a world full of greedy edisons, be a humble Tesla,
Time remembers no oligarch kindly no matter the status.
Only innovators who get engraved in people's heart,
Are the ones who innovate with a humane purpose.
Innovate to bridge the gap, not exploit and cater to disparities.
In a world run by algorithms of greed write a code that helps 'n heals.

Stay Behind (The Sonnet)

While mine owners' kids are packing,
Their mittens to colonize Mars,
How about you stay behind,
To give light as an earthly human star!
I am not here to teach you how to code,
I am here to show you why code.
I am not here to teach you science,
But to humanize the scientific road.
Okay if they don't know the role of science,
You for one, don't walk in their dirtsteps.
You are wise, brave, and above all, human,
Be the practitioner of humanitarian science.
Science is superpower, always use it wisely.
Little science does much harm if used recklessly.

Science is Service (The Sonnet)

Extraordinary technology brings extraordinary recklessness,
Because the human mind hasn't matured like technology has.
We may have developed technology that defies human limits,
Evolutionary predispositions of the mind haven't disappeared.
That's why I say, bigger the power the smaller the mind.
For a wielder without backbone, silicon is but plaything.
Even an ounce of science can do unimaginable harm.
To fathom it you gotta step out of the glare most blinding.
Science 'n society go together, can't have one without the other.
Where there is love for science, there is love for society.
If this simple thing doesn't penetrate the skull of us thickies.
We would be better off without all the scientific glory.
Science is an act of service in the course of lifting all humanity.
Science without accountability is no different from a conspiracy theory.

Genius & Conspiracy (The Sonnet)

Wherever there is extraordinary genius,
There are extraordinary conspiracy theories.
Because the human mind cannot distinguish,
Supernatural mysticism from natural mysteries.
Wherever there is exceptional talent,
There is talk of divine intervention.
Because the mind cannot fathom excellence,
Without involving some good old mystification.
We may tolerate some conspiracies that are innocent,
But those that do harm are human rights violation.
If we can't use it when we need to use it the most,
What's the point in carrying around a lofty brain!
There are times when reason must take a back seat,
Then there're times, ignorance mustn't be given heed.

AI Con (The Sonnet)

Everybody is concerned about psychics conning people,
How 'bout the billionaires who con people using science!
Con artists come in all shapes and sizes,
Some use barnum statements, others artificial intelligence.
Most scientists speak up against only the little frauds,
But not the big frauds who support their livelihood.
Am I not afraid to be blacklisted by the big algorithms!
Is the sun afraid, its light will offend some puny hoods!
I come from the soil, I'll die struggling in the soil.
My needs are less, hence my integrity is dangerous.
I am here to show this infantile species how to grow up.
I can't be bothered by the fragility of a few spoiled brats.
Reason and fiction both are fundamental to build a civilization.
Neither is the problem, the problem is greed and self-absorption.

Evolution & Electronics (The Sonnet)

I know electronic circuitry like the back of my hand,
Yet it's the human mind that fascinates me most immensely.
Fascination in electronics lies in new design possibility,
Whereas the mind is the breeding ground of all possibility.
Our engineering is puny compared to that of Mother Nature,
Each day a new mystery unfolds in the vast organic kingdom.
Our puny electronics work based on cold 'n rigid computation,
Evolution of life in nature is predicated on plastic mutation.
That's why we must never disregard nature blinded by arrogance,
We may have conquered nature's mercy but we're still subordinate.
The moment a lifeform starts to vilify the womb whence it came,
With a single blow creator nature can flatten all our obstinance.
Foster humility and wisdom, before going nuts about technology.
Don't end up yet another fancy stain upon the honor of humanity.

Education Through Excellence (The Sonnet)

During my aimless years I once had an urge,
To learn about jet propulsion engine.
So I wrote content for tech support websites,
To buy a couple of books on aeronautics.
Education means catering to curiosity,
Study to gain excellence not a certificate.
If it doesn't open your eyes to social ascension,
Education only causes the world to dehydrate.
You can stuff entire encyclopedias into your head,
That still will not make you an educated being.
If education was the same thing as information,
Google would be the omniscient superbeing.
Certificate without humanity is a ticket to stoneage.
If it takes away your warmth, it is all decadence.

Confusion (The Sonnet)

Society that confuses competition with education,
Has no idea what knowledge or education is.
Society that confuses memorizing with learning,
Has no idea what learning for wisdom really means.
Society that confuses guns with gallantry,
Has no idea what gallantry is.
Society that tries for peace with bombs,
Earns more contracts for bombs not peace.
Society that confuses luxury with success,
Never gets the civilized sense of success.
Society that confuses materials with happiness,
Keeps drowning in materials away from happiness.
A life well lived is a life lived amidst people.
Any system that creates divide belongs in the jungle.

One Desire (The Sonnet)

I speak most, when I speak nothing,
Light unfolds only in the dark.
Listen to my words, you'll hear my head,
Listen to my silence, you'll hear my heart.
Upon pouring out an insurmountable universe,
Of words into the world, I have but one desire.
I just wanna sit next to someone and say nothing,
While they gently put their head on my shoulder.
Don't know when I'll ever have my long awaited rest,
When I'll have to explain nothing to no one!
Don't get me wrong, I cherish my work greatly but,
There's plenty I never got to cherish with someone.
This is me being human shedding light on human condition.
Even the giant isn't impregnable to life's sweet expectation.

What is Heart (The Sonnet)

The heart wants what the heart wants,
But not always what the heart wants is human.
There's a lot of ways the term heart unfolds,
Sometimes it shelters love, sometimes division.
It is not enough to associate heart with emotions,
It is time we associate heart with wholeness.
Some emotions are expression of sheer prejudice,
Hence, reason must be a part of heart's wholeness.
We often boast a separation between thought 'n emotion,
In reality, it's impossible to tell thought from emotion.
The important thing is not to tell thought from emotion,
But to not behave a savage, be it in thought or emotion.
Human being is whole being, whole being is human being.
If there is no wholeness, we're just a bunch of dumplings.

Poetry Writes The Poet (The Sonnet)

The best poets are the ones,
Who don't know how to write poetry.
Just like the best scientists are those,
Who practice science as everyday curiosity.
The more you focus on the definition,
The more you lose touch with the essence.
That is why I never know what my work is about,
To explain love is to lose love's fragrance.
Painting of a landscape is not the landscape itself,
Depiction must never be confused with the depicted.
I don't know how to do small talk, hence the sonnets.
Poet doesn't write poetry, poetry writes the poet.
The moment I think I am in control, I lose all control.
Craving no control, the river just nourishes the soul.

Enough Analysis (The Sonnet)

Poet knows no poetry,
Sage knows no wisdom.
Lover can't explain love,
Saint can't explain undivision.
Explanation is an act of analysis,
Explanation warrants a lot of division.
Facts and figures can be quantified,
But the mind is beyond computation.
Human is home to the human,
What is there to analyze!
Problem is that we analyze plenty,
But in times of need very little we realize.
When someone's world is crumbling down into abyss,
Practice humanity instead of practicing analysis.

Practical Mindfulness (The Sonnet)

When someone's world is crumbling down,
Reach out to lend a shoulder not analysis.
If the world had more carers and sharers,
We wouldn't need the services of therapists.
Most humans are raised to be selfish robots,
Then they spend their life on a therapist's sofa.
When someone's going through a period of grief,
Only the mindless comments, 'have you tried yoga!'
For the human mind to be whole and healthy,
You gotta empty it of all the unhealthy junk.
And there is no greater junk on the face of earth,
Than the traditions that make us self-centric drunk.
Elimination of coldness is the highest of all wisdom.
Treat the common cold, and you'll treat all descension.

Sapient Selection (The Sonnet)

Some people engineer machines,
I engineer human evolution.
How can we engineer evolution,
Simply by taking accountable action.
This is what I call sapient selection,
When humans choose the path they take.
Sure, nature still has a huge hold over us but,
We have the neurons to override her influence.
It is extremely difficult to conquer nature,
But the important thing is, it is not impossible.
With enough resolve, honor and conscience,
Anybody can tame their inner animal.
Monkeys that walk upright are still monkeys.
Sapiens with hate are but good-looking chimpanzees.

Corazon Calamidad (The Sonnet)

A society that doesn't know the difference,
Between a good-looking chimp and sapiens,
May travel to alpha centauri for all I care,
But will still remain a lifeform of decadence.
If we placed half as much attention,
On the inside as we place on the outside,
We'd be living by now on a planet called earth,
Instead of a graveyard of prejudice and fright.
God's will is whatever the human wills,
Upon your will depends the course of human evolution.
Or you could just lean back and watch the game while,
Intellectual degenerates drag us all into degeneration.
Earth needs no humanity, but ain't no humano sin humanidad.
To build a world suitable for humans,
each heart must stand on guard as corazon calamidad.

47. Esperanza Impossible

Esperanza Impossible Sonnet 1

Earth is but a bedlam,
All the beings are loonies.
We are so engrossed in prejudice,
Integration feels like blasphemy.
We still cannot live side by side,
We want it all for ourselves.
We won't even move a single inch,
When it comes to our opinion and ways.
Selfishness, thy name is Sapiens,
Upon its norm we philosophize kindness.
We invented fancy terms like altruism,
Lest we're infected with common humanness.
Humanity is too alive to be bound by ism.
Dead things can be dogmatized, not expansion.

Esperanza Impossible Sonnet 2

Truth is the pandemic,
Truth is the terror.
My truth versus your truth,
Your truth versus another.
We speak of truth as if it's a constant,
We chase it as antidote to our insecurity.
Most of our truths bring not understanding,
We cook up truth to fan our self-centricity.
Truth, in truth, is the opposite of stagnation,
Contraction repels all hope for understanding.
Truth is not a fixed point, but an act in motion,
Truth is the courageous act of a mind expanding.
Hence, to seek security one must not seek truth.
To seek truth, with security you must cut all truce.

Esperanza Impossible Sonnet 3

Truth doesn't make you calm,
Truth doesn't let you sit still.
If it doesn't make you restless,
It's the soil of fiction you till.
Creation is not an act of order,
Creation is an act of chaos.
Till truth sets the mind on fire,
It stays shrouded by stories fictitious.
A fragile mind must never pursue truth,
For it only turns a beast beastlier.
Pursuit of truth dismantles all prejudice,
Hence it requires a well-built character.
There is no truth, either in past or in the future.
The only place you'll find truth is in the now and here.

Esperanza Impossible Sonnet 4

The first step of practicing truth,
Is not learning something, but unlearning.
If your glass is full with muddy water,
It's irrelevant, how much facts you keep pouring.
You must empty your vessel of assumptions,
If you are to attain any actual realization.
Biologically there's plenty you can't unlearn,
Sociologically there's plenty demanding deletion.
However, behind every social ill there is biology,
Understanding the underpinnings aids the unlearning.
There is no greater sage in the entire world,
Than the one who has conquered their conditioning.
Wake up and smell the coffee, discarding all kool-aid.
Truth is staring you in the eye, just remove the veil.

Esperanza Impossible Sonnet 5

Our whole life we're taught to live behind the veil,
It is forbidden to even dream of removing it.
To really seal the deal society calls this tradition,
So that we feel guilty if we cross our ancestral limit.
This is how habits are proudly passed on as heritage,
And bigotry as the highest form of enlightenment.
Thus, integration is deemed as the ultimate treachery,
And peace remains a matter of armchair amusement.
If you are to choose between tradition and humanity,
I say, treat your ancestors as children not sage.
Those who pass on division and discrimination,
Deserve neither seriousness nor allegiance.
Truth is not the journey from one veil to another.
Truth involves peeling the veil one layer after another.

Esperanza Impossible Sonnet 6

Our sight will never be without veil,
I am talkin' about our predispositions.
Veils are the glasses through which,
The world is recorded in our perception.
Till the brain finds a way to perceive,
The world independent of perception,
There is no objective truth to begin with,
It is all but subjective interpretation.
What we can do is rid our subjective truth,
Of as much primitivity as mentally possible.
In time we just might taste some objectivity,
In time, we might stumble upon truth impossible.
And, if we don't get a grip over our ominous inkling,
The veil on our eyes will be the nail on our coffin.

Esperanza Impossible Sonnet 7

We live in a world where the pursuit of truth,
Has sustained the status quo of bloodshed.
We live in a world where in the name of truth,
Savages have enslaved and tortured the innocent.
Ignorance has filled the graveyards with corpses,
As a glorious declaration of honor and truth.
If this is what truth looks like on planet earth,
I'm glad to be an idiot with no sense of truth.
Truth that makes you a narrow and nefarious nutter,
Is also truth, sure, but only that from the stoneage.
If the horizons of truth don't expand with time,
It is but poison upon the fabric of our sentience.
Liberate your truth from the shackles of the past.
Only then instead of creating drag, it'll lift up the world.

Esperanza Impossible Sonnet 8

Some make bombs for domination,
Some make bombs for survival.
Either way someone pushes a button,
Innocents wind up dead as collateral.
We are all mere scientific monkeys,
Walking upright headed for the cliff.
Some alpha monkey tells us to jump,
And we all rally into the abyss.
We call ourselves civilized beings,
We call ourselves an advanced species.
Some rich kid boasts about space travel,
We happily ignore the bats in our belfry.
Conquer yourself before you go gallivanting around space.
A species without self-control is nature's greatest mistake.

Esperanza Impossible Sonnet 9

It ain't enough for humans to live in the world,
Each human must be the home to the entire world.
Until the world courses through our very veins,
Of peace and harmony we'll have only the talks.
Peace is byproduct of a kind, nonsectarian mind,
It has nothing to do with fancy acts of diplomacy.
In fact, diplomacy is the very antithesis of peace,
No world is made serene with such pretend amity.
Attending peace conference to represent a nation,
Is like attending freedom conference to represent a prison.
They don't attend peace conference to speak for peace,
But to blabber, how their tribe is better than another one.
There is no world peace till the world is actually our priority.
Keep your nationality if you must, but not above humanity.

Esperanza Impossible Sonnet 10

Nationality is not the trouble, real trouble is nationalism,
And nationalism is the super weapon in a politician's arsenal.
When nothing works, peddling nationalism works every time,
For insecure citizenry can't tell nationality from nationalism.

So in practice, all the wars of the world are caused by citizens,
But it feels good to blame the bad things on politicians.
Once the citizens grow up to not be swayed by nationalism,
No authoritarian nincompoop can make them dance.

Nationality is a tool, what it is not is a badge of supremacy,
Just like culture is a tool, and not a badge of authority.
If we must dance, let us dance to life, not to baseless fright,
If we must take a step, let's take a step towards humanity.

Borders exist to aid the functioning of the fabric of society.
They are not some olympian designation of your identity.

Esperanza Impossible Sonnet 11

What kind of a creature values borders over beings,
What kind of a creature values culture over compassion!
What kind of a creature prefers tradition to transformation,
What kind of a creature values stagnation over ascension!
Boarders of planet earth, beware of all borders!
Once you give them control, you'll drift away from order.
I'm talkin' about the order of wholeness, not some puny law.
Society lacking wholeness, despite law drifts into disorder.
Health and happiness come through people, not pills.
Order comes through oneness, not division.
Intolerance repels all illumination,
For illumination comes through integration.
Peace, health and progress are byproducts of assimilation.
Where there is assimilation, by nature there is illumination.

Integration is Illumination (The Sonnet)

Asato ma sad gamaya*,
Benevolence is bismillah.
Tamaso ma jyotir gamaya**,
Mind is the mightiest menorah.
Luz, lux, noor - light by any name,
Brings the same illumination.
And what is this mythical light,
If not an act of collective ascension!
Light is not the absence of darkness,
Light is the absence of indifference.
Darkness is symptom, coldness is the sickness,
Once we treat coldness, we'll treat all darkness.
I repeat, light by any name brings the same illumination.
If not now, when will we put an end to this dehumanization!

(*Let's rise from ignorance to truth. **Let's rise from darkness to light.)

Uncomfortable Illumination (The Sonnet)

Barbarism, thy name is Britain.
Racism, thy name is America.
Regress, thy name is Turkey.
Intolerance, thy name is India.
Superstition, thy name is East Europe.
Megalomania, thy name is Russia.
Snobbery, thy name is West Europe.
Shallowness, thy name is South Korea.
Only "humans" living in these lands,
Will realize the truth in these words.
Whereas the practitioners of prejudice,
Will blow steam out of their ears.
Ignorance, thy name is Sapiens.
Illumination begins with illness acknowledgment.

Freedom from Freedom (The Sonnet)

Obedience was yesterday's opium,
Opium of today is freedom.
And freedom is just as dangerous,
If there is no self-regulation.
Fanaticism of freedom is a slippery slope,
It makes savages out of thinking beings.
Faith fanatics are blindly drunk on control,
Freedom fanatics blindly defy everything.
Misbehavior and craven disregard for society,
Are not the signs of an actual sapiens.
What we need is freedom from freedom,
Just like we oughta be free from obedience.
Defy norms that are obsolete, not norms in general.
Society without norms exists only in fairytale.

Sonnet of Norms

It is not patriarchal to hold the door for a lady,
It is not cowardly to leave your seat to the elderly.
But it is barbaric to harass a breastfeeding mother,
And prehistoric to force a woman carry a pregnancy.
There are norms that nourish the societal fabric,
Then there are norms out of touch with age and times.
Beyond both freedom and obedience as a whole being,
You ought to realize where and how to draw the lines.
The problem is that most do not know when to rebel,
They rebel out of boredom to seek adventure not justice.
They commit reckless vandalism in the name of activism,
And feel proud while committing the most heinous deeds.
Norms require careful scrutiny, not headless rebellion.
Hence, quite often rebels become the new face of oppression.

Vandalism Ain't Activism (The Sonnet)

Systemic change is a slow and tedious process,
It doesn't happen overnight by vandalizing society.
If vandalism and activism were one and the same,
Our jungly ancestors would've been the ideal humanity.
Change habits, change yourself, submit to no primitivity,
The change that you dream of, be the epitome of that change.
Obstructing traffic and refusing to let an ambulance pass,
You're not fighting any crisis, but being a crisis yourself.
Go fly a kite, it is good for the mind as well as body,
Get lessons on common sense before appointing yourself king.
The line between activism and terrorism is so thin that,
Often many go astray without having the slightest inkling.
I repeat, systemic change is a slow and tedious process.
The more you rush with recklessness, the more you digress.

Esperanza Impossible Sonnet 17

The road of revolution is a moral mine field,
You gotta take each step with extreme caution.
It is easy to feel righteous about your drive,
What's difficult is to regulate a biased emotion.
This is why you cannot afford to lose your head,
The moment you do, you'll end up causing harm.
Let the heart take reins of your life for sure,
But keep the head as brakes to your assumptions.
As I put my most powerful ideas in words,
I feel like walking on the edge of a cliff.
One false move nudged by subconscious bias,
Lo, I go hurtling down into a bottomless pit.
The next sonnet will make it clear what I mean.
The main thing is to be aware, we don't turn fiend.

Esperanza Impossible Sonnet 18

Clothes or the lack of it, don't make,
A person obscene, only behavior does.
Who are you to judge someone's expression,
But, here there are plenty grey areas!
Problem is, when obscenity becomes expression,
Misbehavior is deemed declaration of independence.
Too many people confuse attention with admiration,
And a stunt as some wonderful achievement.
Accepting obscenity as freedom of expression,
Is like showing tolerance to intolerance.
Posing butt naked on instagram, unless you're pornstar,
Is like barging into capitol with a flag confederate.
We must find a balance between comfort and conscience.
Civilization falls apart when we can't tell the difference.

Esperanza Impossible Sonnet 19

Even a gentle caution against obscenity,
Is bound to offend some as body shaming.
Just like a study of colonial inhumanity,
Offends some bigoted brits as anglophobic.
Be careful who you idolize, those you idolize the most,
Are turning you into a walking wreck from the inside.
If you need to see someone naked, to feel empowered,
It's not power you lack, you just lack a decent mind.
Often times obscenity is but an outburst of insecurity,
By empowering obscenity we empower mental imbalance.
Health and sanity do not rise by erasing all moral lines,
Key to psychological health is finding the right balance.
A healthy society is born of healthy minds without psychosis.
Or just keep pampering psychosis like they deny climate crisis.

Esperanza Impossible Sonnet 20

Those who love you for your looks will puke,
At your face at the sight of your first wrinkle.
Those who go gaga over your curves and crevasses,
Will forget you just as easily when aging hail,
You may feel empowered by exposing your every inch,
That's okay if it strengthens you in life's walk.
But remember, once the fake glisten starts to fade,
All that'll matter is how many hearts you've touched.
I am a monk, what do I care about clothes and fashion!
The real menace is the world's shallow self-obsession.
Everybody yells, it's what's on the inside that counts,
Very few practice it when it demands self-regulation.
In talk only, it's what's on the outside that matters.
In action we drool for attention by exposing the curves.

Melons & Dongles (The Sonnet)

It is one thing to embrace one's imperfections,
But there is nothing empowering in popping melons.
It is one thing to fight for equal pay rights,
Totally another to fight for the freedom of nipples.
On the other side, nobody wants a dongle in their inbox,
Only the dumb and callow care about your greek abs.
Men who are concerned more with grooming than behaving,
Raise a red flag to those with character and heart.
It is one thing to stay healthy through regular workout,
And totally another to worship one's body in the mirror.
All that packaging isn't worth even a confederate bill,
If inside all you have left is stinky narcissistic vapor.
So I say, stay healthy, but embrace your imperfections.
Once the packaging is gone, what'll be your contribution?

Esperanza Impossible Sonnet 22

Clothes are identity of the shallow,
Curves are identity of the savage.
Behavior alone is identity of the human,
All else is but expendable appendage.
You don't need glamor to be gentle,
True glamor is your innocent twinkle.
You don't need to be cast in the MCU,
To be the light in someone's struggle.
Light requires neither abs nor racks,
Light requires no attire, no etiquette.
We've wasted enough time on trivialities,
It's time to light a candle not cater to darkness.
Power is intrinsic to the mind, independent of constructs.
Breaking out of the prison of beauty, it's time to grow up.

Myths & Comics (The Sonnet)

Some modern superheroes are green in color,
Some ancient superheroes are blue in color.
Some worship hulk, ironman, captain marvel,
Some are fanatics of Zeus, Poseidon, Krishna.
Mythologies are but comics of the old days,
Just like comics are nothing but modern myths.
Fiction is okay in its place, but trouble begins,
When life is belittled and fiction is worshiped.
Inspiration can come from anywhere, real or not,
But all is useless, if it produces mindless savages.
Even I've written fiction to explore some situations,
Though based on reality, some of it is highly exaggerated.
If it brings you back to life, only then it's worth it.
Fiction is supposed to enhance reality, not enslave it.

Esperanza Impossible Sonnet 24

An imaginary friend that lifts you up is far better,
Than all the real people around who just don't care.
But make sure that the imaginary friendship doesn't turn you,
Into another apathetic soul disconnected from social welfare.
Little escapism on occasion is good to charge up the veins,
But a life of escapism is a waste of our neural batteries.
Escapism thrives on the absence of empathy in society,
More we grow apathetic, more we'll need escapist fantasies.
That is why, instead of trying to take away people's deities,
Be a simple human 'n sow some empathy with humane action.
It is apathy that we oughta focus on eliminating from society,
Once we do that, escapism will aid not impede our ascension.
As of now it's about diverting the mind away from real society.
We need escapism that brings our attention back to humanity.

Esperanza Impossible Sonnet 25

I don't write to sell books,
I write so each mind becomes its own book.
During each crisis I asked you not to buy them,
And begged you to help those on life's hook.
This is why I have told you, I am not a writer,
For writers have to think about making a living.
I don't care about living, for I am a revolution,
I come from nothing, I can survive even scraping.
If I wanted to make money from the books, I'd have,
Written a couple, and milked them the rest of my life.
Instead, no sooner have I released one work than,
My attention falls on the next humanitarian light.
Books are merely vessel to carry a light through time.
Reformer does not pen words, reformer writes time.

Esperanza Impossible Sonnet 26

I hate guns and grenades,
Backbone is superior to all weaponry.
Reformer's CSF contains enough C4,
To blow up Alpha Centauri.
Bullets feed on ignorance and fear.
Where the mind is without fear,
and the head is held high,
Bullets are but relics of yesteryear.
Get hold of the granite in your heart,
Every inch of you is pure dynamite.
Why do you bother with tribal toys,
When the greatest power is right inside!
Brain makes bullets, brain can end bullets.
Brain with character makes supersapiens.

Esperanza Impossible Sonnet 27

Don't go bonkers over the idea of supersapiens,
I only used it to refer to a well-built character.
Be a simple sapiens with character, that is enough,
For without character it ain't sapiens but disaster.
We coined a term to depict the human species alright,
But we never took the responsibility seriously.
To us acting sapiens is more of an option than duty,
We are just happy to be sapiens in appearance only.
That is why we obsess over philosophy so damn much,
So that we never have to take ethics as everyday life.
We argue over intellect, law and policy - all for show,
No sooner have the doors been closed than we turn uncivilized.
Sapiens are those alone who act civilized without an audience.
If we need law to behave human we are but homo savages.

Esperanza Impossible Sonnet 28

I am not here to teach you human behavior,
I made myself the human I want to see fly.
I am not gonna force anyone to be like me but,
Every bird by nature is drawn to the open sky.
Soft power is the way to conquer the world,
Gone are the days of irrefutable obedience.
Heart that lays itself down to lift up others,
Gets placed on a pedestal of highest significance.
But concern yourself not with the pedestal,
Your duty is your purpose, not petty hiking.
Let others climb the greasy pole all they want,
You just keep on working, working and working.
To spread a message you gotta be the walking message.
No world is reformed by conformity or rebellion, but by conscience.

Esperanza Impossible Sonnet 29

I don't know how to write poetry,
Because I am the poetry.
My life is my lesson to you,
I am the human I dream to see.
I don't have any message,
For I am the message.
My legacy is not my literature,
My legacy are the Gods I raise.
Foster the will, o brave 'n mighty gods,
The will to be makers of a unified planet.
Be free, be fervent, be whole with humanity,
Foster not rebellion, rather realize oneness.
Counterfeit freedom brings only apathy.
True freedom brings responsibility.

Esperanza Impossible Sonnet 30

There is nothing free about your will,
All of it is conditioned to the hilt.
If you are to foster any original will,
A lot of soil you've got to till.
Perception is not observation,
Perception is prediction.
The brain doesn't care about observing,
It only puts forward a self-serving illusion.
Your will is but puppet to that illusion,
Which means you are but a puppet to evolution.
You do have the brain power to take control,
But it'll take a lot of inconvenient self-correction.
If you can do that, you shall rise as sapiens.
Or you'll just end up as compost in nature's garden.

Esperanza Impossible Sonnet 31

Do something human with your life, so that,
You don't end up as compost like other animals.
Live a life that does justice to the title human,
Never compromise on character coerced by dumbbells.
Life is never flawless like a hallmark movie,
And definitely not as exciting as Marvel movies.
If you can walk through imperfections undisheartened,
Then you shall be able to cherish life's mysteries.
Life begins when you embrace it all wholeheartedly,
Without showing resistance to occasional upheaval.
But accepting all doesn't means accepting bigotry,
Just like you welcome dawn, embrace the nightfall.
There have been times when fear crippled all my senses.
I let the tears run, but did not withhold my footsteps.

Esperanza Impossible Sonnet 32

If you do not feel pain,
It's not strength but coldness.
Strength may attract people but,
Vulnerability builds attachment.
You gotta be extremely selfish,
To be happy when you have nobody.
Your mind is always healing itself,
So it's okay to not be okay occasionally.
Beware of psychics and non-psychics,
Who say they can coach you through life.
We're meant to be each other's keeper,
But not some authoritarian guide.
Life's prime directive is to live without harm.
Everything falls in place if the heart is its own norm.

Esperanza Impossible Sonnet 33

A heart that is its own norm,
Isn't swayed by habits of history.
A mind that writes its own path,
Isn't blinded by arrogant logicality.
There is more to faith, family & tradition,
Than white, straight and christian.
If you are still too medieval to get it,
You're everything of which Christ cautioned.
Norms are meant to provide a nourishing footing,
They must never be taken as irrefutable gospel.
Be the new paradigm, something original and humane,
Be a civilization unto yourself, bold yet humble.
Each generation must think, feel 'n behave one step further.
Where there is no inner evolution civilization will wither.

Esperanza Impossible Sonnet 34

I've said before, civilization is a process, not a place,
A process of questioning the past while reshaping the present.
In short, civilization is but a manifestation of evolution,
The only manifestation that does not rely on nature's grace.
All this time we've been using the term civilization wrong,
We have stupidly equated civilization with industrialization.
Now that industrialization has become the bane of sapiens life,
With no ethics at the foundation it keeps causing degeneration.
Then again we mustn't judge the first industrialists too harshly,
They did what they felt to be the right way of advancement.
Problem is that we continue to pamper their unethical practices,
With no firm will to self-correct as it demands greedlessness.
Upon conscientious acts of self-correction civilization unfolds.
Animals gotta live by instincts, we can't choose the same road.

Consent & Manhood (The Sonnet)

Better deemed a coward than forward,
For there is too much at stake.
Stand ready to wait till infinity,
Without violating her personal space.
She's not your bonerville,
Until she gives you consent.
Remember, consent is the line,
Between a baboon and a sapiens.
Expose your feeling with your gestures,
Earn her trust without forcing yourself.
Keep your libido down, below your knee,
Till you are asked to strip all restraint.
It is no man that turns a beast at the sight of woman.
Real Man is a father, friend and lover - all in one.

Esperanza Impossible Sonnet 36

Do you think it makes me happy,
To write about such animality!
I feel sick to my stomach,
To even think of such bestiality.
But if the janitor abandons the dirt,
Because he feels rather squeamish,
The filth will keep on piling up,
Till the world becomes a giant dung heap.
Likewise if the reformer ignores their duty,
All light of justice and equality will vanish.
Despite battling a thousand typhoons inside,
I shall keep on typing prescriptions till I perish.
Janitor cleans the streets, reformer cleans society.
If either one turns lazy, then you shall know calamity.

Esperanza Impossible Sonnet 37

I am nothing but a social janitor,
Because I wanna flood the world with such.
If every nation had ten social janitors,
UN officials could enjoy a good baseball match.
United Nations does not reflect united nations,
United Nations reflects disunited nations.
Cause of that disharmony is our age-old habit,
Of relying childishly on external institutions.
All the wars of this world have been caused,
By tribal chiefs peddling subscriptions.
Still we keep fanning the tribal fire by refusing,
That internal troubles warrant internal solutions.
Each civilian must pick up the broom as janitor,
And sweep the opportunists right out the door.

Esperanza Impossible Sonnet 38

United Nations reflects a disunited world,
Unity comes from the heart, not Geneva or Rome.
Guided tour may work at fictitious Disney world,
In the real world you are the light of your own.
I had the scriptures for breakfast,
All I developed was a headache.
Then I looked up to help another being,
Lo and behold, I found divine grace.
There is no grace in religious institutions,
Order is never found in political buildings.
Real grace and real order are born of the mind,
Stand up 'n let the light out of your nerve endings.
The world is but a mirror that only reflects your light.
The world is in darkness because of the darkness inside.

Esperanza Impossible Sonnet 39

I need a religion,
With less pomposity and more simplicity.
I need a religion,
With less noise and more tranquility.
I need a religion,
With less pollution and more sustainability.
I need a religion,
With less malnutrition and more magnanimity.
I need a religion,
With less citadels and more sidewalk.
I need a religion,
With less barking and more footwork.
Yet when I look around I get choked with all the pollution.
Perhaps the religion I seek doesn't exist, for I am my religion.

Ethics & Prototypes (The Sonnet)

Take morality out of science and,
All you've left is one big conspiracy theory.
Abundance of facts doesn't make something right,
If it has no regard for the supreme fact of humanity.
Just because we can innovate, doesn't mean we should,
Science can no more be measured by the query of could.
In future we'll be able to pre-edit a newborn baby,
But just because we could, doesn't mean we should.
Only a true scientist will realize the truth in this,
A mind that can look past the pomp into the purpose,
While counterfeit tech giants try to turn the world,
Into a giant lifeless robot made of bolts and nuts.
So better keep radical designs hidden from public eyes.
Some prototypes must never ever be commercialized.

More to Technology (The Sonnet)

Some prototypes must never be commercialized,
Not till we learn to look beyond monetary value.
Write some fiction instead without revealing schematics,
If you want the possibility to survive through.
Technology is a stupidly predictable phenomenon,
What one person can imagine another can rig together.
All it takes is an infinite supply of persistence,
Voila - fiction of today turns reality centuries later!
So I say again, ask the question of "should" not "could",
If you want some tech to bring light not silent regress.
Because once you put the schematics out into the world,
All your brilliance will fall short to undo the damage.
There's more to technology than startups 'n entrepreneurship.
Power without responsibility causes disparity not uplift.

Esperanza Impossible Sonnet 42

The only worthwhile contribution of the Marvel Universe,
Is the statement, with great power comes great responsibility.
Yet the fundamental of responsibility has gone missing,
From the greed infested fabric of innovation industry.
It's time we place humanity at the core of our innovation drive,
Gotta make sure, innovation don't turn worse than ignorance.
If with innovation we only change the shape of suffering,
Then what is the f-ing point of all that so-called advancement!
Innovate your soul before you go innovating fancy machines,
There's nothing sadder than savages building machines.
If you can't tell good technology from harmful technology,
You are just a new kind of tribal with automated javelins.
Be the help, not hindrance - be the aid, not ailment.
Blinded by grandiose, don't you drift into derangement.

The Himalayan Sonneteer

Anybody can be extraordinary,
If they are born into privilege.
But only the ones with no background,
Can exude the impossible radiance.
Some lights are far too bright,
For an amateur species to see.
Just like we can't hear above 20 kHz,
Humanity fails to fathom impossibility.
That's why they idolize artificial lights,
Because the sun is beyond comprehension.
If they ever stare straight at the sun,
They'll go blind for sure, there is no question.
So they celebrate little hills with skin-deep charisma,
While it takes the world centuries to fathom the Himalayas.

I Forgive You (The Sonnet)

Those who mock me today,
Their children will thank me tomorrow.
Those who cuss me today,
Will be cussed by their kin tomorrow.
Those who laugh at me today,
Will be laughed at by their children.
Those who find me worthless,
Will be ridiculed by their descendants.
It is easy to worship phonies like Edison,
While it takes time to warm up to Nikola.
Shakespeares come and go by the dozens,
But there is no peer to the sun of Mevlana.
I forgive you, for you know not what you do.
It's your prerogative to crucify me,
while my duty is to forgive you.

Esperanza Impossible Sonnet 45

You don't analyze the sun,
You just bask in its radiance.
You don't analyze the Everest,
You just drown in its magnificence.
Little things constitute pop culture,
Because little things can be analyzed.
Giants never climb the billboard charts,
For analysis is the act of little minds.
Let all your guards absolutely down,
Stand naked at heart in front of the sun.
Let its vibrance wash your whole being,
With its vigorous rays let each pore be overrun.
Now the question is, where do these rays come from?
Nowhere else, o sun, but your own innermost fathom!

Esperanza Impossible Sonnet 46

You see ghosts because you believe,
You see God because you believe.
Yet the world around lays in darkness,
Because in your own light you don't believe.
We are too used to look for light outside,
We are too used to look for solution outside.
That is why we never find any lasting solution,
That is why we never find any lasting light.
You are the light that you seek,
You are the beacon to the meek.
If you get carried away by the fears of others,
Who else will be the rock and the peak!
But, if you say that is none of your concern,
Then I have nothing to say to such imitation human.

Esperanza Impossible Sonnet 47

When we take biases as common sense,
That is the end of all common sense.
When we take disparity as progress,
That is the end of all progress.
When we take selfishness as life,
That is the end of all civilized life.
When we submit to the convenience of darkness,
That is the end of the possibility of light.
When we take the self as the center of the world,
That is the end of the world as well as the self.
When we take the world as the center of the self,
That is the beginning of the world as well as the self.
A world conditioned is born of a self conditioned.
A world liberated is born of a self unconditioned.

Esperanza Impossible Sonnet 48

Is it possible to have an unconditioned self?
The factual answer is no, it is not possible.
However, it is possible to question them plenty,
Thus loosening the grip of their influence.
The point is not to be empty of conditioning,
But to be aware of all that conditioning.
With awareness comes the capacity for correction,
With correction come all things civilizing.
But do not think of this as some sort of battle,
There is no mind without conflict and dissonance.
Just be aware of the whole being that you are,
And you shall know how to behave, where and when.
Most times belief and desire drive human behavior.
But it's behavior that oughta drive belief 'n desire.

Esperanza Impossible Sonnet 49

Behavior is the key, not belief.
Make behavior your identity, not belief.
Traditions make identity for the vermin,
Humans make identity with their deeds.
Behave yourself, and in time,
The whole world will learn to behave.
May be not in your lifetime,
But for sure, sometime along the way.
The paradigm changes by your behavior, not belief.
The world changes by your action, not opinion.
A new physical world starts with a new psyche,
A new kind of society starts with a new kind of human.
First we gotta rid ourselves of all mechanical coldness.
Once we do that, only then shall we understand progress.

Naskar and Abi (The Sonnet)

Ask me about the strangest secrets of human behavior,
I would ramble on and on without stopping for hours.
But try to make small talk with me as a cold stranger,
And I would struggle to put a single thought in words.
Only force that breaks my autistic barrier is attachment,
I only remember of one person with whom I could be me.
When she left I let the God complex blow at full throttle,
So that Naskar survives even if nobody gets to see Abi.
Perhaps that is why without even knowing I invented Abi,
So that the real Abi finds expression, at least in fiction.
Thus, if and when the strain gets too heavy I could escape,
The vastness of Naskar, without escaping the conviction.
There is no rock of ages without some everyday weakness.
It is the weakness that keeps us grounded as sapiens.

Esperanza Impossible Sonnet 51

What you call God complex,
I call a sense of duty.
Some may leave all to fiction,
But I'm aware of my responsibility.
Then there are fruitcakes who don't care,
What happens to the society.
They ain't qualified to pass judgment,
Even on the dust under my feet.
Point is, to take the world on shoulder,
It's imperative to have some God complex.
Besides, if it makes you a better human,
What's wrong in having a little God complex!
Look inside your heart, you'll find the second coming.
If you don't believe in your strength, there is no resurrecting.

Esperanza Impossible Sonnet 52

We must be able to see the world,
Whenever we look into the mirror.
The world is but our reflection,
We're the light that makes it shimmer.
Or rather, the world is but a mirror,
We see what we are.
Once we feel it in our bones,
All barriers will disappear.
Most times we end up mirror to the world,
We reflect what we receive and perceive.
This won't do when the paradigm is cruel,
We gotta be the mutation that alters the species.
Be a real life mutant that alters the course of progress.
There is no greater mutation than that of selflessness.

Earth Ranger (The Sonnet)

There is no selflessness,
There is only humanity.
There is no charity,
There is only humanity.

There is no Christ, only compassion.
There is no Naskar, only nobility.
There is no Buddha, only benevolence.
There is no MLK, only equality.

Every generation needs a janitor,
Every era needs an exterminator.
Every tierra needs a transformer,
Every generation needs a generator.

We are the wildlife, we are the poacher.
We are the humans, we are the ranger.

Esperanza Impossible Sonnet 54

One ounce of alum is enough,
To clean up a bucket of water.
One grain of goodness is enough,
To clean up the social water.
We are the ones who make the mess,
We are the ones to make amends.
We are the ones who jump the cliff,
We are the ones to rescue ourselves.
Enough with the delegation already!
Delegation ends up causing degeneration.
We'd do anything to not be held accountable.
Representation is code for civic hibernation.
Thus, ours is a perfect paradigm to foster greed.
No wonder the predators rule in a world of sheep.

Takeover Twattery (The Sonnet)

Oligarchs don't even care about the welfare of their employees,
And you want them to care about social welfare! Keep dreaming!
Oligarchs have no regard for the struggles of human life,
And you think they'll transform the world! Keep dreaming!
I thought Mark was bad for not treating facebook's health issues,
But the chief twat makes Zuck look like an incompetent simpleton.
Oligarchs are poster boys for regress, not crusaders for freedom,
Better to have a CEO without answers than one who answers to none.
However, like corrupt politicians, oligarchs are made by people,
If anybody is to blame it's the morons who put them in pedestal.
If you had the common sense to question your pavlovian attraction,
Spoiled brats could never treat society as daddy's mine of emerald.
Now more than ever it is imperative to ban large scale takeovers.
Moreover, it is vital to legally shun the rise of billionaires.

Esperanza Impossible Sonnet 56

At the end of the day, it all comes down to people.
There's no mess big enough we the people cannot treat.
It's not capacity that we lack, what we lack is backbone.
We are not lazy either, we're just used to celebrate greed.
Our world has a habit of turning backbones into boneheads,
Our society has a habit of turning human veins super vain.
And it is quite easy to revolt against society altogether,
What's difficult is to grow original without being cruel 'n lame.
Rebellion takes no courage, even an animal can do that,
Human is to rebel for the right cause without causing harm.
Take charge, not so you could walk around like the new owner,
But so the world could usher into a new age holding your arm.
This does not mean that you won't feel helpless at times.
To help others even while feeling helpless is the sign of life.

Esperanza Impossible Sonnet 57

Every time I am crippled by fear,
I turn off the light and sit in the dark.
With no other light to hold on to,
From the deepest fathoms light comes up.
Darkness brings the light out,
Crisis brings character out.
When there is nothing but darkness,
By osmosis mind's dormant light pours out.
There is no light at the end of the tunnel,
Because the very tunnel is an illusion.
Embrace the tunnel as part of life,
And you shall find your illumination.
Mind is the source and the sink of all light.
Where the mind gives in, there's nothing civilized.

Esperanza Impossible Sonnet 58

Civilization is just another name for unsubmission,
Unsubmission to the instincts that keep us slave.
So it is not only your life that is at stake here,
Rather what's at stake is the entire world's fate.
Your life could be a turning point for civilization,
Or it's just another number, breeding more numbers.
You have to decide what do you want your life to be,
A breeding ground of just babies or a world virtuous!
Mind you, I'm in no way patronizing the desire for family.
Heck, to have it myself someday, I would give anything!
Just make sure that that's not all that you contribute,
Make the world expand in heart not just in next of kin.
Be the reason for a humane world, o brave one,
Not just a more populated one.

Esperanza Impossible Sonnet 59

Populating a planet with people is easy,
Humanizing a planet for the humans, not so much.
Making love to a person by penetration is easy,
To make a person feel loved, not so much.

Spreading genes is easy, spreading virtue, not so much.
Behaving horny is easy, behaving humane, not so much.
There's nothing glorious in acting on age-old instincts.
Glory is when the society shines by your midas touch.

There's nothing amazing in penetration 'n reproduction.
Breeding babies is easy, raising human beings, not so much.
Anybody can raise a family, biology is programmed so.
Raise a family that stands as beacon to this world of ours.

In short, reproduction is not the same as raising a family.
Reproduction requires nothing, raising family requires humanity.

Esperanza Impossible Sonnet 60

Blood makes no family,
Bond makes it so.
And now more than ever,
We gotta let the bond grow.
We gotta bond with the whole world,
Not just our immediate family.
Politicians can rip this world apart,
Because we don't see the world as family.
In a world where the courts 'n congress,
Are filled with a bunch of cocks 'n cunts,
Civilians must take back the reins,
And stand up bold, without bent and arms.
When politics and law fail to reform the world,
Civilians must become guardian of this global dorm.

I Hate Guns (The Sonnet)

Please don't hold a gun to my head,
Because firearms terrify me to death.
When I am scared stiff due to stupidity,
Nothing can keep the beast from outbreak.
I battle every day to keep it tamed,
I dread the moment the beast finds release.
Mock me, hit me, I assure your safe return,
Hold a gun, and be torn apart limb from limb!
So, I implore you, o savage most refined,
Please show some mercy, and give up your guns!
Or be a stupid moron, and carry in secret,
Just not stupid enough to draw at my loved ones.
Committing primitivity even God won't escape the Ravager.
Bullets work on two-bit terrorists, not natural disaster.

Esperanza Impossible Sonnet 62

I am not proof of a violent spirit,
I am the proof of self-restraint spirit.
I am not a vessel of cold narcissism,
I am the drive for accountable uplift.
I am not a sample of lawlessness,
I am the specimen of accountability.
I do not need law to tell right from wrong,
For I am the maker of all righteous legality.
I am the sign of the animal aware,
I am the manifestation of human conscience.
Driven by biases we are but organic robot,
Be aware, and you'll know human sentience.
I am not a person but civilization incarnate.
I am but reflection of every mindful sapiens.

Esperanza Impossible Sonnet 63

Mindfulness has nothing to do with mysticism,
It is just the mind being aware of itself.
From this awareness come all things civilized,
It's the difference between animal 'n human sentience.
Some might ask, don't animals have their own awareness!
Yes they do, just enough to ensure self-preservation.
But unlike humans they lack the brain capacity,
To forge the course of their evolution and expansion.
Among over 8 million species on earth only one,
Can question the nature of their existence.
If you still don't get the gravitas of such life,
Even a billion pounds of intellect breed ignorance.
Being a human is a great responsibility.
Without that awareness, it's all foolery.

Esperanza Impossible Sonnet 64

Buildings carry more virtue than beings,
Billboards bear more character than backbones.
If this is your idea of a civilized world,
Don't disgrace me by posting me on billboards.
If you must keep me somewhere,
Keep me in your heart, not on walls.
It is nothing short of tragedy if virtues,
Are nowhere to be found except on walls.
Real virtue is walking virtue, all else is myth,
Footsteps are the lifeforce of virtue 'n ascension.
Ten selfless steps walked in the course of virtue,
Are worth more than a billion billboards of promotion.
This is why I have never cared for promoting my work.
Truth surpasses the shortsightedness of a populist world.

Esperanza Impossible Sonnet 65

Truth will find a way,
Despite lacking endorsement.
Lies thrive on promotion,
Truth is its own certificate.

I could live inside a cave,
Still would reform the blue rock.
It's not exposure that graces light,
It's light that graces the world.

If I cared for exposure 'n publicity,
I could've never become impossible.
My universe of ideas are infinite,
Because I don't dance to pop jingle.

There is no such thing as pop culture.
You can either have populism or culture.

Esperanza Impossible Sonnet 66

No belief is beyond scrutiny, except truth,
But the point is, all truth is but belief.
Some truths bear more facts than others,
Still all talk of truth is talk of belief.
But it's also true that we need something,
At the core of our everyday existence,
That is too grand for logic to explain,
Nor can it be contained by fairytales.
But it is not really that complicated,
Being human is the core of a human being.
What's there so much to theorize,
What's with all the philosophizing!
Humanity first, everything else second,
Including logic, belief and tradition.

Esperanza Impossible Sonnet 67

More we argue over logic and belief,
More impotent logic and belief become.
The presence of a lot of policy,
Indicates the lack of internal reform.
If the heart lacks real will for reform,
Law, logic, belief, policy, all are fake.
Purpose of law is not to control humans,
Purpose of law is to keep animals in check.
So I say, instead of raising policy,
Raise citizens who need no policy.
Instead of turning and overturning law,
Turn the children into judge and jury.
The point is not to depend on law and policy.
Focus should be on raising a lawless society.

Esperanza Impossible Sonnet 68

Lawless society doesn't mean the absence of law,
Lawless society is the absence of the need for law.
Now the question is, can we raise such a society!
To which I say, the very question puts me in awe.

We don't need law to tell us how to breathe,
We don't need law to tell us when to drink water.
Yet when it comes to fundamental acts of humanity,
We behave like the lawmakers are creature superior.

In fact, it's more likely for a schoolteacher to be,
Wiser than the entire lot of lawmakers.
And if we talk of order, cops are the last people,
To have any idea of actual, lasting, genuine order.

So I repeat, society is ours, its problems are ours.
Whether cops come or sleep, civilians are the keepers.

Esperanza Impossible Sonnet 69

We need a world less legal and more human,
We need a world less logical and more human.
We need a world less intellectual more human,
We need a world less partisan and more human.
We need a world less religious and more human,
We need a world less spiritual more spirited.
We need a world less theoretical more practical,
We need a world with less badges, more benevolent.
All this time we've been focusing on the wrong things,
All this time we've been a lot of things but human.
All this time we've been told, be this, be that,
But rarely ever anyone speaks of becoming human.
Human being and human world won't drop from the sky.
We just need to be the heart less learned and more alive.

Esperanza Impossible Sonnet 70

All things ethical begin with the individual,
All things collective begin with the individual.
When the individual fails to realize their duty,
That's when the world has to face political turmoil.
Contrary to popular belief, politics is not the problem,
The real bane of a democratic society is partisanism.
Because politics involves interest of the people,
Whereas partisanism involves interest of the politicians.
The point is, partisanism thrives on civilian insecurity,
In a way, civilians are to blame for crooked politicians.
But here it is of no use to bicker over who to blame,
I only mention it to point out the root of degeneration.
In short, we are the pigs who put the pigs in power.
If we wanna change that, we gotta build our character.

Esperanza Impossible Sonnet 71

My principles are more important to me than my life,
If there is no principle, there is no character.
And the one principle that matters to me the most,
Is that people come first, principles later.
Before you learn science you gotta learn,
Why do you want to learn science?
Before you run for congress you gotta know,
Why do you want to run for congress?
Before you learn medicine you gotta learn,
Why do you want to learn medicine?
Before you become an engineer you gotta know,
Why do you want to study engineering?
Whatever you wanna be in life, first know the purpose.
And if it's disconnected from humanity it's all hogwash.

Real Human (The Sonnet)

You are either pro-guns,
or pro-human, you cannot be both.
You are either against abortion,
or pro-life, you cannot be both.
You are either intolerant,
or religious, you cannot be both.
You are either anti-semite,
or sapiens, you cannot be both.
You are either homophobic,
or human, you cannot be both.
You are either islamophobic,
or civilized, you cannot be both.
Tolerating intolerance is sign of an animal.
Integration is what makes humanity human.

Esperanza Impossible Sonnet 73

Integration is the cure for terrorism,
Integration is the cure for prejudice.
Integration is the cure for stereotypes,
Integration is the cure for ignorant malice.
A world without integration,
Is a world of degradation.
A heart without integration,
Is a breeding ground of descension.
Intellect, faith, heritage, all are useless,
If the heart lacks some basic warmth.
If a person reeks of intolerance,
It is no person but a walking dump.
Integration is the cure for intolerance.
Integration is the manifestation of sapience.

Esperanza Impossible Sonnet 74

Naming ourselves sapiens,
Doesn't make us sapient.
As of now it is nothing,
But a word without consequence.
We gotta focus less on isms and logies,
And focus more on wordless realization.
We gotta step across the barrier of language,
If we are to find the light of unification.
Today term-dropping is nothing but narcissism,
Nobody practices the fancy terms they drop.
Perhaps by blabbering a ton of fancy words,
They find meaning in an existence most flop.
Inventing a ton of words with no accountability,
Is but a fool's idea of a learned society.

Esperanza Impossible Sonnet 75

Never make the mistake of memorizing my ideas,
Without fully considering the context.
If you have no grasp of the underlying context,
You'll have no practical grasp of the message.
And I say to those who wanna trap me with my own words,
If I want, I could find logical error in everything you say.
But I don't have patience to respond to crocodile query,
Particularly when I can smell fake interest a mile away.
If you are interested in a genuine conversation,
I would love to jabber with you without judgment.
But if all you want is to prove me wrong then,
Please find a like-minded fake with time to waste.
Life is too short to be wasted on judgmental whim.
Put your judgment aside, and have some ice-cream.

Esperanza Impossible Sonnet 76

Life is short,
Assume less, ask more.
Breath is short,
Chase less, cherish more.
In the battle between heart and head,
Go look for the backbone instead.
If heart and head are constantly boxing,
It means both are in need of nourishment.
When heart and head get fused together,
That is the manifestation of wholeness.
Little dilemmas will always persist but,
The big ones are born of dualistic nonsense.
Life is short, live like your life depends on it.
Bring your head, heart, spine, all to use,
without resisting any of it.

Esperanza Impossible Sonnet 77

Get rid of those half-baked clichés,
Notions born of insecurity not wisdom.
Take charge of your life and society,
Stepping across all stagnant imagination.
The world seems like a wonderful place,
When you don't know what's going on in it.
Witnessing the darkness yet choosing to smile,
That's what defines the illuminating spirit.
Throw away all beliefs that keep you oblivious,
To the darkness by feeding you myths of light.
If you want there to be real light in the world,
You must expand beyond your ancestral sight.
Illumination requires observation beyond imagination.
Foster imagination that brings expansion not stagnation.

Stagnation & Expansion (The Cognitive Sonnet)

There is not one but two imaginations,
One causes stagnation, another expansion.
It's okay to have a little bit of stagnation,
But stagnation as life causes degeneration.

A stagnant mind raises cognitive defenses,
To guard the stagnation against radical ideas.
An expansive mind brings down their defenses,
To expand perception by embracing new ideas.

Stagnant minds revolting against new ideas,
Are like impressionable kids throwing tantrum.
It's not their fault that they despise expansion,
Ascension takes a huge toll on minds in stagnation.

So when stagnant souls laugh at your expansion.
It is sign that you're moving in the right direction.

Esperanza Impossible Sonnet 79

Please don't waste your life laughing at me,
To belittle me it does absolutely notin'.
People are threatened by equals or superiors,
But definitely not by their children.
You are all my children, o haters,
Your hate is my treasured possession!
The more you hate me, the more you think of me,
I'm flattered that I'm always in your contemplation.
So, next time you feel like laughing at me,
Remember, it only makes me more significant.
Every mockery directed at me,
Drowns the mockers into insignificance.
Now hear ye all my equals - o humans!
When children go astray, be their firm guardian.

Esperanza Impossible Sonnet 80

Enough with the nonsense of free speech!
It's time we replace it with human speech.
If free speech is just code for hate speech,
It's time we replace it with heart speech.
Free speech is a matter of human society,
Which means that it applies only to humans.
And hate is the utter antithesis of humanity,
Hate speech is free speech only for the animals.
In short, there is not one but two free speech,
One applies to humankind another to animalkind.
Free speech is hateless speech for the humans alone,
Whereas hate 'n bigotry are affairs of animalkind.
So the question is not whether free speech matters,
But, whether we're talking about humans or animals!

Esperanza Impossible Sonnet 81

Freedom has a price tag,
Which reads in bold "accountability".
If we cannot afford to pay that price,
We do not have the right to liberty.
Liberty is an easy enough concept but,
Things get murky when it comes to practice.
Some of the cruelest horrors were born of liberty,
Liberty often maintains the glory of prejudice.
Everybody loves to shout about freedom,
But ask them what it means in practice,
And all they can think of is that,
They are free to do whatever they please.
It is not liberty if it not helps but harms others.
Liberty involves the collective uplift of all humans.

Esperanza Impossible Sonnet 82

Before we start yelling about freedom,
We gotta learn how to use freedom wisely.
If we can't tell human from animal freedom,
Such freedom is but a highway to new inhumanity.
When the notions of human rights were still vague,
We but had to focus on the pursuit of liberty.
But the time has come to take the movement further,
And place our attention on accountable liberty.
In short, we oughta focus on accountability,
And the right kind of liberty will come on its own.
When the human is aware of the duties of the title,
Civilized liberty at long last will be honed.
Democracy, civilization, society, all shall come,
When we're aware of the duties of designation human.

Esperanza Impossible Sonnet 83

Who is human, who is not,
I don't know so much theory.
I only know what is civilized,
The act of taking responsibility.
Like, do you know what the word VOTE means?
It means Vanguard Of Transformational Earth.
So get your ass to the polling station,
Your inaction only empowers the bigoted dirt.
But then again, just voting is not enough,
You gotta foster a transformational spirit.
Your responsibility does not end at the ballot,
Ballot is a part of democracy, not the whole of it.
In the end, it's not about raising a democratic society.
It is about discovering individuality in collectivity.

Esperanza Impossible Sonnet 84

There can be civilization without democracy,
But there is no civilization without collectivity.
There can be civilization without philosophy,
But there is no civilization without accountability.
There can be civilization without political science,
But there is no civilization without civic duty.
However, don't go googling the definition of civic duty,
It's just a fancy way of saying, humans oughta have humanity.
Too many terms, too little meaning - this is the problem!
Trouble is - too many sciences, too little alliances!
Theories are supposed to aid and empower practice.
Yet we have plenty theories, but no practical significance.
In short, ethics and existence are not affairs of partisanism.
Party, ideology, allegiance, all are expendable, but not humans.

Esperanza Impossible Sonnet 85

The only civilized politician in the world,
Is the one with no party allegiance.
All else are but rabid dogs just waiting,
To make their corner of the world infected.
Here I am not talkin' about affiliation,
The choice of party affiliation is up to you.
Just use your affiliation to help the people,
Not for abusing people to help your crooked crew.
If the situation demands, pretend like,
You care a lot about party welfare.
In practice, place all attention on people,
This is called "diplomacy two point whatever".
Honesty is not necessarily the best policy.
In social reform purpose justifies trickery.

Esperanza Impossible Sonnet 86

To trick the tricksters for greater good,
Is not only righteous but humanitarian.
If you don't put the savages in their place,
They'll only keep impeding social ascension.

Mark you, I mean trickery, that is, use of reason,
I am not talkin' about resorting to inhumanity.
You just need to use your head as well as heart,
And you are bound to overthrow all bigotry.

A reformer must never give in to naive idealism,
We gotta keep our head active as well as the heart.
Run for congress or not, our society is our duty,
Once we realize it, what can the baboons do to us!

With the heart as the brain and brain as the brawn,
We shall usher our world into a civilized dawn.

Esperanza Impossible Sonnet 87

It is not enough to have a kind heart,
You must nourish the brain to outwit inhumanity.
Sometimes inhumanity is too powerful for your heart,
That's when you gotta resort to your brain capacity.
Killing the inhumans is easy, all it takes is brutality but,
We must restrain inhumanity while preserving the life.
It is more reason to nourish the head as well as the heart,
For the heart often turns us brutal in vengeful strife.
We gotta use the head, not because we lack the heart,
We gotta use the head so that the heart doesn't turn blind.
So, never give in to the cliché duality of heart and head,
You're a living being - live whole with light, sight 'n might.
Kindness is to guide our wit, wit is to empower kindness.
When all things human come together,
that's when the magic happens.

Esperanza Impossible Sonnet 88

Don't live as a half-cocked human,
Lacking in either head, heart or spine.
Leave the childish dualities to the children,
You for one, be the human that undivides.
Human is a gargantuan force that contains,
Capacities both fathomable and unfathomable.
Human is nameless, formless and timeless,
Human is the last term to be ideological effable.
Human is the only term that is not a term,
It is an entire universe by itself.
If you think you can contain it with clichés,
You, my friend, are in dire need of help.
Every human can be the first of our kind in some way.
When whole, each of us is the herald of a civilized day.

Civil Liberty (The Sonnet)

Policy is not the precursor to civil liberty,
Civic duty is the precursor to civil liberty.
If there is no civic duty, there is no civil liberty,
If there is no civic duty, civilians are but catastrophe.

Contrary to unwritten political law of abuse,
Civilians are not the doormats of democracy.
Civilians are the doors, civilians are the buildings,
Civilians are the whole of the social anatomy.

Problem is, it's more convenient to live life as doormat,
Than take responsibility and turn politicians obsolete.
The war-mongers know this uncivilized tenet of the apes,
Hence they can turn living beings into moronic nationalist.

So I repeat, civic duty is the alpha and omega of civil liberty.
Till we realize this, there is no peace, justice and equality.

Esperanza Impossible Sonnet 90

Civic duty is the foundation of civilization,
Without it all dialogue is mere wind-baggery.
Law and policy are mere fallacious attempts,
To bypass the requirement of civic duty.
All we have is a world fancy on the outside,
Inside it reeks of prehistoric primitivity.
Policy only changes the shape of human pretense,
It does nothing to instill internal civility.
There is no external way to instill internal change,
All we can do is be the first when there is none.
Invent policies and laws as much as you like but,
Don't be stupid to think, that's how you change the world.
Actual lasting change is independent of law and policy.
Change reliant on policy has a very short life-expectancy.

Esperanza Impossible Sonnet 91

Never confuse change with policy,
Unless of course you're as stupid as a neonazi.
Policy is but temporary fix for a deeper problem,
A problem that is rooted in self-centricity.
If we want to bring any lasting change,
We have got to alter the paradigm totally.
We've got to expand the confines of the self,
And contain the entire world community.
When your local power grid is down,
You use candle to light up the room.
But today can you imagine living life,
Only and only in a candle-lit room!
Law and policy are but stand-ins,
yet you mistake them as power-grid.
Because you are oblivious to the real cure,
dormant in your heartbeat.

Love-Abiding Law (The Sonnet)

Love is the master-key to social troubles,
Law is but an inferior and cheaper stand-in.
Instead of obsessing over cooking up more law,
Let's shift the focus on loving and caring.

Do you think love is nothing but a commercial object,
With your olympian authority which you can legalize!
Who do you think you are that you'll legalize order!
You can legalize toys, telephones, not love and light.

Know your place, o puny apes, on a puny little blue dot,
Before standing as authority bearing your badge of law.
There are more things in the vastness of time and space,
Than dreamt up in your paleolithic construct of law.

An ounce of love brings more change than a 100 pounds of law.
What we need is not law-abiding love, but love-abiding law.

Esperanza Impossible Sonnet 93

There is no future, there is no past,
There is only present - here and now.
The only way to change the obvious future,
Is to become the walking future here and now.
Be the citizen of the future that doesn't exist,
Be the human of the future that the apes are not.
All space and time are contained in the present moment,
Action will pour out, once you realize you ain't a robot.
Realize the gravitas of the situation, my friend,
Because you are the world's first and last resort.
I don't know how much more simply I have to say it,
For you to realize, our family is the whole world.
Time begins where action begins - no act, no time.
And there is no act as potent as being the lifeline.

Esperanza Impossible Sonnet 94

The scientist in me says, time is an illusion.
The human in me says, who the fudge cares!
The neurobiologist in me says, reality is illusion.
The human in me says, who the fudge cares!
Who the fudge cares whether reality is real or not,
All that matters is that we live it with humanness.
Who the fudge cares whether time is real or not,
All that matters is, we use it to carry goodness.
Plenty are the facts, plenty are the theories,
First and foremost, we gotta value everyday life.
All the knowledge of the universe is useless,
If they do not aid in expanding our humane sight.
So, argue less, understand more - that's the human way.
Read and memorize all you like, first throw all nonsense away.

Esperanza Impossible Sonnet 95

Science says this, science says that,
This won't make the world kind.
If you genuinely want to bring change,
Be the specimen of humanitarian science.
Bible says this, bible says that,
This won't bring light into the world.
If you genuinely want to bring change,
Start by simply loving your neighbors.
Any woodworm can be a mouthpiece for a box,
It takes a human to live past the box.
Any bookworm can yell passages from books,
It takes a human to crack life's locks.
Stop all, "science says this, scripture says that"!
Grow up and pay attention to the things that matter.

Esperanza Impossible Sonnet 96

Science does matter,
But only as underling to love.
Scriptures do matter,
But only as underling to love.
Technology does matter,
But only as underling to uplift.
Law and policy do matter,
But only as underling to life.
Dialogues do matter, but only,
If they are not debate in disguise.
Advancement does matter, but only,
If it does not make humans more uptight.
The place of the path is beneath human feet.
The moment we put the path on pedestal, we're dead meat.

Esperanza Impossible Sonnet 97

Problem is, we often take our path,
As more important than people.
Thus we end up behave like,
A bunch of ideological sheeple.
It is never really mind versus mind,
Rather it is always path versus path.
If we ever valued people over path,
No reason or fiction could tear us apart.
In short, we are the roadside romeo who,
Fell in love with the road and forgot about juliet.
It is time to break free from the spell,
Long enough from people we've been distant!
So I say, people before path, not path before people,
If in us there is even an ounce of anything honorable!

Esperanza Impossible Sonnet 98

Path is honored when people are honored,
Path with no regard for people is but dry rot.
Head is honored when heart is honored,
Head with no regard for heart is but an empty hut.
Lover is honored when love is honored,
Lover's salvation is in annihilation for love.
The living is honored when life is honored,
A living being with no regard for life is but dirt.
Mi casa no es su casa, porque no tengo casa.
Mi casa eres tú, yo soy tu casa.
When each human becomes home to another,
That is the birth of an impossible esperanza.
The reformer is honored when people are honored.
The human is honored when humanity is honored.

Esperanza Impossible Sonnet 99

Salvation of the reformer is the people,
Salvation of the human is the people.
Salvation of the scientist is the people,
Salvation of the self is the people.
Salvation of the philosopher is the people,
Salvation of the person is the people.
Salvation of the monk is the people,
Salvation of the mind is the people.
Salvation of the engineer is the people,
Salvation of the individual is the people.
Salvation of the politician is the people,
Salvation of the civilian is the people.
The fact is really simple and plain.
We are but each other's salvation lane.

Esperanza Impossible Sonnet 100

Often the truth is so simple that,
We are too pumped up for thrill to see it.
Often truth hangs right smack above our head,
Yet we are too busy chasing shadows to see it.
Simple things like love don't appeal to us,
So we chase lesser shadows like humanitarianism.
Even if the world opens up in front of our eyes,
We won't accept it till we can explain it with isms.
We have an age-old habit of prioritizing,
The painting over the scenery.
Why do you think we have so many isms,
Yet so very little humanity!
To engineer the world we gotta engineer ourselves.
Then again, only machines can be engineered,
so let's just be each other's help.

48. Mukemmel Musalman

Aum Amen Assalaam
(The Interfaith Sonnet)

Jo bole so nihal - honest, brave 'n nondual!
Ain't no human run by divisionism.
You may say Merhaba, or Hallelujah,
Smiling I respond, Walaikum Assalam.
Every human greeting is an act of peace,
Language differs, not the emotion.
Yet we keep bickering over language,
Overlooking all loving unison.
Chag sameach say some of us,
Some say happy holidays!
Across the words, into the heart,
We'll find the flame of happiness.
Underneath every version of felicidad,
there is a sense of illumination.
Aim of all Aum and Amen - is unification.

Goodness (An Interfaith Sonnet)

Not every christian is a good human,
But every good human is a christian.
Not every muslim is a good human,
But every good human is a muslim.
Not every jew is a good human,
But every good human is a jew.
Not every hindu is a good human,
But every good human is a hindu.
Not every buddhist is a good human,
But every good human is a buddhist.
Not every humanist is a good human,
But every good human is a humanist.
Goodness is universal, vessels may vary.
Some call it water, some agua, some pani.

Mental Por El Mundo (The Sonnet)

Mental por el mundo,
Mental por la gente!
Sin mentalidad de servicio,
No podemos seguir adelante.
Some are mental por dinero,
Some are loco por la ropa.
Let them be as they please,
Estoy loco por la humanidad.
A promise was once made,
He asked me to unify the world.
Ever since, I have been on duty,
My life isn't mine but of the world.
If I fail, you cross off one human.
If I succeed, you witness civilization.

If Hate is Holiness (The Sonnet)

Civilization is a civilian in action,
Standing unbent against all charm.
This is called civilized activism,
The will to stand up without harm.
If vandalism were activism,
Insurrection was patriotism.
If Jan 6 is deemed patriotism,
9/11 was divine intervention.
If 9/11 is deemed a divine act,
Hate is but an act of holiness.
If hate is ever deemed holiness,
That is the end of all common sense.
To witness civilization you gotta be civilized.
Even God acting on hate is a being uncivilized.

Hate is Not Holiness (The Sonnet)

Hate and holiness can never go together,
If they do, it means we have no religion.
Bookish religion belongs in barbarian times,
Modern age requires religion of unification.
If religion brings no oneness, it is no religion,
Only in fiction authoritarianism replaces amity.
If a god is peddled as an authority of division,
It is a sure sign of a make belief divinity.
This has been the problem all along, my friend,
We've taken doctrines as foundation of religion.
By doing so we separated the soul from the body,
And we got left with trinkets of petty tradition.
So I'll say plain and simple, hate is not holiness.
Any text that peddles hate oughta be torched to ashes.

New Kind of Kin (The Sonnet)

And by the way, I am talkin' here rhetorically,
Why bother with texts as "gospel" anyway!
Keep them as suggestion if they hold some good,
Otherwise just let termites eat them away.
Don't stoop so low as to burning books,
Such primitive acts don't suit modern humans.
But go right ahead and have a bonfire with books,
If you are a bunch of backward barbarians.
For revolution to change the paradigm, it's imperative,
That we revolutionize the paradigm of revolution.
The means is just as significant as the mission,
Medieval habits of rebellion don't constitute revolution.
Ancient maps do not lead us to destinations unforeseen.
To build a new world, we gotta be a new kind of kin.

Proof of Integration (The Sonnet)

Be the proof of integration,
Against all caution ancestral.
Those who peddle division belong
In a sanitarium, not on a pedestal.
Reason takes courage,
Superstition takes none.
Reason takes backbone,
Presumption takes none.
Insight takes awareness,
Assumption is lifelessness.
Curiosity is an act of life,
Prejudice is act of the dead.
Humanity is the highest heritage,
which we cannot inherit as family heirloom.
We'll find it in collectivity defying all prejudicial doom.

Unlikely Vessels (The Sonnet)

Am I talking to the wrong person,
Or are you a human after all!
How will you know what you are,
Since appearance means nothing at all!
You just gotta ask a simple question,
What's your priority, my friend?
If the answer is devoid of humanity,
You need not bother with being sane.
To question sanity you must have some sanity,
Biases make us trade in sanity for security.
Animal mind does not care about being sane,
It only knows to survive by self-centricity.
We are all unlikely vessels of civilization.
Nevertheless, we're the best shot
nature has got at raising civilization.

Conditioned (The Sonnet)

We are conditioned against being civilized,
That's animal nature for you, plain 'n simple.
It's nothing personal, it's just all universal,
That we are still less human and more animal.

We are so animal, we judge character from color,
What's worse, we call it preservation of truth.
We are so animal that we prefer war over peace,
Because war brings much more instant revenue.

We cannot shoot our way to justice,
We cannot lynch our way to liberty.
We cannot nuke our way to peace,
We cannot hate our way to humanity.

The cycle must break now, without further ado.
Seek no approval, just step up 'n make the world anew.

Haters, My Kids (The Sonnet)

I find patronization to be a potent tool,
Just like arrogance can be a force for good.
The difficulty is to use them with moderation,
Once you take the lid off, it's hard to undo.
But I've spent a lifetime speaking in silence,
So keeping my rage in control comes quite easy.
Hence, I can treat all haters as my children,
Thus, on purpose, I fail to hold a grudge if any.
It's better to treat the haters as children,
Than retaliate hate with hate out of impulse.
Be the parent to those who cannot see reason,
And it'll be less hard to embrace their outburst.
Be the guardian to the bigots and cherish their tantrum.
Laugh with them when they laugh,
just keep them from committing harm.

Civil Discourse (The Sonnet)

Be a friend to the just,
But a parent to the unjust.
There is no place for hate,
Restrain the hater, but do not hurt.
The paradigm of revolution needs reform,
We must make it grow out of cruelty,
For cruelty is not the cure for cruelty,
We must treat it with the light of sanity.
It is a sad state of affairs when,
Violence becomes a part of civil discourse.
How can we possibly call ourselves civilized,
If mere disagreement breaks out into violent uproars!
So I repeat, cruelty is not the answer to cruelty.
Work to destroy hate without destroying the human spirit.

Not Evolved For Peace (The Sonnet)

Human mind has not evolved to find peace,
It has evolved to be anxious, insecure and panic.
In the jungle once you let your guard down,
To the predator you shall end up as dinner meat.
Which means to be at peace and to make peace,
We gotta go against our most natural tendency.
We gotta nourish the feeble spark of civility within,
To transform the norm from cruelty to humanity.
Biologically, cruelty is our first nature,
And that's where all the trouble begins.
We gotta know we are more animal than human,
To discover ways to tame the animal inklings.
Human mind may not have evolved to be at peace.
But if we are willing to be the civilized anomaly,
slowly but surely we shall foster all necessary peace.

Against Instinct (The Sonnet)

Peace begins now and here,
When we defy our instinct of insecurity.
Love begins now and here,
When we defy our instinct of judgmentality.
Reason begins now and here,
When we defy our instinct of convenience.
Warmth begins now and here,
When we defy our instinct of indifference.
Equality begins now and here,
When we look out for one another.
Justice begins now and here,
When social welfare is personal welfare.
In civilization there is no welfare social.
Only the civilized will realize, it's all personal.

The Human Animal (A Sonnet)

The civilized know how uncivilized they are,
The uncivilized insist on being deemed civilized.
The victor knows the fallacy of being the victor,
The wise knows there is no such thing as being wise.
The real human is aware of their inhuman predispositions,
While the inhuman fails to acknowledge all primitive bent.
And there is no question of the rise of civilization,
If there is no question of questioning the self.
The animal is animal for it lacks the brain capacity,
For self-correction beyond the need of self-preservation.
But more animal than animal is the so-called human being,
That despite having the brains, fails to act in ascension.
It is no human that does not know how animal they are.
The animal becomes human, the moment it becomes aware.

Animal Aware (The Sonnet)

The day the animal becomes aware,
Is the day civilization becomes real.
The day the sapiens realize there is no sapiens,
Is the day the sapiens become real, for real.
Sapiens is another name for awareness,
And awareness delivers sapience.
Till sapiens and awareness are one in practice,
The struggle mustn't cease even for a moment.
Upon our struggle against ourselves,
Does the fabric of civilization unfold.
But I ain't talkin' about a brutal outburst,
I am talkin' about a warm reform that molds.
Molding of society starts with the molding of self.
When you are molded whole, the road appears by itself.

Enough Awakening (The Sonnet)

If we got no wholeness, we got nothing,
If we are heartless, we got nothing.
If we are still ain't loco por el mundo,
We ain't sapiens, we have achieved nothing.
Nothing in the word happens by accident,
It is all but manifestation of causality.
But no mind is vast enough to fathom it,
Nor do we need to, to live with dignity.
What matters is, we are the cause of humanity,
Let us start the change with little things.
To hell with all that nonsense of higher truth,
Realize the truth of love, that's enough awakening!
We'd do much better to give up all our intellectualism.
There's plenty to be done at the grassroots of non-ism.

Intellect & Ignorance (The Sonnet)

Ignorance has made a mess,
Intellect has made a mess.
Coldness has made a mess,
Cockiness has made a mess.
Intellect isn't necessarily good,
Ignorance isn't necessarily bad.
Sometimes intellect facilitates ignorance,
Sometimes ignorance keeps the heart from going bad.
Knowledge by itself knows no good and bad,
It is love that gives knowledge direction and sight.
Be pak in love, and say, "pak I stand, pak I rise!"
Call it pak, call it pure, sanctity knows no divide.
Sanctity is but an offspring of amor valiente.
Virtues of the world come from the mind most fuerte.

The Humanizer (A Sonnet)

Valor, virtue, honor, integrity,
All are but meant to serve humanity.
But when they climb aloof from the people,
It is time to wipe them all out from society.
Each generation must revise the notions of virtue,
Each generation must renovate the percept of honor.
Any generation that makes non-correction the way of life,
Basically wastes their existence in a graveyard.
The graveyard belongs to our ancestors,
We must never take it to be our home.
If we have no spine to write our own paradigm,
We better pack our bags early and head for a rest home.
Old ways are called history, new ways are the future.
One who brings them together, is called the humanizer.

49. Himalayan Sonneteer

Himalayan Sonneteer Sonnet 1

My science is you, my art is you,
La mañana de mi mente eres tú.
Mi casa tú, mi cielo tú,
La verdad de mi vida eres tú.

People are the truth of life,
Not some beliefs and biases.
People are the magic of my words,
People are the center of my poetries.

People are the beginning,
People are the end.
People are the meaning,
People are the mend.

We lift ourselves when we lift up the people.
When we're each other's rock, we are unstoppable.

Himalayan Sonneteer Sonnet 2

Just like every family needs a pillar,
Every generation needs a rock.
All may sprinkle salt on each other's wounds,
You for one, be the ointment to the epoch.
Be the foundation stone to civilization,
Be the walking measure of human character.
You are the definition of sapience,
You are the very definer.
Let no law define your duty,
Let no scripture determine goodness.
Let no ancestor imprison your identity,
Expand, explore and usher into sentience.
You are the illusion, you are the truth.
When evil hangs heavy, you gotta blow your fuse.

Himalayan Sonneteer Sonnet 3

What is the role of an electrical fuse?
Amateurs will say, conducting electricity.
But the actual task of a fuse is,
To blow itself when the load is too heavy.
Thus the fuse protects the appliance,
Against any electrical irregularity.
Likewise, we gotta blow our fuse,
Whenever inhumanity hangs heavy.
If we stay silent in indifference,
What's the point of all this electricity!
Nerves that carry not vigor but ice water,
Ain't no human nerves but sewers of society.
Human nerves are the life-circuit of society.
If they carry ice water, it is a catastrophe.

Himalayan Sonneteer Sonnet 4

I'd rather burn bright for five days,
And turn to ashes as a spectacular sapiens,
Than flicker through fifty years,
In order to avoid any inconvenience.
Be the citizen justice,
And keep the cops as servant.
Be the citizen justice,
And keep the congress as servant.
Five days of lion's life is worth more,
Than five hundred years of leech existence.
It is one thing to live as a human being,
And another to just look like a sapiens.
For once, take responsibility for the world,
Instead of acting like another mindless convert.

I'm Above The Law (The Sonnet)

Yes, I am above the law,
So is every single world builder.
It's only the apes without brain who,
Are tamed by the medieval lawmaker.
If you are to be a civilized being,
It is your duty to rise above the law.
If you can't tell right from wrong,
It is common sense you lack, not law.
It is nothing but a juvenile democracy,
That is founded on spineless law-abidance.
Civilized democracy instills accountability,
What it doesn't demand is boneheaded obedience.
You have a heart, brain and spine, why not use them!
Stand up o citizen justice, and keep the law as servant.

Himalayan Sonneteer Sonnet 6

There is a difference between a citizen and a prisoner,
A prisoner, unlike a citizen, doesn't need to take responsibility.
There is a difference between a democracy and dictatorship,
Democracy, unlike dictatorship, oughta be founded on civic duty.
There is a difference between a guard dog and a vanguard,
A guard dog doesn't need to use its head, a vanguard does.
There is a difference between a conspiracy nut and activist,
A conspiracy nut doesn't need to use its head, an activist does.
There is a difference between accountability and nonconformity,
Nonconformity requires no common sense, accountability does.
Mere rebellion out of nonconformity achieves nothing civilized,
What's needed is nonconformity driven by an accountable heart.
In a society where war and violence are the basis of all norm,
Be the nonconformist anomaly of peace to our shared dorm.

Himalayan Sonneteer Sonnet 7

A 10 ounce book brings more peace,
Than a 20 pounds machine gun.
A 3 pound brain brings more order,
Than 300 pounds of uranium.

It is a planet for living beings,
Don't treat it as a dumpyard of ur-anus.
As of now we treat our washroom,
With more care than we treat our world.

Forget about utopia, for it is useless,
To build a castle in the cloud of fiction.
We just have to be alive enough to feel,
That the current paradigm doesn't suit humans.

We gotta humanize the world, not utopianize it.
And it is no mission impossible either,
all we gotta do is stand up in service.

Himalayan Sonneteer Sonnet 8

The day sapiens and service become one,
That day I shall call you an advanced species.
As of now, sapiens is code for sectarianism,
What's worse, we actually take pride in it!
Humanity has no so many cultures, and yet,
None of the cultures prioritize humanity.
If this is your idea of civilized culture,
You are the very picture of inhumanity.
Culture doesn't come by obeying the past,
Progress doesn't come by glorifying the future.
Culture and progress both come hand in hand,
When we're mindful of all time, but act now and here.
Law is no sign of progress, tradition is no cultural heritage.
Our heritage is our ever-expanding humanity,
true progress lies in togetherness.

Himalayan Sonneteer Sonnet 9

I don't obey the law,
I write them.
I am the school where reformers,
And public servants learn the rudiments.

I don't follow science,
I am science.
I am the university where scientists,
Shrinks 'n philosophers develop sapience.

I believe in no God,
I am walking Godliness.
I am the cosmic record that makes,
Monks and theologians grow sentience.

I am the end of all half-knowledge,
I am the beginning of sight beyond sight.
Whoever finds me in their heart's mirror,
Can never be tamed by apish fright.

Himalayan Sonneteer Sonnet 10

The individual must become their own culture,
The individual must become their own tradition.
The individual must become their own progress,
The individual must become their own constitution.
Society where the individual can't tell right from wrong,
Is no society of humans but of apes, no matter the law.
If it takes law to maintain order in a so-called society,
It is no society to begin with but a repressed outlaw.
It is rightness that must drive the individual,
And it is the individual that must drive the society.
Yet we've made an absolute mess by pretending to inject,
Rightness in the world by a lot of legal hokey-cokey.
Conscience is my constitution, courage is my law.
Compassion is my religion, thus speaks the living Ra.

Himalayan Sonneteer Sonnet 11

At school, teachers used to ask,
Growing up what do you want to be?
As a kid I used to tell them,
I want to be human with humanity.
I was rather an average student,
So I never made an impression.
If anything I used to be laughed at,
For voicing some naive conviction.
I never wanted to be successful,
I just wanted to be immortal.
I was never impressed by success,
For me death was unacceptable.
So I gave up living as a person pursuing chains,
I turned my existence into a humanitarian statement.

Himalayan Sonneteer Sonnet 12

Naskar is made by Naskar alone,
Not by an industry or a benefactor.
Naskar is made by Naskar alone,
Not by a nation, religion or culture.

You must forge your own identity,
You are the designer of your destiny.
Unless you start acting as human alive,
Despite all background you have no identity.

Background is meant to be built, not inherited,
What you inherit isn't background but illusion.
None of it is supposed to determine who you are,
Nobody can write in stone, where is your salvation.

Only you can be your own rock, pen and paper.
Background is made, not by heritage, but behavior.

Himalayan Sonneteer Sonnet 13

But, why, you ask me, why,
Do I wanna make the world united?
Çünkü, şarkı dinlemekten,
Daha önemli, şarkı söylemek.
Ser la música es más importante,
Que escuchar música.
More important than listening,
To music is being the musical.
Yes it will be painful,
Yes it will be back-breaking.
But that's why you have a backbone,
To lift up the world despite aching.
Pain is what nourishes the backbone,
While absence of pain turns a human into haribo.

No Pain, No Hope (The Sonnet)

Heavier the pain, greater the hope,
But the language of hope is not inaction.
Real hope brings a sense of responsibility,
Whereas imitation hope induces stagnation.

Heavier the pain, stronger the purpose,
But all purpose is fiction without footwork.
Real purpose does not let you sleep at night,
Imitation purpose keeps you aloof from work.

Crueler the punishment, braver the love,
It is no love that avoids punishment.
Only half lovers try to keep pain at bay
Soaked in pain true lovers emerge triumphant.

Crazier the torture, sweeter the memories.
There is no character if there is no crisis.

Himalayan Sonneteer Sonnet 15

What do you think hope means,
To sit and do nothing!
Such is no hope but cowardice,
Real hope gets you walking.

Hope means to take charge,
Hope means unsubmission.
Hope means to not lose sight,
Hope means to cause illumination.

Life is what happens to the human,
Human is what happens to life.
Nature is what happens to the animal,
Human is the animal rising civilized.

I repeat, hope is no excuse for inaction.
Real hope brings emancipation from submission.

Himalayan Sonneteer Sonnet 16

Hope is nature's defibrillator that,
Electrifies the heart to unsubmission.
Hope rescues us from the depths of despair,
Hope drags the being even out of cremation.

Hope lights the way when clouds convene,
Hope brings sight when smog sets in.
Hope is the bird that heralds the dawn,
Hope is the answer to all things disheartening.

Never let intellect trod on the sapling of hope,
When things get rough intellect is first to scarper.
The brain needs backbone to trudge through hardship,
Without hope, backbone is first to lose its caper.

But again, most times inaction sets in, disguised as hope.
Real hope sets you on fire, it doesn't make you mellow.

Himalayan Sonneteer Sonnet 17

We've wasted enough time as marshmallow,
We've wasted enough time leaving things to fate.
Time has come for us to take our rightful place,
Time has come for the sapiens to rise sapient.
We've wasted more potential on division than unity,
We've wasted more potential as animal than human.
To make things worse, we've called it the will of God,
As if there is no divinity outside ancestral fiction.
Authoritarianism has no place in the kingdom of faith,
Yet all along we've confused authoritarianism as faith.
Either you carry the badge of religion or you're religious,
The supreme sin is to spend a life in blind obedience.
I say to you plainly - oneness is godliness in action.
One who is one with others is a walking divine dimension.

Thus Speaks God (The Sonnet)

Ik onkar, satnaam,
Porque, yo soy insan.
Aham bismillahsmi,
Çünkü, benim adım vicdan.
Sarva dharman parityajya,
Giving up all national grave,
Nos haremos vessels of verdad,
Rise we shall as sapiens brave.
Divinidad está en cada cultura,
But no culture is pure divinity.
Human divided is human undivine,
Hatelessness is civilized divinity.
Thus speaks God in tongue beyond tongues.
One vessel isn't enough to contain my neurons.

Poetry and Philosophy (The Sonnet)

Good poetry is but philosophy,
Good philosophy is but poetry.
It is only the majority amateurs,
Who insist on a divided duality.
Poetry is not about the rhyming,
Philosophy is not about profundity.
A warm philosopher is walking poetry,
A gentle poet is walking philosophy.
Poetry is the most potent form of philosophy,
As it brings illumination through simplicity.
Anybody can make things sound more complicated,
Only the best philosophers can write good poetry.
In philosophy, deeper we go, simpler things get.
Philosopher talks of light, poet swims in it.

Himalayan Sonneteer Sonnet 20

Poet who attains excellence,
Can no longer identify with the term.
Philosopher who attains excellence,
Can no longer identify with the term.
Excellence wipes out all differentiation,
The truly excellent work on building bridges.
And the ones who insist on defending the fences,
Are but kindergarteners still wet around the edges.
Good poetry is indistinguishable from everyday life,
Good philosophy is indistinguishable from everyday life.
Good theology is indistinguishable from everyday life,
Good science is indistinguishable from everyday life.
Every field of human endeavor is an interdisciplinary field.
If it is not, it just means it still lacks maturity.

Himalayan Sonneteer Sonnet 21

Age does not bring maturity,
Most grow old without ever maturing.
Maturity comes by the will of maturity,
Maturity means expanding not contracting.
Contraction is an insult on conscience,
Exclusion is an insult on existence.
Inclusion is synonym for society,
Expansion is a better term for ascension.
Age has very little to do with human life,
State of life is measured by the state of mind.
A mind expanding produces a healthy human life,
A shrinking mind facilitates a savage life.
So don't go counting the candles on your cake.
Some kids grow up without knowing
what is a birthday cake.

Himalayan Sonneteer Sonnet 22

Real maturity is when you are no longer,
Indifferent to the suffering of others.
Real existence is when you no longer exist,
Just to satisfy your own whims and desires.

If a tree falls in a forest, and you are not there,
It is okay that you do not hear.
But if a child cries in a warzone, and you are not there,
Is it still okay that you do not hear?

We have made a habit of not hearing things,
Particularly the things that are not convenient.
When human welfare becomes inconvenient to the humans,
That is the beginning of society's decadence.

Are you mature enough to take on the duties of a human,
Or just another dimwit who measures life in numbers!

Himalayan Sonneteer Sonnet 23

In theory loving peace and making peace,
May appear to be one and the same.
In practice there are vastly different,
Like being asleep and being awakened.

Anybody can love peace, so long as,
They don't have to be its reason.
Everybody shouts about peace on insta,
Then they get back to their life of fun.

The opposite of peace is not war,
The opposite of peace is selfishness.
When we stop being selfishly indifferent,
That is the birth of a peaceful planet.

Real love makes you restless, it keeps you wide awake.
When you love the world like you love your family,
That day you'll develop the peacemaker métier.

Thus Peace Begins (The Sonnet)

Peace begins with society,
Society begins with individuality.
Individuality begins with liberty,
Liberty begins with accountability.
Accountability comes from unity,
Unity comes through community.
Community comes through diversity,
Diversity comes through inclusivity.
Inclusivity comes through nonrigidity,
Nonrigidity comes through curiosity.
Curiosity comes through expansivity,
Expansivity comes through evolvability.
Evolvability comes through taming animality.
Animality is tamed when we prioritize humanity.

Good Seed (The Sonnet)

It is existentially impossible,
For all republicans to be inhuman fiend.
But when they violate human rights as daily choir,
It is also impossible to notice the good seed.
It is existentially impossible,
For all republicans to incite hate and violence.
But when a party coddles guns over children,
It is difficult to find anything good in them.
It is existentially impossible,
For all republicans to confuse divinity with division.
But when a party uses bible as an excuse for bigotry,
It is impossible to see the silent vessels of inclusion.
Forgive me, if at times I have been harsh at an entire party!
I know you're there, o good seed -
it is time to grow some greenery.

Himalayan Sonneteer Sonnet 26

It is one thing to have eyes,
Another to have sight.
It is one thing to have arms,
Another to have might.
It is one thing to have feet,
Another to have motion.
It's one thing to have a spinal cord,
Another to have a backbone.
It is one thing to have a head,
Another to know reason.
It is one thing to have a heart,
Another to have emotion.
One thing to have a body, another to have life.
One thing to talk justice, another to answer plight.

Justice is not a hashtag (The Sonnet)

Using a hashtag doesn't make you an activist,
Social media trend is not herald of social justice.
Justice comes when each lives with accountability,
Not when you play pretend justice because it is trendy.
A true activist spends their life working for others,
Occasionally they indulge in some self-charging activity.
Insta-activists spend their life drooling for attention,
Humanitarian crisis is just an opportunity for publicity.
Human rights violation is just a hashtag for most,
So they keep up with the trend by voicing phony endorsement.
Once the trend fades 99 percent of those voices disappear,
Until the next crisis comes, and the vultures hover again.
Violation of human rights is only violation if it is trending.
Society that measures social justice by social media trend,
is nothing but a bunch of hypocritical, bottom-licking ding-a-ling.

Qatar & The West (The Sonnet)

All of a sudden the entire west is peeved at Qatar,
Because only the west has exclusive rights to exposure.
All of a sudden we care about the migrant workers,
The Afghans, Palestinians and Kashmiris no longer matter.
Human rights issue here is, we don't care about human rights,
We only care about filling the air with hypocrisy and mania.
Our poster boy just dumped half his new workforce as garbage,
We buy Oscar, ditch Batgirl, and we diss Qatar for buying FIFA!
We are just peeved that the Arabs are showing off for a change,
Sure it's unacceptable, since showing off is a western tradition.
Yes, it's true that the Middle East reeks with human rights issues,
But it is also teeming with passion beyond western comprehension.
If you really care about human rights
stick to a cause for more than a fortnight.
Otherwise keep your trap shut, lest you open
and be proved a privileged white.

World Domination (A Satirical Sonnet)

White people's pain is pain,
Everybody else's is just discomfort.
That is why you peddle Hitler,
As such a monster.

You don't hate Hitler because,
He wanted to dominate the world,
You hate Hitler because he wanted,
To dominate everybody, including the whites.

The world is but heirloom to the whites,
All other claims are null and void!
Loot like a pommy, rebel like an insurrectionist,
Trod on whoever, just not the fellow white!

World domination is the ultimate white privilege.
Threat to white welfare is the ultimate human rights infringement.

Himalayan Sonneteer Sonnet 30

Enough with the satire,
Now let's get down to brass tacks.
Enough with all this hypocrisy,
Time to discard the bigoted slacks.
It is time to stand up as human,
Not as mindless snowflakes.
It is time to look beyond tradition,
And live as sapiens not just apes.
Conscience captured by culture is nonsense,
Set your conscience free and you'll know life.
Passport is nothing more than a fancy bus pass,
Person defined by passport is but parasite.
Your bus pass doesn't define who you are,
nor does your passport.
Birth-certificate doesn't certify birth,
only accountability does.

Himalayan Sonneteer Sonnet 31

Birth certificate doesn't certify birth,
Passport doesn't determine personality.
Diploma does not indicate education,
The world has plenty educated moronity.

The world is but teeming with passports,
Yet it is so difficult to find a human national.
Nationalism is often peddled as nationality,
Lest the slaves break free and become human.

Hence they peddle notions of guilt and sin,
To keep us trapped by our own imagination.
Learn to question the paradigm as you know,
And the whole facade will crumble into desolation.

Any idea that comes with a cage is actually a mouse-trap.
House with no windows and doors cannot be home to the humans.

Himalayan Sonneteer Sonnet 32

I ask you not to chant my name,
Be free from all such ritual lame.
Hold my hand and come with me,
Together we'll be a timeless flame.

I am basically powerless without you,
For once I am gone I get rooted in you.
Instead of looking for roots in history,
Let us be roots to each other anew.

We look for roots in dead men's custom,
While we should be looking among the living.
How come we never prioritize life over death,
How come we still act as apes, not human being!

Why should life care about us,
when we don't care about living!
Life values those who value the laughter
and loveliness of the living!

Himalayan Sonneteer Sonnet 33

Life favors those who favor life,
Over the dead who favor the living.
If we must be miserable let us be miserable,
Not for the dead but for the living.
So the choice is not between joy and misery,
For there is no life, if there is no misery.
Question is, will we let the dead make us miserable,
Or shall we choose to be miserable in love for humanity.
To live for the living amongst the living is no shame,
Shame is to forget life in memorizing the dead.
One who chooses life over forbiddance is walking poetry,
One who chooses light over obedience becomes timeless.
Slave to tradition is slave to time.
Be your own tradition, and you'll conquer time.

Himalayan Sonneteer Sonnet 34

They say, time and tide wait for none,
Lest the bird learns it can fly.
The best way to control apes is,
To make them feel guilty for their light.
They say, dead men tell no tale, and yet,
We live our lives based on dead men's tale.
It is okay to tell tales if it enhances sight,
But not the kind that produces a walking hell.
There is no divide when we are alive,
Divisions exist only in kingdom of the dead.
We are divided because we are dead,
Come to life, and all divides will be deleted.
Let us write a new tale with the spirit of life.
Instead of celebrating death,
let's celebrate each other's light.

Himalayan Sonneteer Sonnet 35

God is all in the mind,
What's wrong with that!
Art is also all in the mind,
So, is art nothing but dirt!

Yes, plenty harm has been done,
In the name of God.
The same can be said,
About science and art.

Dividers will always divide,
Haters will always hate.
Apes will find one excuse or another,
To justify their authoritarian trait.

For example, 9/11 wasn't religion's fault,
Any more than Hiroshima was science's fault.

Himalayan Sonneteer Sonnet 36

Holiness is fiction, so what,
So is love, romance and attachment!
All of it is just neurochemicals,
Brewing the mind in the human brain.
There are many things we humans do,
That seem to have no logical explanation.
That's the whole point of being human,
To accept each other despite lacking comprehension.
Imagine if we understood each other completely,
That would be a rather boring affair, won't it!
I once said, differences are not failure of humanity,
Differences are the test of our humanity - isn't it!
It is differentiation we must stand up to, not differences.
All difference is good difference, so long as
it doesn't promote hate.

Himalayan Sonneteer Sonnet 37

Some high and mighty intellectual asked me the other day,
'Why do you claim to be black when you're actually brown!'
I smiled 'n said - the very fact, you ask this question shows,
How little your head fathoms the issues of the ground.
In the mythical world of the bookish intellectual,
Black is black, brown is brown, white is white.
But in the real whitewashed world run by bigotry,
Save white skin, all else is black, and quite not right.
You shall never know the torment of discrimination,
By using mere intellect disconnected from real life.
Born to privilege doesn't mean born to riches,
Greatest privilege in a whitewashed world is to be born white.
For once, stand up as an ambassador for the whole humankind.
Trash those chains disguised as roots that desecrate your human light.

Himalayan Sonneteer Sonnet 38

I'm not saying, it's your fault that your ancestors,
Built the world for you on the bones of everybody else.
I'm not saying, it's your fault that your ancestors,
Made all their fortune torturing everybody else.
You don't have to make it up to anyone,
You don't have to feel guilty.
You just need to stand up as human,
Electrified by the will to end disparity.
A human discriminated is a species discriminated,
Prejudice faced by one is prejudice faced by all.
I don't care whether you're white, colored or martian,
If you're indifferent to human suffering you ain't human at all.
It's time to make those stupid divides disappear for good.
We cannot do that if we're too fragile to
acknowledge historical truth.

Himalayan Sonneteer Sonnet 39

Give me your hand,
I have something to tell you.
Look into my eyes, please,
And listen, what I say to you.
I may make many mistakes,
I ask you to tell me if I do.
I may assume something that is not true,
I ask you to tell me when I do.
It is not inhuman to make mistakes,
What's inhuman is not acknowledging.
Mistake acknowledged brings us growth,
Mistake overlooked is another nail in our coffin.
I stand ready to break the bias, starting with my own.
Will you give me a hand, my friend, because
when we grow together, that's when life is honed.

Himalayan Sonneteer Sonnet 40

Growth is only growth when we grow together,
Everything else is but decay in disguise.
Selfish growth is the root of unsustainability,
If you wanna grow, first denounce self-centric pride.

If my growth does not lift another,
It is a growth I could do without.
If my light does not light another,
It is a light I could do without.

Just because nobody lent you a hand,
Doesn't mean you gotta hog all growth for yourself.
If nobody lends you a hand that's more reason,
For you to reach out in help.

So I repeat, we grow only when we grow together.
Upon our collectivist spirit unfolds the world's future.

Himalayan Sonneteer Sonnet 41

Upon your collectivist spirit,
Unfold all things civilized.
Upon your youthful spirit,
Unfold all things alive.
Youth is not what you think,
Youth is not a matter of numericity.
Youth is the celebration of life,
Youth is the spirit of discovery.
Youth is not about age,
Youth is but a spirit,
The spirit of unsubmission,
The spirit of selfless uplift.
Youth of body is just a passing cloud.
It's the youth of sprit that makes us live out loud.

Women Ain't Hood Ornament (The Sonnet)

Why should women have to give up,
Their name when they get married,
As if they are not real people,
But hood ornament to their husband!
Why should a child be identified only,
By their father's name, not mother's,
Who by the way is the root of creation,
Who is the actual almighty creator!
It is a sad state of affairs when,
Morons peddle moronity as tradition.
Shame on us for sustaining such savagery,
As we do not put our backbone to action!
Each couple must determine the parameters
of their relationship, not some ragged tradition.
Only norm that matters is love, for in love lies emancipation.

She is Crown (The Sonnet)

Love her for all she is,
Not just when she can please.
She is the crown of your life,
Not the fly of your jeans.

Love her for all she is,
Even when she hates herself.
If you can't be the rock to her,
It is you who needs help.

Love her for all she is,
Be the cushion to her failure.
While all celebrate her triumph,
You celebrate her even in disaster.

Death can't do you part if you're never two.
Love is what turns two minds into one truth.

I Am Here (The Sonnet)

Look into my eyes,
I wanna listen to your silence.
Tell me of the storms unpassed,
I wanna be your expression express.
Tell me what you have been through,
Tell me of the heartaches unhealed.
Speak the pain you could never utter,
I am here, I am near, you are my priority!
I cannot promise you all the happiness,
Nor can I promise you eternal peace.
But if and when the sky crashes,
I shall be your human shield.
It's okay if you come late to me.
I am here, I am near, I have come early.

Himalayan Sonneteer Sonnet 45

Love is the norm supreme,
In love lies emancipation.
They say love is blind,
I say, love is what gives us vision.

If love is blindness indeed,
It's the blindness that brings us sight.
If love is but an utter illogicality,
It's the illogicality that breathes life.

Pay less attention to tradition,
More to conscience and compassion.
Put less focus on maintaining custom,
And more on achieving amalgamation.

Give me ten lovers who value love over tradition,
And I shall give you a world without discrimination.

Himalayan Sonneteer Sonnet 46

Humans are supposed to be,
Carriers of love, not tradition,
Particularly those traditions,
That peddle nothing but division.

None of us is raised to carry life,
We're all raised to carry disease 'n hate.
But we are not here to live our ancestors' life,
Why don't we live our life our own way!

Love not only turns two minds into one truth,
In love humanity is supreme truth of humankind.
Enough with obedience that ruins our humanness,
It's time for each human to be a humanitarian tide.

I set myself on fire with this drive at an early age.
And I shall keep on burning so long as
there is a single responsible sapiens.

Neighborhood Humanitarian (The Sonnet)

They ask me, why do I never run out of ideas!
It is because I never dwell in one culture.
Sometimes I'm North American, sometimes Latino,
Sometimes I'm South Indian, sometimes I am Turk.
When I run low on charge, I listen to Español,
When my sight gets foggy, I watch Cary and Jimmy.
Whenever I feel homesick, I listen to some Telugu,
Whenever my heart bleeds, I run straight to Turkey.
It is sort of a perpetual motion engine,
I empower the cultures, the cultures empower me.
If I am the world's not-so-secret hometown human,
The world is my secret to my infinite electricity.
How, do you think, I became the neighborhood
humanitarian to every single person on earth!
It's because I never glorified one culture over another.

Himalayan Sonneteer Sonnet 48

These four cultures have contributed,
The most in the making of Naskar.
But they are not the only cultures,
For assimilation must continue forever.
Each culture is fodder to my fervor,
Each culture is muse to my poetry.
Each culture makes marrow in my bones,
Each culture is corpuscle to my capacity.
Every pore of my anatomy is saturated with,
Molecules of majesty from every corner.
The reason I could create a timeless legacy,
Is because I never was a sectarian prisoner.
I am not one human, I am one humanity.
I am life, I am justice, I am expandability.

Himalayan Sonneteer Sonnet 49

I am one humanity,
Not one human being.
I am life, I am justice,
I am sentience expanding.
I live through your hands,
My motion lies in your feet.
To find me, look in the mirror,
For I am oneness most naive.
Family is world to most,
To me the world is family.
Your triumph is my triumph,
Your suffering is my tragedy.
We are not people, but vessels of possibility.
Peace, love, all is possible, when we take responsibility.

Unsocial Media (The Sonnet)

Never, I repeat, never,
Post family pictures online.
It is a total jungle out there,
In every corner predators are lurking.
There's no such thing as privacy settings,
Internet and privacy don't go together.
Privacy is bad for social media business,
Social media thrives on screwing social welfare.
Anxiety is the currency on social media,
More anxious you are, more money they make.
You are the product they sell to advertisers,
So they need you to spill all without restraint.
Social media is programmed to monetize depression.
Unless you're careful, what awaits is devastation.

Himalayan Sonneteer Sonnet 51

When I raise caution on technology,
They call me technophobic.
When I raise warning on climate crisis,
They call me alarmist.
When I point at colonial barbarism,
They call me anglo-phobic.
When I point out discrimination,
They call me anti-white.
You cannot stand for justice,
Without pissing off a lot of cavemen.
It ain't their fault, they hate integration,
They're just scared stiff by the thought of change.
Reform mustn't stop no matter how many apes are pissed.
We cannot stand accountable without offending a few pricks.

Need Teachers Not Cops (The Sonnet)

The world needs less cops and more teachers,
While cops enforce law, teachers instill accountability.
Thus law enforcement only produces an illusion of order,
It's the teachers who can create a crime-free society.
If students are the future, teachers are future maker,
So be civilized and focus on lifting teachers and students.
Government of baboons invests in police 'n defense contracts,
While a truly civilized government invests in education.
Arm the teachers with books and students with sustenance,
Then watch them accomplish the impossible future,
A future of true lasting order, reform and harmony,
Which a billion police cannot achieve in a billion years.
Society that empowers teachers empowers peace.
Society that empowers police empowers malice.

Himalayan Sonneteer Sonnet 53

Stop being the prehistoric idiot,
Who seeks answer to every social ill from law.
Law is not the answer, law is the question,
The answer to all ill is an accountable outlaw.
The question is not what the cops,
Are doing to defend the society?
The real question is, what we the citizens,
Are doing to protect our planetary community?
Love the world like nobody does,
Love the people like nobody does.
Live the life like nobody does,
Burn to cinders like nobody does.
Why – because, your ashes are your greatest boon.
Your ashes hold the answer to your wounds.

Himalayan Sonneteer Sonnet 54

You may think your achievements,
Are the crown of your life.
But it's your failures,
That make you shine bright.

Burn, my friend! Burn so bright,
That the haters go blind.
Rise alive till you drop dead,
Purpose of life is to be alive.

Measure of life is not,
How many breaths you take.
Life is measured by,
How many lives you illuminate.

So I say, burn till you turn to cinders.
Your ashes are the cement that'll stabilize the universe.

Himalayan Sonneteer Sonnet 55

Difference between life and death,
Is the difference in rigidity.
Difference between sight and night,
Is the difference in rigidity.

Difference between love and hate,
Is the difference in oneness.
Difference between life and death,
Is the difference in oneness.

Difference between wisdom and ignorance,
Is not information but curiosity.
Difference between reason and prejudice,
Is not information but curiosity.

Nobody can make you realize this difference.
A sapiens must be their own sapience.

Himalayan Sonneteer Sonnet 56

Seni seviyorum be insan!
It's okay if you don't get a word I say.
You won't remember the words anyway,
It's the sentiment that makes the way.

There is a bridge from my heart to yours,
But you won't fathom it with all the words.
Oneness is a bridge revealed in silence,
Can you hear the pitter-patter of teardrops!

If you can't hear the teardrops of a warzone,
All your philosophies are basically useless.
If we can't light up the forgotten corners,
What's the point in discovering photoelectric effect!

What's the point of all these fancy words and doohickeys,
If human emotion sinks to the bottom of our priorities!

Himalayan Sonneteer Sonnet 57

What are we if we ain't no human!
What are we if we ain't no kind!
What are we if we ain't no help!
What are we if we shine no light!
What are we if we ain't no wise!
What are we if we ain't no brave!
What are we if we ain't upright!
What are we if all we do is crave!
What are we if we see no injustice!
To not see injustice is to endorse injustice.
What are we if we hear no prejudice!
To not hear prejudice is to perpetuate prejudice.
See all, hear all, then act as the first human being.
Our ancestors might have taught us more to hate than love,
But we have all the neurons needed to be a decent being.

Himalayan Sonneteer Sonnet 58

Life is but a laughing matter,
Better die laughing than live crying.
Life is but a matter of love,
Better die loving than live hating.

Life is but a matter of giving,
Better die giving than live taking.
Life is but a cherishable affair,
Better die cherishing than live chasing.

Life is a matter of ceaseless correction,
Better die correcting than live assuming.
Life is a matter of shared liberty,
Better die free than live enslaved and enslaving.

Life is a matter of the dark as much as of light.
Life is but an untamed motion from darkness to light.

Himalayan Sonneteer Sonnet 59

Darkness is not our enemy, if anything,
Darkness makes us more observant.
Darkness doesn't overshadow the mind,
Darkness gets us enlightened.

Darkness has great potential,
To fear darkness is to stay blind.
Only upon making friends with darkness,
Do the eyes open up to magnified sight.

So fear not darkness, my friend,
Darkness exists to empower your light.
And fear only cripples that possibility,
So never let fear cripple your flight.

To see or not to see, it is all in the mind.
Out of the womb of darkness comes all light.

Himalayan Sonneteer Sonnet 60

Darkness not only enhances light,
Darkness actually can produce light.
Rise above your craving for light and,
You'll find strength in the darkest night.

Right now I sit in the dark,
With no light around except of the screen.
Lo and behold the floodgates break open,
All the pain and light start pouring!

Pain does not bring you down,
Your own imagination does.
Hardship does not ruin life,
Only idealism does.

So, live, live and live to the fullest,
rising above all archaic habit.
Smile, laugh and dance it through,
dance through even the worst bit.

Fear No Fear (The Sonnet)

I have zero tolerance for fear,
I don't mean intolerance of being afraid.
Let the fear come and go,
Just never let it make you slave.
Embrace it all, and the grip will slowly loosen,
Then take care of the cause of your fear.
It is quite human to have cold feet on occasion,
Just know, your backbone is your savior.
Fear resisted is fear amplified,
Fear embraced is fear relieved.
Most fears are rooted in imagination,
Observe yourself and all is revealed.
You are the ultimate answer to your own fear.
Study yourself without coldness, and all will be clear.

Himalayan Sonneteer Sonnet 62

To see or not to see,
It is all up to you.
Whether you see and what you see,
It is all up to you.
Whether you hear and what you hear,
It defines the state of your heart.
Hearing it all if you remain quiet,
What's the point of having a vocal cord!
Voice not used for justice,
Is an utter waste of a vocal cord.
Backbone used for collective good,
Is the only and ultimate cosmic vanguard.
There is no almighty concerned of human welfare.
Which is more reason for us to take care of each other.

Himalayan Sonneteer Sonnet 63

Knowing that all the stories of God,
Are nothing but fantasy self-preserving,
Is not the end of all realization,
But the first step towards true understanding.
Having true understanding of the universe,
Is not necessarily necessary to be a good human.
But if understanding the universe is your priority,
Then it is necessary to reject all fake illumination.
True knowledge begins with the end of assumed knowledge,
But I repeat, it is not compulsory for living a good life.
What is imperative however, whether you seek truth or not,
Is that you reject at least those beliefs that cause divide.
To realize all our notion of grand design is all fiction,
Doesn't make us traitor to heritage,
rather it makes us more responsible of our action.

Himalayan Sonneteer Sonnet 64

To realize there is no grand design,
Doesn't make us traitor to heritage.
It only makes us more alive to life,
It makes us infinitely more responsible.
Does that mean, those who believe in God,
Don't feel responsible for their action!
I too believe, my late teacher watches over me,
But this fiction is yet to cause me inaction.
In the end, it all comes down to the individual,
One with backbone will act responsible no matter what.
It is only the shallow who try to brush off civic duty,
Regardless of whether they believe in some kind of god.
So the question is not whether there is some grand design!
Real question is, shall we take responsibility for our kind?

Himalayan Sonneteer Sonnet 65

Realization begets responsibility,
Curiosity kills prejudice.
Oneness begets peace and harmony,
Correction reduces malice.
Humankind has made many errors,
In their amateur attempts at civilization.
Civilized beings are to correct the errors,
Instead of admiring them as tradition.
Stereotypes have played a key role,
In human understanding of human society.
It's time we dismantle them altogether,
So we could embrace the whole of humanity.
It is okay if oneness feels like a daunting task.
Let's take one step at a time, by breaking the bias.

Himalayan Sonneteer Sonnet 66

I may not always be correct,
But I am willing to learn.
If you can muster the patience,
To correct me gently if I assume wrong.
Nothing is more important to me,
Than ensuring the integrity of our relationship.
For that I'm ready to admit a hundred mistakes but,
No mistake should be justified at the expense of friendship.
One way or another we all make assumptions,
That is not the problem.
The problem is, once we make an assumption,
We assume it to contain the entire reality domain.
So I say, I'm ready to correct if and when I assume wrong.
Will you give me a hand in my act of self-correction!

Himalayan Sonneteer Sonnet 67

I assume, I'll always assume,
That is my animal conditioning.
But the human in me is always awake,
To never let the animal be overbearing.
But an evolutionary fact of animal nature is,
The human animal is conditioned to overreact.
So it takes a lot of conscience and character,
To restrain our inner animal from running amok.
Hence, the first step towards humanity is,
To grab hold of our universal inhumanity.
The first step towards social serenity is,
To grab hold of our self-centric insanity.
Long enough we've fostered bigotry as supreme sanity.
It is time to be insane with our drive for humanity.

Himalayan Sonneteer Sonnet 68

Human am I, Human are you,
Difference in-between is pure fiction.
Alive am I, alive are you,
Real death of life is in separation.
Put aside the bigotry,
Put aside the tradition.
Real transformation of society,
Comes through self-annihilation.
Annihilate yourself not in obedience,
Annihilate yourself in loving liberty.
Let them call you insane all they want,
Let love be the better name of sanity.
Declare love not with your lips, but with your very life.
There is no greater living than alleviating social strife.

Himalayan Sonneteer Sonnet 69

You don't need to keep me on your lips,
Keep me in your heart, if you must.
You don't need to keep me in your hands,
Keep me in your deeds, if you must.
Declare who you are not with mere labels,
For labels fall short to declare a human.
Human is declared by deeds of humanity,
You are human when you speak through action.
No label has ever brought people together,
Throughout history labels have caused division.
Sense your wholeness beyond those puny labels,
And the world will finally witness some ascension.
We are the gateway to the world's ascension.
Why not act as such, for we are our salvation!

Himalayan Sonneteer Sonnet 70

When the one and the world become one,
That is true human salvation.
When the human is human before all else,
That is the ultimate emancipation.
When the human is caring of the fellow human,
That is the practical kingdom of heaven.
Kingdom of heaven is not some magical place,
It is the reflection of human assimilation.
Forgive me Almighty, if you are out there,
I shall always prioritize humanity over you.
Besides there is no greater act of worship,
Than lifting up the fallen and the destitute.
My holiness is rooted in life and humanity.
Life is sweet, life is holy, when lived for humanity.

Himalayan Sonneteer Sonnet 71

Sweetness of life is rooted in the pain,
You are willing to bear to make another smile.
Happiness of life is rooted in the hardship,
You're willing to bear to invigorate another spine,

Be a lover, be a fighter, be a one person army,
To defend the helpless without lifting a weapon.
Strength of savages lies in the weapons they conceal,
Strength of the civilized lies in their backbone.

Be the unarmed peacemaker, be the nonviolent volcano,
Erupt with all your might whenever a life is threatened.
Threat to the welfare and happiness of one life anywhere,
Is a repulsive desecration of all that is sacred.

We don't build civilization by erecting
one sky-scraper after another.
We build civilization by wiping out
one discrimination after another.

Himalayan Sonneteer Sonnet 72

Civilization is not a place,
Civilization is a process eternal.
The process of treating savagery,
The process of eliminating discrimination.

Nuts and bolts do not constitute advancement,
Heart and help constitute true advancement.
Freezers are good for preserving dead meat,
To preserve life we need a warm environment.

Then again too much heat is bad for health,
Just like too much coldness destroys life.
We gotta find the right blend of warmth and cold,
If we are to ever raise a society civilized.

How do we find that right balance, is there a handbook?
No there isn't, that's why each mind must be its own guidebook.

Himalayan Sonneteer Sonnet 73

You are your darkest night,
You are your brightest dawn.
You are the might to the mightless,
You are the inspiration when all goes wrong.
It's easy for animals to mock others' failure,
It takes a human to be the source of courage.
Anybody can draw courage from a hundred people,
Greatness is when from you a hundred draw courage.
Courage is a strange force that multiplies by giving,
We grow stronger by encouraging others.
Whereas the smaller we act in self-centricity,
The more we grow weaker.
So, never try to drag another down, upon their victory.
Little envy is okay, but never let it ruin your humanity.

Himalayan Sonneteer Sonnet 74

We are human not when,
We have no inhuman tendency.
We are human when we are,
Not run by inhuman tendency.
We are at peace not when,
We have no inner conflict.
We are at peace when we come,
To terms with our conflicts.
We come from the animal kingdom after all,
Hence it's impossible to wipe out the animal.
But we have developed enough brain capacity,
To put the animal on leash and act responsible.
We are civilized not when we don't behave uncivilized.
We are civilized when we know when we behave uncivilized.

Himalayan Sonneteer Sonnet 75

It is not about applying Neuroscience in society,
It is about knowing, we are human with unused humanity.
It is not about creating a science-literate society,
It's about having the common sense to erase prejudiciality.
What is there so complicated about it,
Why can't we still tell illumination from superstition!
Because we have not evolved to pursue illumination,
We all evolved as apes to chase a self-serving illusion.
But these illusions have turned into a horror story,
They have made us commit unimaginable primitivity.
What's worse, we are never awake to recognize it as such,
We're too high on heritage to tell what's benevolence what's bigotry.
All this time we have taken the side of tradition against humanity.
For the first time ever, let us be human and stand with some dignity.

Himalayan Sonneteer Sonnet 76

There is no lord,
If there is no life.
There is no life,
If there is no mind.
There is no mind,
If there is no brain.
Healthy society comes,
From a healthy brain.
Brain is the alpha,
Brain is the omega.
The day the brain falls,
Is the apocalypse of dunya.
Neurons make us savage, neurons can humanize.
Neurons aware, are the force that make us civilized.

Himalayan Sonneteer Sonnet 77

Neurons aware are neurons of heaven,
Neurons untamed are neurons of hell.
If you ask, who is to tame the neurons,
Only neurons are to tame themselves.

But it is no slavery training,
I am talkin' about an aware awakening.
When individual neurons wake up to themselves,
That is the first step of social awakening.

Neurons run by nature's autopilot,
Simply follow the instinct of self-preservation.
Whereas neurons aware enhance themselves,
Neurons aware take charge of their evolution.

Possible and impossible all are neurological constructs.
So, it is up to you to push every single envelop further.

Himalayan Sonneteer Sonnet 78

Where is that impossible human?
Where is that impossible light?
Where is that insane sanity?
Where is that inane sight?
Where is that impossible sapiens?
Where is that walking gospel?
Where is that humane anomaly?
Where is that hateless dumbbell?
Where is that illiterate seer?
Where is that uneducated sage?
Where is that civil sentience?
Where is that uncultured poet?
Seer, o seer, wherefore art thou blind, o brave seer!
Cast insecurity aside, for the world's suffering grows severe.

Himalayan Sonneteer Sonnet 79

Who believes you or not,
That is not your business.
Keep your eyes fixed only,
On collective development.
Social welfare is human welfare,
Even in the midst of mockery.
No triumph is cherished truly,
Unless it comes with some mockery.
Cherish the mockery more than applause,
Mockery makes pure steel out of fragile iron.
Whereas applause often gets to our head,
Which then wreaks havoc on our conviction.
Most of all, hate none, no matter how much you're despised.
To retaliate hate with hate brings only our own demise.

Himalayan Sonneteer Sonnet 80

External noise makes us observant,
Of the music within, if we care to listen.
External mockery makes us observant,
Of the might within, if we care to listen.

External stagnation makes us observant,
Of the ascension within, if we care to look.
External prejudice makes us observant,
Of the illumination within, if we care to look.

External indifference makes us observant,
Of the strength in our shoulders, if we care to muster.
External difference makes us observant,
Of the unity within, if we care to foster.

External crisis makes us observant of the character unborn,
If we just once grab hold of the reins of dawn.

Himalayan Sonneteer Sonnet 81

If we treat people,
Like we treat currency,
That is the end of the world,
That is the end of society.
Currency is a social construct,
So, its value varies based on geography.
Humanity is the foundation of our existence,
How can we be human if we value people like currency!
North, South, East, West, humans are the best,
Mind not location, human life is worth just the same.
Appearance may differ across geography,
But our innate humanity is one and the same.
So I say, a nation's value lies not in its currency,
But its regard for the welfare of all humanity.

Himalayan Sonneteer Sonnet 82

Worth of a land lies not,
In the value of its currency.
Worth of a land lies solely,
In its regard for humanity.
Advancement of a nation,
Is not revealed in etiquette.
Advancement of a nation is revealed,
In its intention to be integrated.
People are measured,
By the bridges they build.
Animals are measured,
By the lives they kill.
Regardless of whether a currency drops or climbs,
We must never cease to work on being humanized.

Himalayan Sonneteer Sonnet 83

Even the darkest night,
Is no match for the rising sun.
Even the falling currency,
Is no match for the brave human.
Even the cruelest norm,
Is no match for a bold kindness.
Even an indifferent world,
Is no match for an accountable sapiens.
All the armed forces are no match,
For one unarmed peacemaker standing unbent.
All the corrupt bureaucracy is no match,
For one bold and uncorrupted citizen.
The struggle isn't over till the last drop of tear is wiped out.
We shall rise human when we rise human unbound.

Himalayan Sonneteer Sonnet 84

Unbound by tradition,
Unbound by biases,
Unbound by belief,
Unbound by loyalties,
Unbound by logicality,
Unbound by assumption,
Unbound by selfishness,
Unbound by argumentation,
Unbound by intellect,
Unbound by ignorance,
Unbound by arrogance,
Unbound by indifference.
This is how we rise human,
This is how we find communion.

Himalayan Sonneteer Sonnet 85

They'll call you traitor,
They'll call you infidel.
They'll call you a lot of things,
Because you act human not animal.
That is the way with the animals,
They despise being reminded of their animality.
You gotta be prepared to be unpopular.
If you want to practice your humanity.
We are an utterly infantile species,
We still don't realize how infantile we are.
Every time one of us raises any kind of concern,
All the kids naturally cannot handle the idea.
Awake, arise, and stand for justice
even if you're branded traitor.
If you never foster the guts,
you're perpetuating an ominous future.

Himalayan Sonneteer Sonnet 86

It is a world of wolves,
And they want you to be one.
The question is, will the human give in,
Or struggle till death to keep the light on?
It is existentially important that you don't give in,
Because your struggle is the struggle of our species.
That is why we are still so much uncivilized,
While most never join the fight, plenty never finish.
No matter how loud the wolves howl,
They are no match for a humble elephant.
Be like the elephant, my friend,
An unstoppable gentle giant!
If you give in, the jungle gains another predator.
If you stand firm, the world gains a transformer.

Himalayan Sonneteer Sonnet 87

If we want to reform this predatory world,
We gotta do away with our self-centric ways.
If we want conscience and compassion to be the norm,
We gotta lay ourselves to pave the way.

There is no sunrise without sacrifice,
There is no unity without inclusion.
There is no love without conviction,
There is no justice without unsubmission.

No sewage is ever sanctified without sewage-workers,
No society is ever civilized without reformers.
No mutation ever occurs without an anomaly,
No world is brought to life without love-laborers.

You are the messenger, you are the message.
But you'll feel nothing till you feel the seriousness.

Himalayan Sonneteer Sonnet 88

Do you realize how serious the situation is,
Are you aware of the lives ruined by cruelty?
Because if you stay aloof in your cloud castle,
All talk of humanity is but a tale of fantasy.
Can you tell the real from the unreal,
Can you tell facts from fantasy?
I am not talkin' in terms of neuroscience,
I am askin' you as a human, of human responsibility.
We can argue about the nature of truth all we want,
But that won't alleviate the suffering of society.
So the question is, do you know the worth of life,
How far will you go to preserve another's serenity!
Does human welfare overpower your insecurity?
Or is the self still separate from society?

Himalayan Sonneteer Sonnet 89

Self disconnected from social welfare,
Digs its own stinking purgatory.
Society disconnected from individual welfare,
Heads for an astronomical catastrophe.
In a civilized world self and society are one,
In a civilized world norms involve welfare of all.
Civilized norms are the ones that keep evolving,
Norms that don't evolve only make a society fall.
In a civilized world, triumph of one is triumph of all,
While tragedy of one is the tragedy of all.
That is why it is human to have each other's back,
While it is prehistoric to wish for another's fall.
Collectivity is not a philosophy, collectivity is civilization.
It doesn't mean thinking same, it just means ascension in unison.

Himalayan Sonneteer Sonnet 90

Peer pressure has no place in civilization,
Peer pressure is the antithesis of collectivity.
The idea of collectivity is to listen without judgment,
If we can't do that, it's no different from current primitivity.
The idea is to overpower primitivity with civilized sentience,
Not simply to replace one primitivity with another.
If we ostracize each other for varying views,
That is not civilization but a galactic disorder.
We oughta stand up to hate and discrimination,
Not to anything and everything that appears different.
Differences will not destroy the world,
What will is our indifference.
So I say to you plainly, it's good to be different,
What's not good is to be indifferent.

Himalayan Sonneteer Sonnet 91

It's good to be different,
What's not good is to be indifferent.
Differences are not our failure,
Our difference is our greatest strength.

What we need to do is,
Humanize our notion of difference.
The first course of action is to differentiate,
Between discrimination and difference.

We must be very clear on,
What is difference, what is discrimination!
If we accept discrimination as a mere difference,
Then we end up in a death loop of degeneration.

And how do we tell discrimination from difference?
All we gotta do is scrutinize each situation with conscience.

Himalayan Sonneteer Sonnet 92

There is nothing more beautiful,
Than a heart that beats for others.
There is nothing more ugly,
Than a heart that hogs all pleasures.

This is not a matter of political ideology,
It is a matter of common humanity.
This is not a matter of charity either,
It is just a matter of community.

Sharing is not socialism,
Caring is not catholicism.
Helping is not humanism,
Reform is not partisanism.

Problem is, we still value ideology over humanity.
How 'bout we put aside our intellectual ideocracy!

Himalayan Sonneteer Sonnet 93

Problem is, we want every single act,
To have some sort of ideological allegiance.
How about we just act humans for a goddamn second,
Forgetting all high 'n mighty, puny-minded obedience!

I have a distinct distaste for ideological blindness,
They bring nothing but heartache for the self and society.
No ideology is human enough to sustain civilization,
Yet all pretend to have answers to all social inquiry.

Replacing religious bigotry with political ideology,
Is not progress but simply refurbishment of prejudice.
If you really, genuinely, actually care about progress,
Grow up to life stepping out of your ideological crib.

My ideology vs yours, your ideology vs another's,
It has been going on like this since time began.
Isn't it time yet to actually be a whole human!

Can’t Handle Freedom (The Sonnet)

Whole human is the first human,
All else are but wannabe.
Designation human says it all,
Yet why do you chase terminology!
Even when you broke free from religion,
You could not handle that utter freedom!
Like a rightful new descendant of divisionists,
You chained the word "human" with an "ism".
It is like you can't handle being free,
You have to stay enslaved by one ism or another.
They used to keep the world apart with religions,
Today the same is done by new-age dividers.
Human, human, human - that is all we ever are.
Not humanist, not socialist, just carers of each other.

Himalayan Sonneteer Sonnet 95

We don't want to behave human,
We just want a cheap ism to define our point of view.
We don't want to cause peace and harmony,
We just want an ideology that talks a lot about virtue.
In short, we don't want to put in the effort,
The effort that actually transforms a world.
We just want to show off amongst our peers,
‘Look, this is how my belief debunks all others!’
We just want to find an intellectual label,
That defines perfectly what we believe.
And to hell with our actual contribution,
In the transformation of a civilized species!
Ideologies are a hypocrite's way of begging for attention.
Real reformers only care about society,
not ideological castration.

Himalayan Sonneteer Sonnet 96

Ideologies are the hypocrite's way,
Of begging for attention.
Real reformers care about change,
Not about admiration.
Admiration or no admiration,
You keep on doing your duty.
Duty of what, you ask -
Duty of a caretaker of humanity.
Learn from all the isms, but obey none,
Because obedience is decadence.
Be a life-long learner, but never slave,
There is no learning in enslavement.
You are no slave, you are no master.
You are simply a civilized humanizer.

Himalayan Sonneteer Sonnet 97

You are no slave, you are no master,
You are a vessel of civilized sentience.
Master, slave, these are archaic concepts,
That don't belong in a world of sapiens.
There are a lot of these concepts around,
We gotta scrutinize each one carefully.
Then whichever does not apply to our time,
We gotta leave behind without rigidity.
It may feel difficult at times but,
It is imperative that we carry it through.
Because those who fail to filter the past,
Will go to bed without ever knowing life anew.
Criticize no past, glorify no future,
Just have the common sense to tell dawn from disaster.

Himalayan Sonneteer Sonnet 98

Learn from the whole of time,
Without the slightest rigidity.
And nature will adorn you with the capacity,
To observe and act in the interest of humanity.
Learn from everyone everywhere,
Without the slightest resistance.
Only then can you observe all of society,
Only then can you mold the society with sapience.
And how do you mold a society at your will?
You don't - if you did, that would again be prejudice.
What you are to do is be the first original sapiens,
So that the world around transforms through osmosis.
I'll say to you plainly - be the future you do not have.
And you shall be the turning point of the universe.

Himalayan Sonneteer Sonnet 99

Nothing will be civilized,
If we are afraid of change.
No world will be humanized,
If humans are afraid to be human.
Difficulties only strengthen the feet,
Burdens only strengthen the shoulder.
Once you get the hang of accountability,
Indifference will feel like disaster.
If you can't take the world on shoulders,
Take the responsibility of your neighborhood.
It's not the size of your duty, but your unsubmission,
To indifference that reveals your humanhood.
Start small and keep on walking, no matter the mockery.
Little everyday acts of justice end up transforming society.

Himalayan Sonneteer Sonnet 100

It's the little everyday acts of justice,
That bring most change in society.
It's the little everyday acts of justice,
That actually eliminate inhumanity.
One big revolution in five years,
Brings no lasting change.
But one small act of uncompromise everyday,
Makes the whole world gain conscience.
Hence, reformation of a nation isn't measured,
By how many big revolutions it has to face.
Reformation of a nation is predicated on,
How many citizens it has who refuse to bend.
So I say - break the chains, take off the blinkers.
The whole world awaits, for it needs to be tinkered.

Made in the USA
Columbia, SC
14 April 2023

cb3b37f8-43da-46a8-bbb2-488c20d142bdR01